THE GENERAL'S WIFE
THE LIFE OF
MRS. ULYSSES S. GRANT

ISHBEL ROSS

First published by Dodd, Mead & Company in 1959.

Copyright © Ishbel Ross.

This edition published in 2018.

TABLE OF CONTENTS

ACKNOWLEDGMENTS	5
PART ONE	8
CHAPTER I: WHITE HAVEN	9
CHAPTER II: A PLANK BRIDGE PROPOSAL	26
CHAPTER III: ST. LOUIS BRIDE	44
CHAPTER IV: JULIA'S SIXTY ACRES	63
CHAPTER V: HARDSCRABBLE	74
CHAPTER VI: GALENA	88
CHAPTER VII: THE GENERAL'S WIFE IN JEOPARDY	104
CHAPTER VIII: THE GUNS OF VICKSBURG	125
PART TWO	139
CHAPTER IX: MRS, GRANT MEETS THE LINCOLNS	140
CHAPTER X: RETURN OF THE VICTOR	157
CHAPTER XI: FIRST LADY	171
CHAPTER XII: LONG BRANCH	191

CHAPTER XIII: PENELOPE FOLLOWS ULYSSES   209

CHAPTER XIV: A MANSION OFF FIFTH AVENUE   231

CHAPTER XV: DEATH ON A MOUNTAINTOP   247

CHAPTER XVI: "AS THE NEEDLE TO THE THREAD"   261

ACKNOWLEDGMENTS

I am much indebted to Princess Cantacuzene, Mrs. William Pigott Cronan and Major General Ulysses S. Grant, 3rd, for all the aid they have given me and the interest they have shown in the preparation of this biography of their grandmother, Mrs. Grant. Their personal recollections have been invaluable, and I am especially grateful to General Grant for the time and effort he has devoted to rounding up fresh material, and for his unfailing cooperation in checking facts and looking up references. He put at my disposal family letters, papers, scrapbooks and photographs, all of which were of great value in tracing the life story of Mrs. Grant. The General also was good enough to let me glance through his grandmother's unpublished memoir, not to draw from it in any way, but to give me fuller understanding of her character and personality, I am also grateful to his daughter, Mrs. John S. Dietz, for her good offices and interest in this work.

Princess Cantacuzene, who was born in the White House and has many affectionate memories of her grandmother, most generously evoked for me incidents from the past that shed light on Mrs. Grant's character and family relationships. She and General Grant are the children of Frederick Dent Grant, who was the first son born to Ulysses and Julia Dent Grant. Mrs. Cronan, the daughter of Jesse Grant, their youngest son, was kind enough to give me letters, manuscript material and her personal recollections of her grandmother. These family links have served to give insight to the true nature of Mrs. Grant, in addition to supplying essential facts in her history.

Mr. and Mrs. Delbert Wenzlick, who now own White Haven, her early home close to St. Louis, passed on to me many echoes of the Dent-Grant occupation of the lovely old homestead where Mrs. Grant was born. Mr. Wenzlick's father, Albert, collected material on the family, and the house is rich in Dent associations. Miss Shirley Seifert, whose novel Captain Grant deals with the early years of the Grants, was generous in indicating local sources.

The Missouri Historical Society proved to be a fountainhead of intimate material on Mrs, Grant. There I studied the manuscript of her younger sister, Emma Dent Casey, who described in detail their early days at White Haven and the courtship of young Ulysses S. Grant. I am most grateful for the aid given me by the Society's director, Charles van Ravenswaay, and by Mrs. Ernest A. Stadler, archivist; Mrs. Benjamin D. Harris, Mrs. Eileen J, Cox and Miss Marjory Douglas.

Homer Clark, of the Anheuser-Busch estate, which now embraces the old Grant farm, showed me over Hardscrabble, the log cabin built by General Grant. It is not open to the public, la the surrounding acres and along the banks of the Gravois, where Ulysses Grant courted Julia Dent, it was possible to picture their physical environment in the days of their youth. Another period of their life together was made manifest in Galena, where the streets, houses and stores, as well as the De Soto House, have enduring Grant associations. Their old home on the hill has on exhibition furniture, china and intimate possessions that suggest their daily existence there. Many of the citizens of Galena had stories to tell about the Grants, and I am especially indebted to Mrs. Charles Allen, custodian of their old home; to Mrs. Lutie Asraus, director of the Galena Historical Museum; and to Miss Edith Cleary, whose family had associations with the Grants.

The cottage at Mount McGregor, where General Grant died in 1885, remains much as it was when the family occupied it for the last agonizing weeks of his life. Its custodian, Mrs. A. J. Gambino, gave me friendly assistance on my visit there. Mrs. Delia H. Pugh, of Burlington, New Jersey, guided me to local information on the months spent there by Mrs. Grant and her children in the closing days of the Civil War. James M. Babcock, chief of the Burton Historical Collection at the Detroit Public Library, was particularly helpful in indicating material on the life of the Grants in Detroit. Miss Helen Reynar, of Cobourg, Ontario, supplied me with facts on the summers spent by Mrs. Grant at that lakeside resort. Samuel Charles Webster, son of Charles L. Webster, who published General Grant's Memoirs, was good enough to give me family letters, pictures and some recollections of Mrs. Grant.

I am indebted to officials of the National Archives, the Smithsonian Institution and the Library of Congress for generous aid in assembling material on my subject. The Manuscripts Division of the Library of Congress was an excellent source of Grant documentation, some of it restricted, but opened to me by the courtesy of General Grant, and I should like to express my warmest thanks for the unfailing cooperation and interest of David C. Mearns, chief of the division; Robert H. Land, acting chief; Dr. Joseph C. Vance, Edwin A. Thompson, Dr. Elizabeth G.

McPherson and Miss Kate Stewart. Miss Virginia Daiker, of the Prints and Photographs Division, was most helpful on pictures.

Although not as zealous a letter writer as General Grant, the name Julia Dent Grant shows up in a number of manuscript collections. She corresponded with such men as Theodore Roosevelt, Grover Cleveland, Andrew Carnegie and W. H. Vanderbilt. I cannot begin to list all those who have aided me in libraries and historical societies clear across the continent but I should like to mention in particular Mrs. Shirley Spranger, of the American History Room, and Robert W. Hill, Edward B. Morrison and Miss Jean McNiece, of the Manuscript Division of the New York Public Library; Miss Sylvia Hilton, Miss Helen Ruskell and other stall members of the New York Society Library; Clyde C. Walton, Illinois State Historian, and S. Ambrose Wetherbec, of the Illinois State Historical Library at Springfield; Frederick Anderson, assistant editor of the Mark Twain papers, University of California; R. N. Williams, 2nd, and Miss Catherine Miller, of the Historical Society of Pennsylvania; Miss Mattie Russell, curator of manuscripts, Duke University; and Miss Blanche Jantzen., of the Chicago Historical Society.

In tracking down Grant material I have been generously aided by the staffs of the New York Historical Society, the Chicago Historical Society, the Illinois Historical Society, the Massachusetts Historical Society, the Clements Library, University of Michigan; the Burlington County Historical Society; Rutgers University Library; the Henry E. Huntington Library and Art Gallery, San Marino, California; the Free Public Library, Philadelphia; and the American Antiquarian Society, Worcester, Massachusetts.

I. R.

PART ONE

CHAPTER I: WHITE HAVEN

SMOKE CURLED FROM the wide stone chimneys of White Haven as Ulysses S. Grant reined in his horse on a spring day in 1844 at the rambling homestead that shimmered through a grove of locust and spruce trees. The young lieutenant walked up a zigzag path to the house, sure of the welcome he would receive from the family of Colonel Frederick Dent.

Eight-year-old Emma ran out to meet him, her ringlets bobbing over her shoulders. She had news for Lieutenant Grant. Her oldest sister Julia had returned from a stay in nearby St. Louis and now he would meet her. He had been riding over to White Haven from Jefferson Barracks twice a week for two months but had yet to see the sister most admired by young Frederick Dent, his classmate at West Point. He was already devoted to Emma, and to sixteen-year-old Nellie, a sparkling brunette who did her best to flirt with him.

When Julia moved forward demurely to welcome him he saw at a glance that she was the plainest of the three Dent sisters. But she greeted him with such grace and warmth that she made an instant impression on Grant. She had flawless skin and bright coloring, whipped up by the outdoor life she led and her daily horseback rides. Her dark hair, thick and glossy, was drawn back smoothly into a chignon. She was barely five feet tall and was delicately fashioned, with the smallest hands the lieutenant had ever seen in a girl.

Julia was equally interested in him, Fred was her favorite brother and he had pictured Grant as a fine fellow, the champion horseman of West Point, He had visited Ulysses' home in Bethel, Ohio, and had asked his family to make the young lieutenant welcome at White Haven. Meanwhile, Fred had left for the West with his regiment. Studying the shy youth on their first meeting, Julia could understand Emma's observation that he "looked as pretty as a doll" But she viewed him with more perception than her romantic little sister, whose recorded impression of him might have astonished the future commander of the Union forces,

Like Emma, she noticed his porcelain complexion and how readily he flushed. He seemed sensitive and silent by comparison with the lusty officers from the barracks, who were apt to swashbuckle a little as they swung her around the dance floor. She soon learned that he did not dance and had avoided most of the social intercourse in which the young officers of West Point indulged. This did not dismay Julia. She saw that he was radically different from all the men she had met up to that time, and her interest in him was quickened at once. He bore small resemblance to her stoutly built brother Fred, or to handsome James "Pete" Longstreet, the cousin who often came to call at her home and escorted her to dances.

Young officers were no novelty in Julia's life. Her parents kept open house for the soldiers stationed at the whitewashed barracks on a 1,700-acre estate a few miles from White Haven, With three daughters growing up, and a son already in army service, the Dent hospitality was an accepted fact, and the officers relished the good meals, the homelike surroundings and even an occasional argument with Colonel Dent. Julia had been to dances at the barracks and she knew some of the most dashing officers circulating around St. Louis in the early 1840s. At the age of nineteen she was already sought after, both in the city and at White Haven. She was known for her good manners and amiable disposition. She was an excellent dancer, an expert horsewoman, and she sang and played effectively.

Julia and Ulysses were in sympathy from their first meeting, although both were successful at hiding their growing interest in each other. Only Emma and Nellie detected the fact that their oldest sister moved around in an unusual state of preoccupation, and that her hair got special grooming and her ribbons extra twists when Lieutenant Grant came to call. She laughed at Emma's insistence that he was her own sweetheart; that she had seen him first when he rode up to the turnstile one day and called out; "How do you do, little girl Does Mr. Dent live here?"

"The whole picture of him and his sleek, prancing steed was so good to look upon that I could do nothing but stare," Emma recalled in later years. "His cheeks were round and plump and rosy; his hair was fine and brown, very thick and wavy. His eyes were a clear blue, and always full of light. His features were regular, pleasingly molded and attractive, and his figure so slender, well formed and graceful that it was like that of a young prince to my eye . . ."

This was Emma's view of him. Julia's observations went deeper. His composed manner was soothing to her in the restless mood that beset her that spring. His blue eyes were contemplative as he listened to her light chatter. He had a straight, stubborn mouth and firm chin, which would be concealed by a beard for most of his life, but was clean-shaven when Julia first saw him. A heavy crop of russet hair ringed an uncommonly wide forehead. His hands were muscular and graceful as they gripped his horse's reins.

Grant told Emma years later in the White House that it was love at first sight with him where Julia was concerned, and that he had never had "but the one sweetheart in his life." Emma, always the sentimentalist, added her own deduction: "Not even the boyish amours that usually precede a young man's real passion had ever been his. His wife was the lady of his dreams, I the heroine of his romance." But she may well have been wrong about this. Although it was known that Grant had gone through West Point without any entanglements, he was not indifferent to girls. He was merely too shy and lacking in social grace to make headway in the romantic field. "I have now been here about four months, and have not seen a single familiar face or spoken to a single lady," he wrote to his cousin, McKinstry Griffith, in 1839, shortly after he entered the Military Academy. "I wish some of the pretty girls of Bethel were here, just so I might look at them . . ."

But if Grant had any passing interests they all faded when he met Julia. He quickly showed an insatiable taste for her company and rode over to White Haven as often as four times a week. He frequently stayed for supper, then galloped back to the barracks, where he was stationed with the Fourth Infantry. Julia often went part way with him at twilight, and the woodland paths, scented with late spring flowers, had their own beguilement for the young pair falling in love.

Their horsemanship was a genuine bond, and Grant, awkward in the ballroom, here was at his best, leaning forward in the saddle, his fair skin flushed, his blue eyes glittering, his whole being intent on what he was doing. He rode a blooded horse he had brought with him from Ohio, and Julia was quick to appreciate his horsemanship. Her own mount was a Kentucky mare named Missouri Belle. A Negro groom later recalled that she touched her toe to Lieutenant Grant's hand and sprang to her horse's back "like a bird flitting from one tree to another."

When he stayed overnight they raced before breakfast. Julia had intimate knowledge of the countryside. She had ridden through its groves and over its gentle undulations for years. She knew where the tall ferns and the trailing vines were thickest; where streams flashed like silver on their way to the Mississippi; where the rarest plants and the most uncommon flowers might be found. It was fashionable at this time for girls to botanize, and

Julia, in her practical way, took a magnifying glass and needles with her to analyze the flowers on their trips. There were romantic moments, too, although their love for each other was not yet in the open.

Grant carried back to his post flowers that Julia picked in the woods and he read to her from Sir Walter Scott as they sat on the banks of the creek on a languid day late in spring. Although he was not a bookish youth he had been studying the works of Scott, Irving, Marryat and Cooper. At the moment he was reading history, an occasional novel, and was reviewing his West Point course in mathematics. He had worked out a program for himself at the barracks, expecting to become a professor. William Conant Church, head of the mathematics department at West Point, had given him encouragement and he had applied for a post there as assistant professor. He was promised first consideration should a vacancy occur. Had the Mexican War not intervened, Julia might well have been a professor's wife.

Grant had no real love for army life and did not intend to stay in the service. He disliked military routine and had no taste for drills, parades or regimental bands, which were discordant to his tone-deaf ears. Julia soon learned that his pet abomination was music, and particularly military airs. He did not know one tune from another, although when she sang her ballads he hung over the piano, his brooding eyes focused on her with an expression that baffled Emma as she twanged a guitar across the room from the deeply engrossed pair.

The Dents had town and country houses, but White Haven was Julia's special delight, a spacious farmhouse that stands today, skilfully restored and privately owned. The estate originally was more farm than plantation, although Colonel Dent had brought the traditions of the Maryland plantations with him and kept his slaves up to the day of emancipation. The land was actively farmed and here Julia had practical preparation for her early married years as a farmer's wife. They were not rich, according to plantation standards, but they were well-oil until Colonel Dent had severe losses shortly before Julia's marriage. In her girlhood days there was no lack of good living at White Haven, and she was surrounded by the choice possessions that went with the pillared mansions of the old South. This, too, had its effect on her, so that no matter how bare her homes in the early years of her marriage, or how extreme their poverty, she was always able to create a setting that suggested taste and fastidious training.

Although her father had close to a thousand acres and thirty slaves, the girls were schooled in the domestic arts by their thrifty Pennsylvania mother, <u>Ellen Bray Wrenshall Dent.</u> They made jelly and preserves at the big stone fireplace in the basement kitchen. They baked cakes and knew how to brew punch and apple toddy. They watched their mother manage her home resourcefully as they prepared themselves for the inevitable goal of matrimony. When their tasks were finished, they rustled into billowing frocks, made from materials brought from New Orleans. Often they tucked jessamine in their hair or roses in their sashes before settling themselves on the porch to await callers, Julia made most of her own gowns and her small white hands were deft with ribbons and frills. She fashioned many a poke bonnet of straw or silk, and helped her mother to sew for the other children. As she grew older she spent more time at the piano, Her sweet voice, singing Southern ballads and old Scottish airs, could be heard all through the house on summer afternoons and as far away as the turnstile, where visitors reined in their horses when they came to call.

White Haven, stoutly built by William Lindsay Long, had stood since 1808. A one-story cabin, put together with vertical logs in the French style and dating back to the late eighteenth century, was moved into place to enlarge the white frame dwelling as it stands today. The beams supporting the basement still have their bark, and the pegged rafters and stringpieces of the sloping attic are of heart oak. The banister of solid black walnut remains as it was when Julia and Ulysses used the stairs. When the Dents occupied the house, narrow windows gave the family a shifting seasonal vista of trees and rolling meadows.

Julia valued White Haven and its historic echoes. As she rambled over the place with Ulysses she told him that Ann Lucas Hunt, sister of Charles Lucas, who was killed by Thomas Hart Bentem in a duel, was a tenant with her husband Theodore for several years, retreating there before the scandal that enveloped the family at that time. Hunt, a sea captain, built a "deck" at the back of the house, with an oval roof fashioned to resemble shipboard. Benton was a friend of Colonel Dent's, and Julia knew his daughter, the fascinating Jessie, although neither she nor Ulysses would ever learn to like her husband, John C. Fremont.

Steep steps and an irregular path through the locust grove led to the woods, where lindens, elms, maples and oak trees composed a graceful forest, not too dense for the sun to penetrate or shadows to play on the woodland paths. As children they all wandered through the locust grove on their way to the stream, where they waded, fished and picnicked. With so many brothers Julia was an agile tree climber and had shared in many hunts for birds' nests. Nearly a score of whitewashed cabins to the rear of White Haven housed the slaves, and Emma usually went about with a train of colored children in her wake. She had four of them Henrietta, Sue, Ann, and Jeff in tow on the bright afternoon early in 1844 on which Grant first rode into their lives.

Snowballs, orange blossoms, acacia and other shrubs bloomed in season around the house, and Julia spent many hours in the garden, working over her flower beds. She soon discovered that Ulysses shared her love for growing things and both had the amateur botanist's knowledge of the subject. Like horses, it was one of the tastes they shared in common. Altogether, it proved to be an enchanted spring for Julia and Ulysses. When they were not riding they took woodland walks or went fishing along the banks of the Gravois, a stream that rippled over snowy pebbles and divided the Dent property in two. At times the water between the banks would not run a coffee-mill, in the words of Ulysses Grant. Again, there were floods that swamped the nearby land. Julia forded the Gravois hundreds of times on horseback and knew it in all its phases.

By degrees Emma discovered that Julia and her young lieutenant preferred to be alone and at the slightest hint she and the Negro children skipped off to round up grasshoppers for bait. In their absence the young pair soon wandered off along the river bank and into a world of their own. But Ulysses still played with little Emma and teased her. Since he was well used to small sisters of his own, he carried her around on his shoulders and sometimes kissed her in jest. She resented this, considering herself "too big a girl for such things," Emma attended the log schoolhouse half a mile from White Haven and he sometimes whisked her up on his horse and rode her to school. On one occasion he exclaimed teasingly: "They're looking at us, Emmy. They're saying 'Look at Emmy Dent! She's got her sweetheart with her.'"

"More like sister Nell's beau, you mean," she retorted and the lieutenant blushed furiously.

At the time no one was quite sure which sister fascinated him most. He told the story of her indignation years later at a White House dinner and Julia shared in the laughter at Emma's expense. But he quickly reminded his youngest sister-in-law that she knew him best because she had known him longest. They had remained good friends over the years, even though she had stood with her father on the rebel side when war broke out, and her brother John had been a prisoner of war.

Ulysses' earliest memories of Julia involved Emma and her little train of Negro children dogging his footsteps around the Dent property. He took a keen interest in the farm and was more ready to discuss the animals and the crops than he was to argue political issues with the Colonel. He visited the stables and stock pens behind the house and approved the Dent horses. Grant was already a farmer at heart and loved the land. He and Julia found adventure in the woods, too, and one April evening they rode to the rescue of an elderly Negro who had severed an artery in his foot with an axe. With deft movements Grant staunched the blood, cut some clean oak bark with an axe, bruised it to a pulp on top of a stump and applied it to the wound, while Julia held Ulysses' handkerchief in place. The man's vest was ripped apart to hold the bandaging in place. Julia was not a girl to faint at the sight of blood. She comforted his wife and children when they arrived, weeping bitterly. Grant put the old man on his horse and rode him to his cabin.

The lieutenant had to hurry off for a dress parade but Julia and her sisters visited the injured man to see that he was resting comfortably. Grant rode over the following day from Jefferson Barracks with the regimental surgeon. He had brought a new vest for the Negro, and Julia arrived with a basket of invalid fare. She took the two officers home with her, and the surgeon remarked as they had refreshments afterward on the piazza that she should belong to the army she had stood the baptism of blood so well.

Julia's parents soon found that there was no gush about this young officer, an inescapable conclusion where Grant was concerned. The older girls appreciated the temperate way in which he discussed politics with their inflammable father. They approved his "rare common sense" and the "quiet, even tones" in which he spoke, without gestures or affectation. Ulysses' modest bearing made an immediate impression on Mrs. Dent. Emma remembered her mother saying on many different occasions and in several different ways that Grant would be heard from some day. "He has a good deal in him," she said on one occasion. "He will make his mark." But Colonel Dent was less enthusiastic. He was ambitious for Julia and he did not consider Grant a man of substance. He found him a silent fellow who kept his views to himself and failed to spark up on national causes like "Pete" Longstreet, or Robert Hazlitt, another young officer who rode over from the barracks with Grant. "Pete" was a whirlwind, then as later. Grant stood firm and still. He was not articulate on public issues, although mighty currents were then stirring the nation.

He, in turn, found the Colonel a formidable figure. His steel-gray hair stood out in a shock around a beardless, furrowed face. He had a healthy complexion and his eyes glinted fiercely under overshadowing brows. He had abandoned his ruffled shirts and wide beaver hat for the long dark coat, dark trousers and high stock of the era. Grant thoughtfully observed Julia as she waited on her choleric father, who spent the greater part of the day in his rocking chair on the front porch. He smoked a churchwarden pipe and he seemed always to be reading, when he was not mowing down his opponents with dogmatic political utterances. It was understood in the family that he never failed to listen attentively to what his oldest daughter had to say and she acknowledged in her old age that she was "petted and spoiled" to the point where it was generally thought on the plantation that she "ruled papa."

Colonel Dent traced his ancestry to Thomas Dent, who had come from Yorkshire, England, in the middle of the seventeenth century and had settled in Maryland, where he bred sons who held public office and prospered in the new land. From her earliest years Julia had heard tales of soldiering and adventuring on the frontier. Her father had made enough money in fur trading by the time he was twenty to buy the tract of land that he later developed into the White Haven property. Ho named it after an ancestral Dent home.

Although the Colonel seemed formidable to many, Julia took a bland view of his eccentricities and loved him dearly. He was prone to file a lawsuit or start a quarrel, and Dr. William Taussig, a local physician who knew his family well but admittedly did not like him, pictured him as grim and stubborn, "masterful in his ways, of persistent combativeness and, where foiled, inclined to be vindictive." To others he seemed courtly, a man of gifts and strong convictions. He was a Jacksonian Democrat, hostile to the Whigs and bitter about the abolitionists who were beginning to make themselves heard.

Julia inherited her spirit from her peppery father, and her good sense and practical wisdom from her mother, a slender woman with calm gray eyes, who could soothe her husband in his most explosive moments. Grant was charmed by Mrs. Dent, an "elegant woman," both fascinating and affable, in Julia's opinion. She was stately in appearance and sweet in manner, and her friends took note of her equable approach to life's problems. She was handsomer than her daughters and gave careful attention to her princess gowns and snowy caps. She presided with true serenity in a home where babies arrived with regularity and were brought up with a light-handed blend of order and indulgence.

Julia was the fifth of her eight children. The oldest was John, who was born in Pittsburgh in 1816. The others arrived either at White Haven or at the Dent town house in St. Louis. John was followed by George. Then came Fred, the brother who went to West Point and led Grant to Julia's door. By this time he was a huge, good-natured officer, who always hunted in the White Haven woods when he was at home. Louis was the fourth son. Then four daughters were born in succession — Julia Boggs; Ellen Wrenshall, who was always known as Nellie; Mary, who died in childhood; and Emily Marbury, who was more often called Emma. She was the last of the Dent children and was ten years younger than Julia. In the years to come she would record and leave her recollections of their childhood and of Grant's courtship of her sister.

Ulysses was a sturdy boy of four growing up in a small house in Ohio when her four older brothers welcomed Julia into the world on January 26, 1826. The land was silvered with frost and great log fires roared at White Haven on the day of her birth. The Dent home suggested affluence. The Grant cottage, standing close to the tall oaks that yielded bark for the family tan-yard, was austere by comparison. Yet the two young people whose paths now crossed had much in common. Although coming from, different backgrounds, both were born to opinionated fathers and sage, quiet mothers. Both were of vigorous pioneer stock and had soldier ancestors. Both had a hardy childhood.

All of the Dent children in turn attended the log schoolhouse buried in the woods near their home until they were old enough to be sent in to the city. Julia often rode to school on horseback behind her stalwart brother Louis, and he sometimes carried her on his shoulders through the snow. She had little zest for learning but she was popular with the boys and girls who sat on backless benches, stared through the open door on sunny spring days and yearned to skip rope or go fishing.

From her earliest years Julia was generous and warm-hearted, qualities that were noted in her later life and were cherished by Grant in his wife. Her friendly spirit served her well when she became a pupil at the age of ten at a private school in St. Louis run by the Misses Moreau. The academic standards were not exacting. Julia cast a bright beam on them with her own comment: "Being allowed to select my own studies, I devoted myself to history, mythology and the things that I happened to like. I had a sweet little voice and I took both instrumental and vocal lessons," It may be assumed, too, that she had some drilling in English composition. Moreover, like Grant, she had a definite taste for sketching. While he was drawing horses in school she was busy with flowers and water-color landscapes.

Whatever she may have learned during these early years, Julia's later experiences and travels gave rich texture to her life. She developed into a well-informed conversationalist, as ready to express herself as her husband was to show reserve in public. By the time she had reached full maturity she was a shrewd observer of men, but her primary passion all through life was her home. Her husband and children were rarely out of her thoughts. The warm current of life circulating in the Dent household may well have stirred up this depth of family feeling that was to be her most notable characteristic. As a family they were all as demonstrative, affectionate and impulsive as the Grants were silent, reserved and patient

Ulysses soon was aware of another strong influence in Julia's upbringing. Mrs. John J. O'Fallon, Colonel Dent's cousin, loved her as she did her own daughter Carrie. The O'Fallon mansion in St. Louis, where Julia was staying when Grant first arrived at White Haven, was a second home to her. "She was the beautiful angel of my childhood," Julia wrote to young John J. O'Fallon when his mother died in 1898. "So many acts of kindness, so many kind words of hers fill my heart's memory. Do you know your dear mother brought me my beautiful wedding gown; and with such sweet, kind words they still linger with me."

Mrs. O'Fallon injected a good deal of worldly wisdom and a touch of the philanthropic spirit into the life of the growing girl. Her husband was a Kentuckian who had made a fortune in railroads and real estate, which he turned to account in helping to build up St. Louis. He had attended school with Zachary Taylor and, like him, had later fought the Indians. He was a widower when he married Ruth Caroline Schutz the year after Julia's birth. Caroline was a Baltimore belle of twenty-three at the time. With a fortune at her disposal, she soon became noted for her charitable works, as well as for her looks and style, her social grace and goodness of heart.

Julia spent a great deal of time at the O'Fallon home and caught vistas of the larger world as she moved in and out of Caroline's parlors, conscious of the Italian statuary, the imported French furniture, the somber paintings.

In her late adolescence she dreamed by the hour at the lace-curtained bay windows that overlooked the formal garden; or sat straight-backed in a Regency chair by the fireside straining her weak eyes as she read verse by candlelight from limp-leather volumes. Best of all, she had a chance to use the fine new piano owned by Caroline, which was later sent to White Haven for Julia's special enjoyment. These were happy days, although it was soft cushioning for a girl destined to know hardship and deprivation.

Young men flocked to the O'Fallon home, and its hostess, in Paris gowns, with jet and diamonds flashing at her throat and wrists, by degrees introduced Julia to a more cosmopolitan world. She gave Julia dresses, some of them imported, that tended to transform her plain portegee into a fashionable figure. But Julia was always content to get back into her homemade poplins and to settle down to the simpler pleasures of White Haven. In the spring of 1844 she longed for the freedom of the farm. She had finished with school in the previous June and was feeling out of sorts. One of her suitors, a rich young man approved by Mrs. O'Fallon, was becoming urgent in his attentions and she did not care for him. She was not responsive to his smooth ways, his Parma violets and his extravagant compliments. Finally Caroline, with true understanding of her adolescent mood, put Julia and her boxes into the largest O'Fallon equipage and together they drove to White Haven over roads deeply rutted with spring mud.

Julia announced to her mother that she had returned to stay. It was only a matter of days after that until she and Ulysses met. Mrs. Dent already had him in tow, for she was inclined to mother him and treat him as she did her own sons. Grant was far from well at this time. For the six months preceding his graduation he had suffered from an illness then known as "Tyler's grippe," He left West Point weighing only 117 pounds, not an ounce more than he had been when he enrolled, although in the intervening years he had grown six inches and was now five feet eight. The Dents, like the Grants, did not fuss about health, but Julia's mother was alarmed by the young lieutenant's exhausting cough. She urged him to eat well and to take the medicine she prescribed for him.

Bit by bit Julia learned more about him. His brilliant horsemanship at West Point was an old story, told first by Fred, then by Longstreet and other officers who had watched his cavalry maneuvers and high leaps with something approaching awe. It was a profound disappointment to him that he had been appointed to an infantry rather than a cavalry command, where he clearly belonged. Julia was well aware that his special genius lay with horses, and that although most of his academic work was undistinguished, he was also brilliant in mathematics.

Except for this subject, in which he shone without effort, Grant had been lazy and careless in his studies, running hastily through his texts but doing passably well in his recitations, Disliking tactics, drill, parades and ceremonials, he had a way of ignoring petty regulations. His numerous demerits, which affected his class standing, were all for minor infractions. The restrictions on a cadet's life were stifling to a boy who had roamed the countryside at will. Yet there was general agreement among his associates and teachers that he was most dependable, a youth whose common sense and resourcefulness in an emergency could be counted on; who was gentle and considerate of others, and honorable in his dealings.

He graduated twenty-first on a list of thirty-nine, no better and no worse than a great many others who would be heard of during the Civil War. He was president of the Dialectic Society for a brief term but was otherwise so inconspicuous that Rufus Ingalls, a classmate and lifelong friend, commented that no one would ever have picked out this quiet, unassuming cadet as destined for a conspicuous place in history. But during his years at the Academy the rough edges had been smoothed a little and he held himself better than the slouching youth who had arrived in butternut colored jeans, woven in the backwoods, with stout shoes and a rustic air which was quickly dispelled when he mounted a horse and outpointed them all in style. However, he had done such heavy physical work at an early age that his shoulders were always slightly rounded and he bore himself with a forward thrust of the head.

Although he had failed to dance and chat with the belles who, accompanied by their chaperones, had come to the Academy from New York, they had wildly applauded his high jumps in the barn-like riding school at West Point, "Pete" Longstreet was not the only one to consider him the most daring and accomplished horseman at the academy. Half a century later one of his grandsons would see his name posted at the Imperial Riding School in Vienna as the rider of a horse named York, whose record high jump at West Point remained unchallenged for years.

By the time he met Julia, Ulysses had done some traveling and he seemed worldly in experience to her. She liked to hear him talk of his sightseeing In New York; of the forest of masts, the flat-fronted Dutch houses, and the girls in great niched bonnets who strolled along Bowling

Green, He knew Philadelphia, too, and had lingered for five days there to take in the sights while traveling between West Point and Bethel He had made the strange romantic journey over the Allegheny Mountains by stage, canal boat and railroad. He had seen Washington Irving, Martin Van Buren, General Winfield Scott and a "lots of other big bugs" at West Point. He had learned to button up his coat to his chin; to ignore the fact that his pants "set as tight to my skin as the bark to a tree"; to attend the Episcopal Church; and to admire the hills and the dales, the rocks and the trees close to the Hudson — "that beautiful river with its bosom studded with hundreds of snowy sails."

But the world in which Julia moved with such warmth and confidence was new to Ulysses. There were picnics, dances and parties in the Gravois settlement and the Dents lent their support to most of the neighborhood social events. Political figures came to call on Colonel Dent and the big lumbering family coach went rocking over the rough roads in all sorts of weather. There were lighter buggies for the young people. Homes lay far apart and wagons hitched up with several teams went from house to house, picking up the young. Square dances were the rule, except for an occasional schottische or Virginia reel. In summer there were hay rides, corn huskings, apple and pork parties and occasional camp meetings.

Neither Julia nor Emma ever forgot the night on which they ran into a severe thunderstorm on their way home from a Methodist gathering. They had gone in a farm wagon with a bed of hay to sit on and a few straight-backed chairs for their elders. Pete Longstreet was there with Mrs, Betty Porter, a young widow with whom he was flirting while he waited for Louise Garland to grow old enough for marriage. He towered among them all and gave orders to young Bob Hazlitt when the downpour began. Fork lightning danced around the wagon. There were shrieks from bright faces framed in lacy summer bonnets. The efficient young lieutenants decided to set up a tarpaulin that lay in the wagon, but they needed something to sustain it. Hazlitt, tall and lean, was the victim chosen to serve as tent pole. The girls crouched in a ring at his feet, protected from the slashing rain. Grant and Longstreet settled themselves beyond the range of the tarpaulin, impervious to the weather and happily unconscious of what the future held for them.

Julia always threw herself heart and soul into the camp meetings, an instinct inherited from her grandfather, John Wrenshall, who was one of the English nonconformist preachers who took to the woods and fields to preach and finally fled the country to get away from religious intolerance. He settled in Philadelphia in 1794, and eventually founded an importing business in Pittsburgh, trading in ginseng, tea, silks and other Oriental wares. He helped to establish Methodism in Pittsburgh and was often host to Bishop Francis Asbury, who ordained him as the first Methodist minister west of the Ohio.

Grandfather Wrenshall was solemn and exhortatory, but Julia gathered from her mother that he was also a fine musician and a kind father. He died five years before Julia was born, so that she heard only echoes of his life, but his principles were handed down in the family and they had their effect on her own religious life. Impromptu prayers and Wesleyan. hymns became a familiar tradition to Julia in her early years, although her mother was never a zealot and their home was worldly compared with Grant's, where fiddling and dancing were considered fleshly evils. Nevertheless, Julia was devout and a churchgoer all her life. She was never to lose her early interest in the evangelical tradition, and she was apt to prod Ulysses into churchgoing if he showed reluctance, as he sometimes did. But he always backed her up on church attendance for the children, and he had the utmost respect for his wife's deep-rooted religious feeling.

In addition to all their country pleasures Julia attended the more sophisticated dances in St. Louis homes and at Jefferson Barracks. She danced as expertly as she rode, but she soon discovered that although Ulysses presented himself regularly as her escort, she had to dance with other partners. Neither then nor later did he walk out on a dance floor without embarrassment All the young officers knew and liked Julia Dent but she was constantly teased about Grant. On one occasion when she went to a ball with another officer, Lieutenant Charles Hoskins walked up to her and remarked:

"Miss Julia, where is that little man with the large epaulets?"

It was true that the epaulets seemed enormous on his slim shoulders. Betty Porter in particular teased good-natured Julia about them and General Longstreet liked to tell this story in his later years, commenting at the same time on the tenacity with which she had clung to her young lieutenant and eventually married him.

Grant found it astonishingly easy to talk to Julia. She was not only interested in what he had to say but she had authentic understanding of the military tradition. Through Fred and his friends she knew the terminology of the army. She had often ridden to the whitewashed buildings of

Jefferson Barracks, poised high on a hill and bounded by white fences. Spiked pines ran like a ridge against the skyline in the background. She was familiar with the miles of bridle paths that threaded field and woodland. She knew that the officers had gardens of their own and that in their spare time they played cards, lounged on the broad piazza and discussed their hopes for the future. Most of them at that time were yearning over various belles in St. Louis.

Colonel Stephen W. Kearny, the commandant, gave the officers latitude for social diversion, provided they were punctual for rollcalls and drills. They were much sought after by hostesses with marriageable daughters. But Captain Robert C. Buchanan, president of the mess, was insistent on form and he pounced on Grant for the sort of infraction that had irritated Ulysses at West Point. He noticed the youth's repeated failure to show up for dinner on time, because of his frequent rides to White Haven. It was customary to fine a cadet a bottle of wine for being late. When this happened repeatedly, Captain Buchanan called Grant to account. Usually quiet and self-effacing, the lieutenant spoke up:

"Mr. President, I have been fined three bottles of wine within the last ten days, and if I am fined again I shall be obliged to repudiate."

"Mr. Grant, young people should be seen and not heard," said Buchanan crushingly.

This incident stirred up antagonism that was to have serious bearing on the lieutenant's future when he came under Buchanan's command for the second time. But at this point Grant, Longstreet, Hazlitt and most of the other young officers were swept away from ballroom and barracks to start down the long road that would end in the Civil War and bring them together again, some fighting for the North, others for the South. In May their regiment was ordered South, as war with Mexico threatened. This was not surprising news, since all through their pleasures and social gatherings the shadow of war had hung over the young officers. The political echoes coming from Washington pointed plainly in one direction.

Colonel Dent talked of little else. He backed annexation, which was regarded as an entering wedge for the extension of slavery. Grant had been giving thought to the political issues that burned hot and strong in the early 1840s and he was opposed to annexation. When President Polk finally dropped the boom by asking Congress to declare war on Mexico, Zachary Taylor and his forces were already skirmishing in the disputed territory between Texas and Mexico.

Ulysses had left for a twenty-day leave to visit his home in Bethel when his regiment received orders to move South. Knowing that war was close at hand, he had decided to bid his parents good-by. A message sent after him did not reach him. No sooner had he left, however, than he began to yearn for Julia. He wakened to the fact that he was deeply in love and that she was the girl he must marry. "I now discovered that I was exceedingly anxious to get back to Jefferson Barracks, and I understood the reason without explanation from any one," he confessed in his Memoirs. The thought of going off to war without declaring himself had become unbearable.

His regiment had already gone up the Red River when he returned. He reported for duty to Lieutenant Richard S. Ewell at Jefferson Barracks and received the order to join his unit. But first he begged for a few days more of leave, since nothing must stop him now from going to White Haven to plead his case with Julia. Ewell was understanding and perhaps guessed the reason. Later he would fight on the Confederate side but to Grant he would always have special significance a man "who proved himself a gallant and efficient officer in two wars both in my estimation unholy."

Grant had now known Julia for three months and in his Memoirs he summed up the dawn of their mutual love in the clear, unemotional prose with which he wrote of battles and world events:

In February she returned to her country home, After that I do not know but my visits became more frequent; they certainly did become more enjoyable. We would often take walks or go on horseback to visit the neighbors, until I became quite well acquainted in that vicinity. Sometimes one of the brothers would accompany us, sometimes one of the younger sisters. If the 4th Infantry had remained at Jefferson Barracks it is possible, even probable, that this life might have continued for some years without my finding out that there was anything serious the matter with me; but in the following May a circumstance occurred which developed my sentiment so palpably that there was no mistaking it.

The "circumstance" in question was the departure of his regiment for the South. Julia always considered his comments a flat approach to their love, and in an interview given shortly before her death she mentioned in a jesting vein that she did not think the General had done the subject justice in his book. Characteristically, she recalled their courtship as the distilled essence of romance, and mentioned the fact that her own first Impression of Ulysses was of a "darling little lieutenant." He bore only slight resemblance in 1844 to the stalwart bearded soldier who would dominate her life and impress himself on the pages of American history.

CHAPTER II: A PLANK BRIDGE PROPOSAL

THE MISSISSIPPI was on the rampage in 1844. It was a year of floods and all the surrounding streams were engorged. When Grant rode over from Jefferson Barracks to White Haven to propose to Julia he found desolation and high water along his course. The quiet little Gravois rolled furiously between Its banks. Uprooted trees and the splinters of plank bridges bounced on the waters that roared through the valley toward the Mississippi. Grant knew the Gravois well He had often forded it on sunny days when the water was low. But now, in Emma's words, "the rains had been drenching the earth like a deluge for several days and the creeks were swollen and raging." He paused at the bank to reconnoiter, then decided to go ahead. His determination to propose to Julia without delay controlled his actions. Years later he recalled this decision in a statement that summed up much of his life history: "One of my superstitions had always been when I started to go anywhere, or to do anything, not to turn back, or stop until the thing intended was accomplished ... So I struck into the stream . . ."

When he made the plunge he was quickly submerged. His horse automatically began to swim and Grant felt himself being sucked away by the current. He swam, too, hanging on to the horse at the same time and eventually they reached the opposite bank in safety. When he arrived at White Haven he was soaked to the skin, plastered with mud and scarcely looked like a smart young West Pointer coming to propose to his girl.

Julia had not expected him. She was busy in the garden, stiffening her battered flowers with sticks, when she saw him ride up to the turnstile on his dripping horse. She ran toward him with a sympathetic greeting. Emma recalled his clothes "flopping about him like wet rags." They all laughed hilariously at the sight but the lieutenant took it in good part and he laughed, too. Julia turned him over to her brother John, who gave him dry garments that were absurdly large for him.

It took a second episode with the high waters to give him his chance to propose to Julia. At the time of his return, the Dent family were preparing to attend a neighborhood wedding, and they invited him to go with them. Alert for an opportunity to be alone with Julia, he asked John if he might drive her in the buggy in exchange for his horse. Julia never forgot what followed, and in 1890, when she was sixty-four, she told the story in her own words:

We had to cross a little bridge that spanned a ravine, and, when we reached it, I was surprised and a little concerned to find the gulch swollen, a most unusual thing, the water reaching to the bridge. I noticed, too, that Lieutenant Grant was very quiet, and that and the high water bothered me. I asked several times if he thought the water dangerous to breast, and told him I would go back rather than take any risk. He assured me, in his brief way, that it was perfectly safe, and in my heart I relied upon him. Just as we reached the old bridge I said, "Now, if anything happens, remember I shall cling to you, no matter what you say to the contrary." He simply said "All right" and we were over the planks in less than a minute. Then his mood changed, he became more social, and in asking me to be his wife, used my threat as a theme . . .

There seems to be little doubt that Julia literally threw herself into the arms of a shy young man who was all too eager to have her there. But coquetry was not needed. Both were deeply in love, and the bashful lieutenant had found the opening wedge in Julia's own words, which were prophetic. For forty years she would both cling to him and rely on him, through discouraging days and moments of triumph.

Emma left her comment on the day's event: "Grant was often most slow and hesitant in his efforts to come to a decision, but when that decision was once made it was irrevocable and acted upon immediately," she observed. But this significant moment in their lives received the barest mention in Grant's Memoirs and carried the flat note of suppressed emotion to which his wife objected:

Before I returned I mustered up courage to make known, in the most awkward manner imaginable, the discovery I had made on learning that the 4th Infantry had been ordered away from Jefferson Barracks. The young lady afterwards admitted that she too, although until then she had never looked upon me other than as a visitor whose company was agreeable to her, had experienced a depression of spirits she could not account for when the regiment left. Before separating it was definitely understood that at a convenient time we would join our fortunes, and not let the removal of a regiment trouble us.

Both sat through the midday family dinner in a daze and afterward they went to the garden, to work over the battered flowers and to continue discussion of their plans. Grant sat on a garden stool nearby, thoughtfully watching Julia's delicate fingers weaving their way through twisted stalks, separating tangled blooms. In his slow persistent way he soon returned to the question of marriage. He had told her at the bridge that he hoped they might be married without delay. But Julia now held out for a long engagement, knowing that her father would raise objections. They debated the matter with great intensity and finally her will prevailed. She promised to prepare her father, and Ulysses said he would write to Colonel Dent from camp, stating his case. If need be, he would resign from the army in order to marry Julia.

She tried to sound casual when she said good-by, for only her sisters knew of the momentous thing that had happened to her. But before she had time to pave the way, Grant's letter arrived and Colonel Dent argued hotly with his daughter.

"You are too young and the boy is too poor," he told her. "He hasn't anything to give you."

Julia flashed back at him with spirit: "I am poor, too, and haven't anything to give him."

Colonel Dent was no more anxious than Zachary Taylor to see his daughter marry a soldier and go off to desolate army posts. He thought her too delicate for the rigors and uncertainties of that sort of life. Sarah Knox Taylor's death from typhoid in 1835, three months after she married Jefferson Davis against her father's wishes, was a fresh memory. Moreover, Colonel Dent could see no future for Julia married to a young lieutenant who made less than a thousand dollars a year. Nor did he consider Grant at all outstanding among the young men who called at his home. Julia had wealthy beaux in St. Louis, particularly one who was all too anxious to marry her. He envisioned his favorite daughter comfortably settled within reach of White Haven.

With this shadow now between them he growled at Julia, who responded with spirit and bided her time. But her mother was loyal and devoted to Grant. She read his character in those early days more truly than anyone else, except Julia. Meanwhile, Ulysses, nursing his secret and dwelling with satisfaction on the future that stretched ahead of him, wrote with gentle implication to Mrs. G. B. Bailey, of Georgetown, Ohio, where he had grown up, that on his "forty days journey in the wilderness" one incident had occurred that was "laughable, curious, important, surprising." She must not guess at it, he warned her, for she would be wrong, yet he plainly stated that he had passed four or five good days with friends near St. Louis. It was clear that Grant could scarcely refrain from sharing his secret with Mrs. Bailey, who loved him as she did her own son. She had kissed him warmly when he left for West Point, which was more than his own mother had done. Caresses were not squandered in the Grant home, and it must have amazed Ulysses to observe the affectionate ways of the Dents. However, it never occurred to him that they could defy Colonel Dent on the subject of marriage. Grant recognized him as a formidable figure in Julia's life.

But it took four years — from May 1844 to August 1848 — to put through their plan and there were times when even the faithful Julia felt that Ulysses would be lost to her forever. He was stationed first at Camp Salubrity near Natchitoches in Louisiana, He wrote impersonal letters that she could show to the other members of her family and he waited anxiously for some word from Colonel Dent, but none came. It was a trying period for Julia, although life had taken on new meaning for her, and she could look with indifference at the suave young men who moved in and out of Caroline O'Fallon's parlors. She settled down to sew linen sheets and she started a quilt that Ulysses would always tease her about, for it went with them everywhere and never was finished. Shortly before his death he jested about this in a letter to Nellie. There were many family jokes of this kind between the Grants, particularly about Julia's unpunctuality and her tendency to procrastinate.

Ulysses, who had ignored the more fleshly pursuits at West Point, was no less austere at camp. He concentrated on the thought of Julia and waited anxiously for her letters. She was never as zealous a correspondent as he, but she followed the details of his daily life with close attention. She knew that Ulysses had told no one of his love for her. She kept quiet herself, because of her father's disapproval, but she discussed him freely with her sisters as they sewed on ribbons and stitched hems.

Grant had a foretaste of war's discomforts that summer. Camp Salubrity stood on a high pine ridge. There were crystal springs in the valley below and the air was dry and invigorating. He lived in a small tent, slept on a plank bed and used his trunk and bed for chairs. He was plagued by red bugs, ticks, ants, and occasional scorpions. The swamps crawled with alligators. But he felt remarkably well in the piney air. He developed an appetite and ate ravenously at the mess tent in the woods. His cough left him at last. He put on weight and lost his morbid fear of consumption. Two of his uncles had died of it. A brother and sister both would develop the disease. But camp life hardened and strengthened Grant.

Julia heard next about Fort Jessup, midway between the Red River and the Sabine, and close to the Texas line, where Zachary Taylor's troops guarded the frontier. Grant would gallop over from Camp Salubrity on a frisky horse to take part in the camp sports. He rode with Longstreet, Rufus Ingalls and other officers he had known at West Point. They played brag and attended the five-day races. Grant bet low and usually lost. The Red River planters observed his skill with horses and invited him to their homes, to meet their wives and daughters. However, he did not share their love for hunting. Woodcock and water fowl abounded but he was a poor shot and recoiled from killing animals.

The Presidential election was bitterly fought and the Polk administration began with Texas being admitted as a slave state. The soldiers viewed this move according to their regional backgrounds and political faith. Grant made no secret of the fact that he deplored it. To his last days he regarded the Mexican War as "one of the most unjust ever waged by a stronger against a weaker nation" and he always felt that the Civil War was an outgrowth of the earlier conflict. "Nations, like individuals, are punished for their indiscretions," he commented. "We got our punishment in the most sanguinary and expensive war of modern times."

Marching orders did not come immediately after the annexation bill was signed and Grant obtained a brief leave of absence to visit White Haven. This time he meant to tackle Colonel Dent, who had never responded to his letter. He cherished the hope that he might make Julia his bride in the five days' leave allowed him. Failing that, he hoped to have her father's full approval when he left for Mexico. The longer he was away from her the more certain he was that he could not exist without her.

On a May morning in 1845 he rode up to the familiar turnstile and Julia never forgot how he looked in his new uniform. Camp life had bronzed and hardened him. He was no longer the doll-like pink and white lieutenant they had so unrealistically thought him. He looked older and tougher and more seasoned. By chance Colonel Dent was leaving for Washington that day, and when Grant rode up they were all on the front porch kissing him and stuffing his pockets with notes on things they wished him to buy in the capital.

Grant looked so purposeful that Mrs. Dent quietly led him indoors to the parlor and left him there with her husband. The young people stayed on the porch and Emma posted herself at the parlor shutters to watch what happened next. She listened to every word, leaving a record of the interview.

"The determined young soldier stood straight before my father and looked him in the eye," Emma reported, "'Mr. Dent,' he said, 'I want to marry your daughter, Miss Julia.'

"For a minute the older man did not answer but sat soberly thinking. The soldier boy awaited his answer, unmoved.

"'Mr. Grant,' my father spoke at last, 'if it were Nelly you wanted, now, I'd say Yes.'

"'But I don't want Nelly,' said the soldier bluntly. 'I want Julia.'

"'Oh, you do, do you? Well, then I s'pose it'll have to be Julia.'"

Emma was convinced from the start that her strong-willed sister would have her way. "When Julia wanted a thing of my father she usually got it," she commented. But Julia chose to believe that the balancing factor was her father's haste to get off to Washington. There was no time for argument, and he dearly loved to battle a point. However, the matter was settled with qualifications. The Colonel would not hear of an immediate marriage, but he promised to consider Grant's plea and to give him his answer by letter. The young pair had to be content with this. Emma noticed with surprise that her father was quite good-humored after his talk with Grant. She concluded that the "lieutenant's frankness had pleased him and had, I think, won him over in spite of himself."

Julia had some blissful hours with Ulysses, feeling that an important point had been gained, but in the background was the nagging thought that he might soon be going into battle. The woods and fields were fragrant with May blossoms as they rode under arching branches or galloped over open meadows. The silent Grant grew eloquent in Julia's presence and the hours sped on toward their parting. In the years to come she would often see him off to battle, but this was the first, and perhaps the most painful, of their partings. He was headed now into war, a new experience for both.

The months that followed were anxious ones for Julia. "My soldier lover was in and about Mexico for four years, including the war," she remarked reminiscently in 1890. "Every mail brought me a letter. Every one of them full of sweet nothings, love and war and now and then some pressed leaves and flowers. Some were written on drumheads captured from the Mexicans and others on sheets of foolscap, folded and sealed with red wafers. I read each one every day until the next one came."

Emma took a more realistic view of this correspondence. Perhaps Julia did not read the personal bits to her family but her little sister noted that the letters "generally had more to say about the movements of the army than of himself ... he was never a great hand to talk about himself, nor could he write about himself, either."

Things were quiet at White Haven after the young officers left for Mexico. There were no more balls at the Arsenal or at Jefferson Barracks, and the girls turned to civilian pleasures. St. Louis, incorporated in 1809, was growing fast and its customs were well established by 1845. The population was so mixed that in the year of Julia's graduation the closing school exercises throughout the city were conducted in six different languages. There were great parades on May Day, the Fourth of July, Washington's Birthday, and January 8, the anniversary of the Battle of New Orleans. St. Patrick's Day brought forth the Negro draymen with bands playing and bunting decorating horses and wagons. The most exuberant of all was the Volunteer Firemen's Parade, manned by the bankers, merchants, doctors, lawyers and other local dignitaries. Engines and firemen were smothered in flowers and the day wound up with banquets and balls.

The Dents entered enthusiastically into the life of the growing city. Their town house was at Fourth and Cerre Streets, close to the Sacred Heart Convent and the French Market. It was a narrow building where they all felt cramped after the freedom of White Haven, but Colonel Dent considered his city home imperative for the education of his children and at times they liked to get away from the winter rigors of life along the Gravois Road. Although the mansions of nearby Chouteau Avenue represented the wealth of a city where large fortunes had been amassed by fur traders, steamboat men, explorers and pioneers of various kinds, the Dent city home suggested the simplicity of village life. A white church with a modest spire stood nearby. Wagons drawn by eight oxen obstructed light buggies and carriages. Shade trees lined the streets. Porticoed homes stood in their own grounds, surrounded by lawns and gardens, and each man knew his neighbor. The young girls liked to parade in their new clothes along Fourth, Main, Olive and Market Streets, stopping to chat in music and confectionery shops.

The Dents usually avoided the nearby French village of Carondelet, with its gabled cottages and walled gardens. At the time of his marriage the Colonel had acquired possession of an old Spanish claim which he tried to enforce against the residents of this picturesque village that later became part of St. Louis. He lost his suit and never forgave the villagers. Nor did they warm to him. This situation was the basis of many of his feuds. But Julia had friends in Carondelet, to whom she waved in passing.

The girls went in groups to teas and bazaars in the churches. They shared in the fads and novelties of the day, and took in such sights as Tom Thumb when he appeared at the Jones Museum of Arts, Sciences and Curiosities. The Ohio Fat Girl went on view at Concert Hall and the Scottish Giant and Giantess were an awesome pair. The young people viewed dioramas and shared in the chatter about James P. Espey, the "Storm King" who laid the foundation for weather forecasting. Phrenology was in fashion and animal magnetism and hypnotism were much discussed. From this time on, Julia showed interest in mind reading and "second sight." She was much given to premonitions in the war days and in later years, not an uncommon trend in her generation.

St. Louis had races, circuses and menageries with performing lions in the 1840s, but Julia went most often to the Horticultural Gardens, to study the tropical birds hanging in green cages, and the exotic trees from the tropics. In winter there was skating on the river but, above all, the young set loved the illuminations and turned out to admire the houses, streets, stores and steamboats when they were strung with starry lights and transparencies. It was no novelty to Julia to see bands of Indians doing their chants and dances in the streets at this time. They camped on the banks of Chouteau Lake and were a reminder to the inhabitants that they still were close to the frontier. The Indians gave demonstrations of arrow-throwing in exchange for the vivid paints they obtained from local stores. On summer Sundays, Chouteau Lake was dotted with sail boats and canoes, and its shores were livened by picnic parties, with little girls in pantalettes, and small boys in long trousers, throwing balls and rolling hoops.

Caroline's home was the focus of many interests and, inevitably, Julia was caught in the stream of civic events. She was nurtured in an atmosphere where the fresh breath of the frontier blew across the culture of older civilizations. Celebrities came and went Henry Clay, Daniel Webster, Martin Van Buren, Lafayette, Charles Dickens. Her father always made the girls turn out to hear the orators. Fashionably dressed, with her hair sleeked down to a netted chignon, Julia attended oratorical and dramatic soirees at Lyceum Hall, and concerts and parties at the newly opened Planters House. With its strong German background the city was music-conscious from its beginnings, and part of her education was this inflow of good music in her early years.

With her lover far away Julia went through the usual round of New Year festivities in 1846. She was now twenty and could share in adult entertainment. The holiday was more fervently celebrated in St. Louis than Christmas. On New Year's Eve Julia attended a ball in a handsome dress given her by Caroline O'Fallon. Sipping broth between the numbers in the fashion of the day, she listened dreamily to compliments but with her thoughts far off. On the following day there were illuminations, eggnog parties and suppers, with great venison roasts and spun-sugar confections on display. The visiting from house to house was formidable. With three girls in the Dent home, a stream of young men came calling from nine in the morning until midnight. Nellie was now the family belle, being courted by a succession of youths. In her letters to Ulysses Julia passed on all such family chitchat and he took note of it in his replies. He was never to lose his interest in Julia's younger sisters. They were always part of the family picture to him.

Mrs. Mary Robinson, the intelligent Negro maid who spent most of her life in the service of the Dent and Grant families, watched hopefully for some sign of friendliness on the part of Colonel Dent toward the absent lieutenant. "Auntie Robinson" was always on Grant's side in family disputes. She had watched him from his first visit to White Haven, and thought him an "exceedingly fine looking young man."

"Old man Dent was opposed to him, when he found he was courting his daughter and did everything he could to prevent the match but Mrs. Dent took a great fancy to Grant and encouraged him in his venture," Mary recalled, echoing Emma's observations. "Mrs. Dent used to say to me, 'I like that young man. There is something noble in him. His air and the expression of his face convince me that he has a noble heart, and that he will be a great man some day.'"

"Auntie Robinson" understood the nagging anxiety that beset the girl when her father failed to write to the young lieutenant as he had promised, and when he scowled every time Grant's name was mentioned. But Julia held her ground. She was maturing rapidly under the pressure of events. She was now putting together things for her married home and was studying the way in which her mother ran the household. She shopped for her in the French Market and learned to economize. Soon her knowledge of the absent soldier was enlarging through his letters. They were soldierly, detailed and precise, except when he injected the personal note and wrote of his longing for her. His opinions emerged clearly in this correspondence. He felt sorry he had enlisted. He was not enamored of war. He did not believe in the conquest of Mexico.

Grant had admired General Winfield Scott since his West Point days, but now he had a new hero in Zachary Taylor. From Camp Salubrity he had moved to Corpus Christi, where he had ample opportunity to study the rough-hewn warrior of the frontier. Taylor gave him another conception of what makes a soldier besides fuss and feathers. Although he considered Scott one of the "immortals" as a commander and a master strategist, he viewed Taylor as one who had little concern with army maneuvers or the blueprints of battle, but was a true soldier in every sense of the word and a man to follow.

Julia read eagerly of the adobe houses of Corpus Christi and the encampment on a green slope covered with mesquite where Ulysses passed that winter away from her. Game abounded and the officers fished and hunted. Grant saw deer, mustang and antelope, and his friends came in laden down with ducks, snipe and turkeys. In spite of his reluctance to use a gun, he at last went out among the pecan trees, planning to shoot wild turkeys. Instead, he stood and watched their flight with fascination, returning to camp convinced that he would never be a sportsman.

In March, just as the snow began to melt at White Haven, Grant started for the Rio Grande and soon was encamped in a field of green corn within range of the guns of Matamoros. On the second anniversary of his meeting with Julia, he was on his way to Point Isabel. On May 8 he was involved in the battle of Palo Alto, followed by a second engagement at Resaca de la Palma.

Immediately after these two battles he settled down to write to Julia. His desk was a captured Mexican drumhead. He had little to say of his own part in the fighting, although a shell had come close to ending his career. "There is no great sport in having bullets flying about one in every direction but I find they have less horror when among them than when in anticipation," he wrote. Then, with a switch to the personal note, he added: "Now that the war has commenced with such vengeance, I am in hopes, my dear Julia, that we will soon be able to end it. In the thickest of it I thought of Julia. How much I should love to see you now to tell you all that happened . . . When we have another engagement, if we do have another at all, I will write again; that is if I am not one of the victims. Give my love to all at White Haven and do write soon my dear Julia."

Back in St. Louis, she had read with breathless interest of the first engagement long before Ulysses' letter reached her. The war was on in earnest now and the papers were filled with praise for the warriors who had fought the battles of Palo Alto and Resaca de la Palma. On May 12 Julia sat down and wrote what Grant considered a "sweet letter" when it reached him early in June. She told him how much she wished that they had been married before he left. She said she would willingly share his tent, or his prison — should he be taken prisoner. She wrote that she often saw him in her dreams.

Grant had longed to hear from her. He had received only four letters in six weeks, which he conceded was better than she had done in the past. He reproached her gently in an affectionate and revealing letter written from Matamoros on June 5, 1846. She would scarcely know him now, he wrote, for the climate had changed his appearance, if not his love for her. He felt equally sure that her emotions had not changed, for his Julia wrote "such sweet letters when she does write."

Actually, she was never as good a correspondent as Grant, who wrote affectionately to all members of his family over the years. Even at this age her eyes troubled her considerably. She had a mild case of strabismus, a defect common enough in the early nineteenth century. She could not sew for any length of time. It tired her to do much reading, and she did not like to write when she could avoid it. All through their married life the General tried to save her eyes when he could, reading to her, writing letters that normally would fall to her, and helping her in sundry small ways. It was a quiet and sympathetic acceptance of a handicap to which they did not often refer; nor did it disturb her seriously until Ulysses became a famous General and she was exposed to public scrutiny. Then she began to worry about her squint, and to pose self-consciously in profile for her portraits. But as yet she gave little thought to the matter

In his letter of June 5 Ulysses referred directly to the situation with her father and urged her to let him know when next she wrote if "your Pa ever says anything about our engagement and if you think he will make any farther objections." He felt from what Colonel Dent had said to him the previous spring that he would not, but "he has not written to me as he said he would do." However, he hoped that before many months went by he would be able to talk over this matter without the use of paper. General

Taylor planned a march on Monterey, "a beautiful little city just at the foot of the mountains, and about three hundred miles from this place." That taken, they would have in their possession all the Mexican territory east of the mountains and "it is to be presumed Mexico will then soon come to terms," Ulysses wrote optimistically.

Both had been considering the possibility of her joining him in Mexico and Julia had ardently promised to go anywhere with him. Grant now responded warmly: "How much I do want to see you again, but I know you would not recognize me ... Julia if the 4th Infy. should be stationed permanently in the conquered part of Mexico would you be willing to come here or would you want me to resign? I think it probable though that I shall resign as soon as this war is over and make Galena my home. My father is very anxious to have me do so."

He was still unhurt and free, he assured her. She need have no fear for his welfare, since the greatest danger was from exposure to rain, sun and dew in a very warm climate. He was never sick and had become quite acclimated to the south.

Julia treasured this letter. It was more personal than most of those that reached her from Mexico. She began to think about living there, and she picked up every scrap of information she could about the country. Some of her friends also were getting letters from their beaux, and they all maintained a lively exchange of news. They studied maps and read about Mexican customs, The papers blazed with war news. The excitement in St. Louis, as in other parts of the country, was intense.

By September 6, writing from Ponti Agrudo, within six days' march of Monterey, Grant's impatience to see Julia again was self-evident in his letter:

Julia aren't you getting tired of hearing of war, war, war? I am truly tired of it. Here it is now five months that we have been at war and as yet but two battles. I do wish this would close. If we have to fight I would like to do it all at once and then make friends.

It is now about two years that we have been engaged Julia and in all that time I have seen you but once. I know though you have not changed and when I go back I will see the same Julia I did more than two years ago. I know I shall never be willing to leave Gravois again until Julia is mine forever! How much I regret that we were not united when I visited you more than a year ago. But your Pa would not have heard of anything of the kind at that time. I hope he will make no objections now! Write to me very often Julia. You know how happy I am to read your letters.

His own political theories were developing strongly at this time and the more he saw of the Mexican scene the more persuaded he was that the war was wrong. But he quietly took note of some of the fine points of soldiering and developed a strong allegiance to Zachary Taylor. By September they were camped near Monterey, in the foothills of the Sierra Madre. The turrets and fortifications interested him less than the people, the vegetation, the brilliant landscape and the birds. For years to come Julia and their children would hear about the towering mountains, the tinted cataracts, and the gorgeous sunsets that flooded the Mexican skies. It was a brightly painted canvas, from the brilliant plumage of a bird flashing through tall palms, to the lively concourse of people in the market place, or the cathedral chimes at Monterey,

The march to Perote and then to Puebla through a mountain pass would linger in Ulysses' memory forever and he wrote to his parents, as well as to Julia, with a slightly poetic touch at times. He mentioned the hillsides "covered with tall palms whose waving leaves . . . toss to and fro in the wind like plumes in a helmet, their deep green glistening in the sunshine or glittering in the moonbeams in the most beautiful way." However, he thought that the Mexican birds, with superlative plumage, "beat ours in show but do not equal them in harmony."

Julia at this time was reading in the papers of another aspect of life at Monterey. There was much talk of the fandangos and the beautiful senoritas who entertained the American officers. Nellie and Ben Farrar, a current beau, sat on the porch and chattered about the influences to which the absent officers were exposed. Julia was well aware that Ulysses might take delight in the tropical birds but she knew that a fandango would mean little to a man so resistant to the dance. She did not worry unduly about the charms of the Mexican girls, but she was under heavy pressure from her father. He had done some subtle campaigning against Grant, making full use of his own financial difficulties, which had become acute at this time through the loss of an old lawsuit. He was anxious for Julia to marry well and he felt she was ignoring some excellent prospects while she waited interminably for Grant. Torn with anxiety because of her old loyalty to her father, Julia was actually driven into writing to Ulysses, offering to release him.

On the day after Monterey was taken Grant met an old Georgetown friend, serving as a captain with the Ohio volunteers, and they discussed their forthcoming marriages. Grant told him he was engaged to Julia Dent of St. Louis. Then, incomprehensibly for one so reserved, he revealed that she had offered to give him up because of her father's financial embarrassment. He said that of course he had no intention of doing anything of the sort. The two friends promised to name their sons after each other, and the Ohio soldier's boy, who later went to West Point, was baptized Ulysses Grant White.

But Monterey brought much sadness to Grant, and some of Julia's closest friends died or were wounded in this engagement. Tall Bob Hazlitt, who had served as tent pole on their wagon ride, bled to death while trying to save the life of his wounded captain. Thomas L. Hamer, the Congressman who had backed Ulysses for West Point, died of dysentery. Grant nursed him at the end and wrote home that his death was a loss "which no words can express."

Buena Vista in February 1847 brought lasting fame to Zachary Taylor, but by this time Grant had come under the command of General Scott. When marching orders arrived in January he believed that he might be on his way back to St. Louis. Instead, he found himself on the Rio Grande, mustering supplies for the expedition General Scott planned against Vera Cruz. In the months that followed, his letters to Julia were few and far between as he took part in the siege of Vera Cruz, the battle of Cerro Gordo, the capture of San Antonio, the battles of Churuibusco and Moliao del Rey, the storming of Chapultepec, and the final capture of the City of Mexico.

Molino del Rey, where Fred Dent was wounded, was a long stone mill stocked with grain and used for defensive purposes at the base of Grasshoppers Hill, when Chapultepec was under assault. Grant was there to aid him. His letter home was the first reassurance the Dents had about Fred's condition. The musket ball hit Fred in the thigh as he charged a gun near the gateway. At the same time Captain Robert Anderson, whom Grant would hear of again at Fort Sumter, was hit with a ball in the shoulder. Grant was one of the first soldiers to enter the mill, not knowing that Julia's brother had already been wounded. He found Fred stretched close to a stone wall. Although he was bleeding freely Ulysses saw that his injury was not serious. He heaved him up and laid him on the flat top of the wall, thinking he would be spotted quickly when medical aid arrived. Then he went on his way. But Fred fell off the wall and was badly bruised. In later years he sometimes jested with Grant about this incident, saying that his fall had done more damage than the shell that hit him. But he recovered quickly and was promoted to a brevet captaincy.

It was October 25, 1847, before Grant finished a letter to Julia that he had begun after the army entered Mexico City a month earlier. His yearning to see her was plainly expressed. He found the idea of staying longer in Mexico insupportable. But Julia alone could solve the problem of his discontent. "Just think of the three long years that have passed since we met," he wrote. "If you were here and I in the United States my anxiety would be just as great to come to Mexico as it now is to get out." Exposure to weather and the tropical sun had added ten years to his age and "at this rate I will soon be old."

Back in St. Louis, Julia heard tales of her fiance's skill as a quartermaster. As the first of the officers returned she listened to graphic accounts of his work, and his insistence on getting into battles, even when he did not belong among the fighters. Longstreet observed that on horseback in Mexico "he was a very centaur." In no other manner could an animal unhorse him but by lying down and rolling over. "You could not keep Grant out of battle," he added. "He was as unconcerned as if he were weathering a hail storm instead of a storm of bullets. ... He was always cool, swift and unhurried. ... So remarkable was his bravery that mention was made of it in the official reports, and I heard his colonel say: 'There goes a man of fire.'"

But the two important points to Julia were the knowledge that he had come through the war unscathed, and that her father spoke more kindly of him since the incident with Fred. Moreover, lie had been mentioned in dispatches, and would return home a brevet captain. She was overjoyed when another letter reached her, written on January 9, 1848, anticipating peace within a few months' time. "I hope it may be so for it is scarcely supportable for me to be separated from you so long my Dearest Julia," he wrote.

He had tried for a leave of absence but could not break through the red tape. He had no hope of getting sick leave, since he had not been ill a day during the campaigning. Fred, who had recovered from his wound, was in the same brigade with him and he saw him every day. But now that the fighting was over Grant was intensely bored and longed for Julia to be with him, even for a single day.

Within a month after he wrote this letter the Treaty of Guadalupe Hidalgo brought the war to an end. But it was July before Grant had his last impression of the angelus bells; the cupolas gleaming in the dying sun; the distant ridge of hyacinth-tinted mountains; the volcanic cones and dramatic sunsets; and in the market place the parrots on long poles, the wax figures and huge bouquets of violets.

His regiment returned to New Orleans and then left for New York. He obtained a leave of absence and sailed up the Mississippi River, passing Vicksburg, high on the bluffs, Milliken's Bend, and other points that would figure significantly in his future history. Thirty-nine of the men he had known at West Point had lost their lives in the Mexican War. Julia, awaiting his return on a July day in 1848, was well aware of this, as the seasoned man who had seen so much of bloodshed, of battle, of an exotic life at which she could only guess, took her in his arms and told her that they would be married at once.

At the moment army life seemed more practical for him than a professor's chair. He was assured nearly a thousand dollars a year, with rations for a family and forage for his horses. It was not much to offer Julia but he knew that this was of no real concern to her. Soldiers were in high esteem at the moment, because of the victory in Mexico. The returning troops were met with wild applause and St. Louis entertained its heroes. A war was ended, but many were dead, and there was gloom, too. The Dents moved in to the city for an August wedding, and Julia and Dudy, as she called Ulysses now, were busy with preparations. Grant made a quick trip to Bethel to see his parents and prepare them for his wedding. He took with him Gregory, a Mexican boy he had brought back from the war.

Emma noticed how Ulysses' shoulders had broadened, and how becomingly he wore his double-barred straps. Julia was conscious of a new strength and steadiness in his bearing. His fair skin was deeply tanned; he had lost the feverish look that accompanied his cough. Before arriving he had shaved off the straggly reddish beard he had worn for much of the time in Mexico and was again the clean-shaven soldier, but looking older. His horizons, too, had broadened. He talked thoughtfully to Colonel Dent of political currents and the men who ran the country. Longstreet always said in later years that Grant could be both a voluble and interesting talker when he was with friends, and that his so-called taciturnity after he became famous "was assumed to shut off busybodies — it was only judicious reticence."

Julia had changed, too. Life had not stood still for her. She was now twenty-two and Grant was twenty-six. She was more thoughtful and she laughed less often. She had met a great many men of different kinds in the intervening years and was now a better judge of character. Her father had worked mightily to wear her down on the subject of Grant, but Julia was positive by nature and his resistance had only made her more stubborn. Her mother had sided with her, too, an irresistible combination in the long run, so that there was no further opposition to the match. Both were relieved that the mellowing had taken place, but Julia, watching Grant and her father groping for a common meeting ground in their talks, knew that it was only half-surrender. However, there was no doubt in her own mind about the wisdom of her decision, more particularly now that she had seen Ulysses again and had found him more desirable than ever.

As they walked through the busy streets of St. Louis he observed with amazement the thick melee of assorted vehicles. The buggies and grog shops, the fruit and cigar stores, the tenpin alleys and livery stables had increased in number in the years that he had been away. The scene was strange and unfamiliar after the vivid colors and heightened emotions of the war days in Mexico.

The days passed swiftly at the Dent home. "He showed his future bride the most devoted, yet quiet, attention, and these were happy days for us all," Emma noted. Young people flocked in and out and Caroline O'Fallon gave parties in honor of Julia and her fiance. During Grant's absence she had often taken her proteg6e to Shakespearean and French plays, as well as to the opera, and Julia's experience had broadened in many ways. She had come to love the theater. Now Grant took Emma with them when they went to Ludlow & Smith's theater, where Joseph and Matthew Field were playing. Kate Field, Joseph's daughter, would one day have much to say about Julia and Ulysses in Kate Field's Washington, when she became a well-known correspondent and they were world celebrities.

Julia's trousseau was in readiness long before her suitor came back from war. She had had ample time for preparation, but she was forced to buy with care, for Colonel Dent was no longer the rich man he had been. After Ulysses' return she shed an aura of happiness around her wherever she went. Her small figure, with tiny waist and great ballooning skirts, seemed to float along by Grant's side. To Ulysses, plain though she was, Julia would never be anything but a belle, appropriately gowned and ever pleasing. Shortly before his death he could still write with feeling to their daughter Nellie, in England, that her mother's new dresses were "stunners." Each viewed the other for forty years through the rosiest of mists, which first floated between them at White Haven when Julia was nineteen and Ulysses twenty-three. The illusion never left them but served always to make the good moments better and the bad ones more bearable. There would be plenty of both in the years to come but their love would grow with their trials.

Dr. Sylvester Nidelet, who was courting Nellie at this time, had vivid recollections of the "thick-set, muscular, handsome young fellow" who shared the Dent front steps with him. Nearly every time he called he found Grant and Miss Julia seated side by side on the steps, holding hands and gazing at each other with deep devotion. "They would then be reinforced by the younger Miss Dent and myself," he added. "I remember Grant as a quiet kind of a man who volunteered but little conversation until some topic coming within his experience was referred to, when he would warm up and talk with great interest."

Nidelet remained a bachelor and eventually fought in the Confederate Army, like so many more of Julia's associates of that day. Nellie finally settled down with another physician, Major Alexander Sharp. Emma, still Grant's little pet, circled around them with the enthusiasm of her twelve years. Getting Julia married had become a family topic of prime importance. But there was one cloud in the sky. On his visit home Ulysses had urged his parents to come to the wedding, but they had declined. Jesse Root Grant and his quiet wife, Hannah, abhorred the thought that Ulysses was marrying into a slave-owning family. They did not wish to subject themselves to plantation airs. Moreover, they knew that Julia would soon be visiting them as a bride, and they awaited this event with a chilly sense of expectancy.

CHAPTER III: ST. LOUIS BRIDE

JULIA WALKED DOWN the narrow staircase of the Dent city home on a hot August night in 1848, star candles lighting her way. Ulysses waited in the parlor below, Longstreet towering beside him. Heavy showers had followed a thunderstorm and raindrops pattered on the roof like drum beats. The house seemed too small to contain the girls in hoops and men in uniform who drove up in carriages and crowded into the hallway, leaving their wet wraps in a closet beneath the stairs.

The bride's gown was the gift of Caroline O'Fallon and came from Paris. It was of watered silk with cascades of lace, caught with cape jessamine, Julia's favorite flower then and for the rest of her life. "I never saw a wedding gown I thought as lovely as my own," she commented fifty-three years later, when one of her granddaughters was being married and she was helping to select her trousseau in New York. "Never shall I forget when I came down the staircase that hot August night . . . I felt just as happy at that moment as if I had been married in a church, as girls are now, with a great crowd of people to see me."

Her three bridesmaids — Sarah Walker, Nellie Dent and her cousin, Julia Boggs — wore white, and Ulysses was flanked by trim young officers. Longstreet, Cadmus Marcellus Wilcox and Bernard Pratt would fight with the Confederate forces. All were handsome and full of promise at Julia's wedding. The ceremony was conducted by the Rev. J. H. Linn and was quickly over. Colonel Dent showed little warmth to the bridegroom but was deeply moved to see his favorite daughter take her wedding vows. The most perceptive spectator of all was Emma, dressed in a bell-shaped muslin with dangling ribbons. Young Wilcox teased her about being much in the way and getting herself jammed among the hoops as she rustled about trying to find the best spot from which to watch the bridegroom's face. She and Anna Amanda Shurlds, who would eventually become John Dent's second wife, fidgeted and giggled throughout the ceremony.

"But, at least I sat still long enough to admire my big sister's extreme prettiness as she stood in her bridal dress beside her quiet, self-possessed soldier," Emma noted. "Captain Grant was as cool under the fire of the clergyman's questions as he had been, under the batteries of the Mexican artillery."

Although gas had come to St. Louis the year before, it had not yet been installed in the Dent home. Candles suffused the rooms with soft light. Masses of flowers spread fragrance through the house. Windows and doors were flung wide open to let in the night air when the slashing rain subsided. The military uniforms and bright silks made a picture recalled much later by one of the St. Louis matrons who watched the ceremony:

The bride's dress was really beautiful; and her lovable character and sweet ways made her as much loved as she was admired. I loved Miss Julia so dearly that I was very observant of Lieutenant Grant, though I had met him before. He was a little brown from his three years in the Mexican War, but this made him look more the soldier; and, as he stood beside his bride, clasping her hand (the smallest hand I ever saw on a woman), he in full uniform, I thought I had never seen a better embodiment of a soldier, nor a more charming wedding. Grant's bearing was admirable; he was dignified and polite, with a marked quiet and naturalness. . . . The wedding was attended by a select few of the best people of the city, and the feeling was general that we had never seen two young persons wedding who seemed so happy and so entirely suited to a happy married life.

Julia's intense joy and her diaphanous veil gave her a certain radiance as she clung to her father's arm. When she cut the bridal cake, the ring went to one of her bridesmaids. Afterward there was music. A violinist played and a traveler from Santa Fe did a Spanish dance. The rooms were too small and crowded for the guests to dance but the wedding supper was festive and Julia was toasted by several men whose names would make Civil War history. She felt that she had already tempted fate that day by seeing Ulysses when he made an early morning call. Her sisters had teased her, pointing out that a bride should not be seen by her groom until the hour of the wedding. "He didn't wait, however," she commented. "No, indeed."

Ulysses had waited four years for Julia, and it seemed enough. He had no jewels to give her but his wedding gift was a daguerreotype of himself. Many pictures were taken of Grant over the years as the West Point cadet, the young lieutenant in Mexico, the Civil War warrior, the President of the United States, the world traveler, the dying man at Mount McGregor — but the one that Julia loved and wore into her old age was this picture of her bridegroom, with the thoughtful eyes and stubborn mouth. It was held by a narrow velvet strap at her wrist, the miniature enclosed in a chased gold locket that opened to show his face. All of her grandchildren were familiar with this treasured possession of Julia's, his wedding gift to his bride.

The young pair stayed that night in the family home, then set off next day on their wedding trip in a smother of bouquets thrown after them, Southern fashion, instead of rice. They sailed away in a Mississippi boat, a new experience for Julia. Everything about the expedition seemed dreamlike. She had never been farther away from White Haven than St. Louis and in her old age she recalled that it gave Ulysses pleasure to witness her delight in the changing scenery and the novelty of the river boat.

Like most young brides, she approached her husband's parents with trepidation. She had a strong desire to do him credit and make his family like her, but she and Ulysses at the moment did not feel that anything could darken the sky. She knew that Jesse Root Grant, like her own father, was a man of strong opinions, and that he was as averse to the wedding as Colonel Dent. But Ulysses' mother was still a shadowy figure to Julia. She was well aware that other eyes would be watching her from behind curtains along the single straggling street that made up the settlement of Bethel.

Hannah welcomed her calmly, without the exuberant family embraces to which Julia was accustomed. Ulysses' mother was of medium height, delicately built and with a ramrod spine. A lace cap rested on her hair, which had turned white during the last six months of the Mexican War, when no letters arrived from her son. Her family attributed this swift aging to anxiety, although she had never given a hint of outward concern, but had lived through the war period, as through all her life, with the same impassive air.

Her manner baffled Julia at first until she became accustomed to her mother-in-law's long silences. Nevertheless, Hannah had an alert, inquiring face and Julia warmed to her when she delicately settled her spectacles far down on her nose and stared at the bride appraisingly as they sat having supper. A white kerchief looped at her neck relieved her plain black gown, but Julia felt grossly overdressed in the striped silk she had chosen for this meeting. She knew that it struck a worldly note in these subdued surroundings.

To some of Grant's biographers Hannah Grant's attitude seemed to be one of indifference or eccentricity; to others it suggested deep reserve, self-discipline and a soul at peace with itself. Albert D. Richardson, who knew

Grant well, viewed her as an "amiable, serene and even-tempered woman," speaking ill of none. Julia, a good judge in this instance, led her children and her grandchildren to believe that Ulysses' most sterling qualities — his simplicity, directness and quiet strength of character — came from his mother. Her grandson, Frederick Dent Grant, recalled his grandmother as "one of the most modest and unselfish of women," with deep faith in her son's future and the religious zeal to pray for it.

Julia found the Grants comfortably settled in a good two-story brick house with a tannery along the street and a stage-coach tavern across the way. Studying the family setting it was easy for her to visualize the way in which her husband had grown up — the quiet Sundays with drawn blinds; the lack of excitement in their daily lives; the absence of the small luxuries to which she was accustomed in her own home. There was no overflowing emotion at Hannah's board, although Jesse Grant's emphatic utterances reminded Julia of her own father's verbosity. But with her intimate knowledge of family life in the Gravois settlement she could imagine the young people gathered around the blazing logs on the kitchen hearth, playing fox and geese, morris and checkers, sharing riddles, or roaming the countryside in all sorts of weather.

She felt at home at once with Ulysses' brothers and sisters, although the girls stared at her with some of their mother's candor. This was the girl whom Lyss had been mooning about for so long. They were surprised to find her so practical and everyday. Clara Rachel was twenty and she seemed a trifle stern and disapproving, like her father. Virginia Paine, Ulysses' favorite, was sixteen and she looked charming to Julia, with her blonde hair and gray-blue eyes, like her brother's. The youngest daughter, Mary Frances, was nine. All of the girls struck her as being intelligent, and greatly devoted to Lyss. Samuel Simpson was a thin, good-looking young man of twenty-three, with sharp features and a high color. Orvil Lynch was a merry boy of thirteen with whom Julia soon established jesting relations. None of them seemed to resemble Ulysses closely and Jesse frankly observed that although Lyss had been a beautiful chad he thought the other boys had grown up to be better looking.

By this time Julia was slightly perplexed by the variety of names borne by her husband. Members of his family called him Lyss or Texas. His soldier friends knew him as Sam. He was Dudy to her at this particular time but would soon be Ulyss, the signature he used in writing to her. As the years went on she often called him Mr. Grant and after Vicksburg she sometimes addressed him as Victor, but only if they were alone or with intimate friends. He was endowed with his classical name by Grandmother Simpson, the family scholar who agreed with Jesse, after both had read Fenelon's Telemachus, that Ulysses was a noble-sounding name. Grandfather Simpson had held out for Hiram, thinking it a native, honest name. There were other suggestions but Jesse and Hannah compromised with Hiram Ulysses Grant. However, this added up to HUG when his initials were pounded into his trunk with brass nails as he was leaving for West Point, an obvious invitation to ridicule. Young Grant decided to switch the initials and call himself Ulysses H. Grant. But Thomas L. Hamer, the congressman who signed his formal application, had already made him Ulysses S. Grant, absent-mindedly thinking of the Simpson connection. The complications by this time were so acute that it seemed simpler to adopt the new sequence for life. But this made no difference to the cadets. When they saw U. S. Grant on the bulletin board they called him United States Grant, Uncle Sam Grant, Uncle Sam and, eventually, plain Sam. None was more persistent in this bit of fun than William Tecumseh Sherman, who suffered from the nickname "Cump."

Julia thought Lyss both simple and suitable when she heard his mother use the name. She noticed that he treated Hannah with the utmost respect and did not joke with her as he did with Julia and his sisters. Actually, soon after entering West Point, he had written to the woman who had seemed not to notice his departure: "I seem alone in the world without my mother. There have been so many ways in which you have advised me ... that you cannot tell how much I miss you . . . your kindly instructions and admonitions are ever present with me. I trust they may never be absent from me as long as I live."

But Hannah showed neither joy nor feeling of any kind in addressing him now, and Julia turned with relief to Jesse Grant, who overshadowed them all with his assertive ways and boastful talk. While recognizing the fact that he was thorny and abrupt, she caught the better side of his nature and handled him with tact from the start. It was clear to her that he had the same stubborn qualities as her father, although their convictions were poles apart. She would do much juggling in the future to keep these two aging gentlemen from angry debate, yet still have them moving within the family circle at the White House. Julia knew that Jesse was the one she had to win at this time but she was used to testy fathers.

Grant was tall but had the slightly stooped look that his soldier son also developed. He was of rugged build, with the same wide forehead as Ulysses, high cheekbones, and a thin, determined mouth. His eyes seemed small behind their glasses and he talked in a voluble, rapid way. He could scarcely have been more unlike his silent wife and his reticent son when it came to manner and conversation. He seemed severe to Julia but she knew that Ulysses had never been punished at home, although he had often felt the touch of the beech switch at school. In Georgetown he was regarded as a quiet, well-behaved boy, who had stood out among the others only because of his horsemanship.

Julia realized by this time that although Ulysses bore some physical resemblance to his father, in temperament he was more akin to his mother, who had grown up within twenty miles of Philadelphia and was the daughter of John Simpson, a prosperous Pennsylvania farmer. She was heiress to six hundred acres of good land when Jesse Grant, a penniless young tanner, married her in 1821. He viewed her then as "an unpretending country girl, handsome but not vain." However, it took years for him to plumb her quiet depths, and her stepmother, the bookish Sarah Hare Simpson, thought her a reserved and mysterious girl, with the deportment of a mature woman.

Hannah was of mixed Irish and Welsh ancestry and Jesse, whose family also had moved west from Pennsylvania, was of Scotch-Irish stock. Thus the Celtic inheritance was strong in Ulysses S. Grant, who was born to them in Point Pleasant, Ohio, on April 27, 1822. As the son of Noah Grant, a wanderer and soldier in the Revolutionary War, Jesse was a child of the wilderness, with only five months of schooling in his entire life. But the boy taught himself to read and write and do simple sums, and as he grew older he developed a burning ambition to go into politics. He took lessons in grammar after his marriage to Hannah, and fancied himself as a writer of occasional verse and sketches for local papers. He had an unquenchable instinct for debate and insisted on making himself heard on all public issues.

This pronounced characteristic in Jesse was manifest to Julia as she listened to her father-in-law. They all skirted the question of slavery. Lyss talked in an interesting way about the Mexican War. They discussed family affairs and inevitably came round to the boy's early feats with horses. Hannah blushed furiously when compliments were paid. It was her only show of feeling. The flattering talk of the South was not in accord with her inborn sense of humility. She had been known to walk from a room to avoid hearing compliments paid to Lyss in his presence. Even when he was elected President, the most she would allow herself to say of her famous son was that "he was always a good boy."

It took no encouragement at all on Julia's part to start Jesse talking with pride of small Lyss riding around the circus ring at the age of three; driving a horse and wagon alone at seven and a half; hauling wood with a team when he was eight; riding with one foot on the saddle and balancing himself with a bridle rein when he was nine; and a year later picking up passengers who had arrived by stage coach in Georgetown and driving them the remaining forty miles to Cincinnati. Ulysses ploughed at eleven and did heavy farm work up to the age of seventeen. But however hard he worked there was always time to fish and swim in the creeks, to gather hickory nuts and wild grapes, to roam at will through the woods, to play marbles or skate. His father always insisted that Ulysses had had just as many privileges as any other village lad.

Hannah had never shown the least alarm when neighbors drew her attention to the fact that her small pinafored son was imperiling his life by playing around the horses' hooves and swinging on their tails. She believed in self-reliance. When Ulysses was ill she dosed him with castor oil and trusted to the good Lord and the boy's sound constitution. She watched him leave for West Point without a quiver, and when Mrs. Bailey, their Georgetown neighbor, kissed him good-bye and wept, he exclaimed: "Why, Mrs. Bailey, they didn't cry at our house." It so happened that one of Mrs. Bailey's sons had been killed trying to emulate Ulysses on a horse, and that he was now taking the place of another son, Bart, who had failed to make the grade at West Point. But she did not blame him in any way for his ill-starred relations with her family.

All this was to become legend in the Grant family, as Julia told her own sons and daughter something of their father's early history. Whatever she had failed to learn from Ulysses about his boyhood she picked up during her visit to Bethel and Georgetown. Everyone wanted to tell the bride some anecdote about her husband. She knew by this time that he was an expert swimmer as well as rider. He liked to skate and at the age of ten when his straps were too tight and his feet froze, Hannah had thawed them out with smoking hay. Then she had bound slices of bacon around them as emollient. She also had to cope with the fever and ague that beset Lyss in his boyhood. Dr. Bailey, their neighbor who was both physician and chemist, stocked all the remedies of the day for this malarial tendency, but Hannah believed in simple home remedies for every physical ill, and prayer for the sick soul.

Julia found one common talking point with her in their Methodist background. A meeting house stood close to the Grant home and the circuit ministers found immaculate quarters and good food when they became Mrs. Grant's guests for the night. Card playing was not allowed in their home, and Ulysses had never learned to dance. He was taught from childhood to shun profanity and all his life he was averse to a coarse story or obscenity of any kind. His father insisted that he had never been a quarrelsome boy but that no one could impose on him when he believed he was right. He was shy with girls although he went on sleigh rides with groups of young people. Usually he was more at ease with the mature than with his contemporaries.

After making the round of family calls in Bethel Julia visited the tan-yard and the currier shop, a spot much disliked by Ulysses. Hides were stretched on fences and a strange smell hung over the area. Her husband had never overcome his distaste for his father's occupation after he had been put to work cleaning raw hides with a long knife in the "beam-house." He found the work disgusting and took an active dislike to all aspects of tanning. This was thought to be the basis of his lifelong aversion to rare meat. After handling the hides he would not touch any meat that had a drop of blood exuding from it. Steak had to be burned almost to a crisp or he would not eat it.

Before going to West Point he warned his father that he would never become a tanner. He had considered farming or trading on the Mississippi, but above all he hankered for a good education. His father was sympathetic to this ambition and made the necessary arrangements for him to enter the Military Academy. But Julia could see that Ulysses' education had been as spotty as her own up to that point.

Georgetown seemed charming to her as she strolled along its shady streets, admiring the gardens and plain substantial houses. Oak, maple and ash trees grew up the surrounding slopes. Wherever she went, she made a good impression. She wore her trousseau gowns and all were interested in the vivacious, well-mannered girl from St. Louis. By this time she had heard all about Kate Lowe, Mary King, and the daughters of Senator Thomas Morris, with whom Ulysses had gone horseback riding in his West Point days. He had stirred up Kate Lowe's interest when she traveled west with him and his grandmother Simpson by canal boat from Harrisburg on his first leave from West Point. Kate was impressed by his "clear eyes and good features," as well as by his manners, which she found diffident but not awkward. His gentle attitude to his grandmother impressed her.

Grant called often on Miss Lowe that same summer, and he passed many contented hours with another Bethel girl, Mary King, to whom he later sent a water color done by himself of the majestic scenery surrounding West Point. He always recalled this as the most carefree period of his life and he wrote revealingly shortly before his death: "Those ten weeks were shorter than one week at West Point . . . This I enjoyed beyond any other period of my life."

Now he was back with his bride and the other girls took careful note of Julia Grant. In a sense this was the homecoming of a hero as well as of a young man on his wedding trip. Groups of men gathered around Grant in the street to discuss the Mexican War and seek his opinions on the political currents of the moment. His uniform was now regarded with respect, although it had been jeered at on his return from West Point. He had left the Academy proud of his trappings and intent on showing the girls at home how well he looked in military attire. But after catcalls in the streets of Cincinnati as he traveled west, and some gibes in Bethel, he developed a lasting distaste for uniforms or military show of any kind.

He was still less the dude after his return from the Mexican War. The officers who knew him best concluded that he preferred comfort to show, and that he was influenced to some extent by the vigorous, untidy figure of Zachary Taylor. But Julia was always proud to have him wear his uniform. For the rest of her life she would stoutly fight the legend of careless dressing that first attached itself to him at West Point, then followed him through his array days, and was commented on when he was in the White House — a tendency to leave waistcoat buttons undone, to ignore creases, to wear battered hats and not spruce up, either in military or civilian clothes.

She devoted much wifely attention to this matter, in so far as Grant would listen to her. In bringing her small grandsons up to the mark in standards of dress, she always impressed on them their grandfather's "insistence on clean linen, his liking for good cloth in his clothes and a good tailor when in later life he could afford it." In fact, when a gushing visitor asked him: "What were your thoughts, General, in that sublime moment when you knew that at last Lee would surrender, and the heavens of your glory were about to open?" he replied briefly: "My dirty boots and wearing no sword."

But on their wedding trip Ulysses was intent only on pleasing Julia and she had not yet begun to worry about his attire. Before she left for home she knew that she was at least approved by her husband's family and friends, although there was no way of telling from Hannah's unresponsive face what conclusions her mother-in-law had reached. Clearly, Jesse thought that she was a fortunate girl to have won Ulysses, and that was how Julia viewed it, too. "How happy he was that I liked his family, and his Ohio friends!" she exclaimed. Actually, he had been worrying more about his bride's reaction to them than about their feeling for her. But the marriage was a success from the start, and both found contentment in the new world they had discovered.

They came back to St. Louis as the wild pigeons migrated south, making the woods west of the city their roosting place. The branches of the trees were bruised by this invasion and the hunters had a season of abundance. By this time Grant's leave had expired. His regiment had been ordered to the northern frontier, with headquarters at Detroit. As quartermaster his place was there, but a brother officer who did not wish the bleak and lonely billet of Madison Barracks at Sackett's Harbor on Lake Ontario had Grant transferred to the lesser post while he became acting quartermaster in Detroit. Grant protested but by the time General Scott had upheld him navigation was closed and he was forced to stay where he was until spring.

Colonel Dent's worst prognostications for Julia were fulfilled but she set forth cheerfully on the nomadic life that would be hers for years to come. She was to put together a great many homes in her lifetime, always with loving care, as if each were the last. She took readily to the life of a garrison wife. She was naturally gregarious and went in for social gatherings of all sorts, from a rural quilting party to a ball or masquerade. The stone barracks were half a mile from the lake, which looked gray and forbidding when they arrived in November. Old block houses designed for Indian fighting stood at Sackett's Harbor, which was the naval station in the War of 1812 and had been an important post.

The Grants would always remember the winter of 1848-1849, since it established the pattern of marital happiness that became theirs all through life. These were really the days in which Julia came to know Ulysses and to give him her lifelong devotion. Outwardly it was a bleak winter, yet both recalled it with nostalgia. Their quarters were bare but Julia soon turned them into a home. She had brought a few of her wedding gifts with her, but she and Ulysses bought most of their furnishings on their arrival. She had her own tea and coffee service and china that she treasured. "I knew fine china when I saw it, for my mother's was very nice indeed; but this was my very own," Julia wrote. Her mother's was white and gold. Julia's had a design of hand-painted field flowers. They had two or three carpets, "but all lovely in our eyes."

Proud of his home and his new wife, Grant invited four or five officers to dine with them as soon as things were in place. Julia protested. She must practice a little and have a trial dinner, she said. She had left her slaves in the South and was now on her own, except for a local girl named Hannah, but she knew nothing about her capacities at that time. Grant told her that he could run up a savory mess himself, if need be. He had roasted apples at West Point and had even been known to cook a fowl. But the officers were put off and were asked to come the second day, to give Julia time for a rehearsal. She prepared her dinner party with care, setting out her silver and china, arranging flowers, "seeing that all were properly placed, and remembering with loving pride the well-served table of my father's house."

Ulysses took his friends into his confidence about his bride's apprehension. "How they all loved to tease me ever after when he would ask any of them to dine with us!" Julia commented. "They would timidly peep in at the door, and ask 'Is it all right?' or, 'Shall we come another day?'"

Almost at once the Grants set up a budgeting arrangement, Ulysses giving Julia an allowance for her household expenses. It varied according to his means and their requirements. "I have therefore lived on a lieutenant's pay and spent that of a President," she observed in her old age, "and I must not fail to say that he was more than liberal with me."

The plan was adopted at Julia's suggestion. She bought a small black notebook and kept accounts, but since she did not share her husband's mathematical gifts, they were often in a muddle. When she asked him to help her he would look them over and say: "Excuse me, I cannot make out your mathematical conundrums." He preferred to make up the deficit. But occasionally she came out on the right side of the ledger and by degrees she learned to be an excellent manager. At this time she bought butter for twenty-four cents a pound, coffee for nine cents, brown sugar for six cents, a loaf of bread for nine cents, tallow candles for sixteen cents each, and potatoes for seventy-five cents a bushel She sometimes accompanied

Ulysses to Watertown, the county seat, and went visiting and shopping while he attended to commissary affairs or played checkers and chess with his cronies.

That winter they rode in cutters and grew used to the most extreme cold. Julia was healthy and never complained about physical discomfort, although jugs of frozen water and snow up to the window panes posed some problems for the young couple. Gregory, the Mexican boy Grant had brought back from the war, was with them. He suffered acutely in his icebound surroundings, but he learned to feed the wood box and light the fires. They were snowed in much of the time, but featherbeds, heavy quilts and roaring wood fires made life a little easier at the army post. The young officers liked to drop in on the Grants to play cards, with Julia proudly marshaling the best she could do in the way of refreshments. It was a Spartan life after the comforts of White Haven but she was a happy wife and thought little of the hardships. The ancestors of both the Grants had been vigorous pioneers and possibly Julia liked to think that she was carrying on a tradition.

But as soon as the ice broke, they moved to Detroit, staying at the newly finished Michigan National Hotel until they could find a home. In the spring of 1849 Julia laid her carpets and arranged her hand-painted china in a small frame house at 253 East Fort Street, where they lived for a year. It had a small arbor in front with some wisps of vine that gave them the illusion of having a garden. West Fort Street was fashionable; East Fort Street had a number of immigrants and some tough characters. Grant was warned that he might have troublesome neighbors, but he is quoted — somewhat improbably — as having said: "No matter; if home has a hell outside of it, it ought to be a heaven within." Actually, his closest neighbors were a grocer, a laborer, a bootmaker, a peddler, a lawyer, and two blacksmiths.

Gas had not yet come to Detroit, which then had a population of 21,000, and Julia coped with grease and oil lamps, and the familiar tallow candles. She had a large kitchen, which was the one warm room in winter, and unbearably hot in summer. The bedroom was simply furnished with pine. The rope bedstead had a featherbed in winter and a corn-husk mattress in summer. The kitchen had one of the earliest stoves made in Detroit. With the coming of spring Julia was conscious at once of the magnificent pear trees, fluttering with blossom against the brown, gray and crimson houses. There were only seven stone houses in the city at this time; six hundred were built of brick and more than seven thousand were of wood. Windmills turned slowly with the spring winds. Fish nets hung on reels and the river was strung with gem-like islands. Canoes glided over its glassy surface on still days and Julia and Ulysses took stock of these delights when they drove by the river or walked in the woods. Pond lilies and sweet flag grew along the banks, and as the summer advanced they picked wild strawberries, whortleberries and raspberries. The woods were alive with quail, woodcock and golden pheasants. The wild pigeons were so plentiful that strollers killed them with walking sticks.

The Grants let the game alone but noted the other characteristics of the Detroit woods. Wild honeysuckle and eglantine, Michigan roses, snowberries and locust bloomed in season. Bright-plumaged birds flitted around trumpet vines, and larks and brown thrushes crossed their path as they took their Sunday walks. The woods reminded Julia of White Haven, with their massed oaks and elms, their beeches and hickory trees. But disturbing news was reaching them that year from St. Louis. A cholera epidemic took the lives of more than 8,000 residents of the city in 1849. And a great fire almost destroyed the entire river front. Everyone was talking of the gold rush — in Detroit, in St. Louis, and clear across the country. A number of men whom Julia knew were setting off for California. One of them was her brother, Louis Dent.

By September Grant had full status as regimental quartermaster at the post, although Major E. S. Sibley, of Sibley tent fame, directed this work for the entire lakes department. After the taste of soldiering he had had in Mexico, the chaffering over tents, tent-poles, knapsacks, forage, food and uniforms, wearied Grant as he ordered supplies and directed commissary affairs. He had no taste for forms or desk work and Julia could see when he came home at night how distasteful it all was to him. Friend Palmer, then quartermaster's clerk at Detroit, observed his extreme reluctance to ask for anything, and commented to his sergeant on the unsuitability of so diffident a soldier holding down this executive appointment.

The sergeant, an admirer of Grant, flared up and said that although he was not much good with papers, accounts, returns and office routine, "when you get to the soldier part of it, drill, manual of arms, etc., he could handle the regiment as well, if not better, than any other fellow in it."

The barracks were not inspiring. The wooden buildings stood on open ground and were fronted by a board fence. The sutler's shop and the officers' quarters were nearby, but most of the married officers preferred to live in town, and the Grants were close to the barracks. Julia became a favorite at once at the dances and social gatherings linked to the garrison life. Her excellent dancing delighted the young officers and her thoughtful ways with their wives and children made her popular with the women. At first she never missed the weekly assemblies at the Exchange Hotel, although her husband merely looked on while she danced. Friend Palmer observed that "he used to stand around or hold down a seat all the evening." Sometimes Grant went off for a convivial hour with the other officers but Palmer insisted that he had never seen him under the influence of liquor.

He did attract attention, however, as he raced through the streets on a fast little French pony that he bought for $250 from Jim Cicotte, a local politician. By that time he had raffled off Nelly, the gray horse he had brought with him from Mexico. French ponies ran wild in the fields at this time and they had speed, if not pedigree. Mrs. Eunice Tripler, wife of Dr. Charles S. Tripler, the post surgeon, was among the first to take note of Grant's mad gallops on the Cicotte mare. Her husband had known him for a long time. Dr. Tripler was assistant surgeon at West Point and had been through the Mexican War.

"That's Grant over there," he said to his wife, as they drove along behind their own Vermont Morgan mares. "How he does, drive that little rat of a horse."

On Saturdays he went racing along Fifth Avenue, a favorite course for the horse fanciers of Detroit. When winter came and the River Rouge was frozen, Ulysses took Julia driving over the ice in fast cutters. This was in the old Gravois Road tradition and she found it exhilarating, although she had never experienced such acute cold, except at Sackett's Harbor in the previous winter. As they sped on their way her cheeks had a deep flush; she was bundled up in heavy shawls; her wool-mittened hands were clasped around her husband's arm as he drove; and she felt a rare glow of excitement, because by this time she knew that she was going to have a baby. She had promised her father that she would return to White Haven to have her first-born in her early home. Dent had softened somewhat toward Ulysses by this time and had signed his bond as quartermaster.

The Grants' little house was offered for sale, rent or exchange, in the Detroit Free Press of May 25, 1850, and five days later Julia gave birth to a son in her father's city home in St. Louis. Her mother and Auntie Robinson were in attendance, and she coped with this first great ordeal of her life with a minimum of fuss or excitement. She named the baby Frederick Dent Grant, in honor of her father, and Colonel Dent correctly predicted that some day the child would be a general.

During her absence Ulysses was restless and lonely. He had found Julia a comforting and absorbing presence in his life and he missed her greatly. This was the first of the periods in which he was to find himself aimless and unhappy without her. He was already regarded as a "restless, energetic man, who must have occupation, and plenty of it, for his own good." He behaved in typical army fashion at this time. He consorted with horse-fanciers, smoked incessantly, hung around the sutler's store, played loo (a game resembling euchre), and seemed unremarkable in all respects — even to those who in later years, when he had become famous, tried to enlarge or diminish his reputation. Except that he rode a little faster than anyone else, went to dances but did not dance, kept silent while others talked, he did not create a ripple on the social scene.

By the time Julia returned to Detroit, Ulysses had set up house-keeping in larger quarters on Jefferson Avenue with Captain and Mrs. J. H. Gore. She settled happily into this joint arrangement. The house was rented from W. A. Bacon, a teacher whose little schoolhouse stood to the rear. The country around was comparatively open and they could see pasture land from their back windows. There were no sidewalks, but the soldiers had laid a plank walk to the barracks and Julia became adept at gathering up her petticoats and leaping to dry land on muddy days. Bacon chatted often with Gore and the two army wives but could get little out of Grant. When Richmond fell it took him some time to establish the fact that the hero of the hour was the quiet young captain who had shared the house with the Gores. But he found convincing proof in a window pane on which Grant's name had been scratched with a diamond ring.

Julia usually served supper on the back porch, from which they could now view a garden full of peach trees. Here Ulysses liked to smoke in the summer twilight, while she sat across from him, singing lullabies to their baby. They watched small Fred develop from day to day and Mrs. Tripler observed that whenever she saw Mrs. Grant she had a "great lump of a baby in her arms." But the birth of her baby had not weighted Julia's feet. She danced as lightly and gracefully as ever and Mrs. Tripler next saw her at a large ball given by General Hugh Brady, a veteran of the War of 1812. She then observed: "Most of the time Lieut. Grant was standing rather aloof from the company and uncommunicative with his hands behind his back, impassive. He always gave me the impression of a school-boy who had not learned his lesson, but he was always very devoted and tender to his wife. She, as I think, was his salvation."

Mrs. Tripler was to become a severe critic of Grant, although she had conventional social relations with the Captain and his wife in Detroit, and in the end was forced to extol him. Her cousin, Captain Lewis Hunt, a classmate of his at West Point, had already told her that "there's more in Grant than you think," but it took years for her to revise her original estimate of him. Julia was intensely sensitive to the slightest criticism of her husband and she did not warm to those who failed to appreciate him. From the beginning she would let none assail Ulysses and she scolded him for the way in which he ignored slights. Her pride came quickly to the surface. But he took her proddings as impassively as he did the barbs of his critics. Her quick spurts of anger seemed as amusing to him as her jokes. She soon learned to show tact with the army wives.

Busy though she was with her maternal duties, she resumed her social life to the full. She and Mrs. Gore attended parties together and entertained constantly in the house that they had tried to make attractive. Friend Palmer was impressed by a masquerade they gave and thought it as brilliant an affair as he had attended in Detroit. The two wives illuminated the house with candles speared on deer antlers, and domino masks gave dash to the affair. In addition to the army wives, Julia had friends among the old French families settled in the frontier town. They reminded her of the same social element in St. Louis. Sometimes she missed her piano, and she longed for the music and the theater that had been a part of her life in her native city, but vetting celebrities passed through who aroused her interest. Fredrika Bremer, the Swedish author who championed women's rights, a cause strongly backed by Julia in later years, visited Detroit in 1850. So did William H. Seward, whose name meant little to them then, but would be significant in the future.

Shortly before the Grants left Detroit, Ulysses unwittingly stirred up a storm when he filed a complaint against Zachariah Chandler, the powerful New Hampshire Whig who later became Mayor of the city and eventually a United States Senator and Cabinet officer. The captain had slipped and sprained his leg on the sidewalk in front of the Chandler home. The snow and ice had not been removed, a violation of a city ordinance. Some of the other officers had had similar mishaps when passing the Chandler home on their way to the barracks, and Grant decided to take the culprit to court. His associates appeared to give testimony, and the wives, particularly Julia, were deeply concerned over the result.

Chandler, a man of forceful personality, defended himself. Turning to Sibley, Gore and Grant, he said that the soldiers in general were loafers, living off the community, and added: "If you soldiers would keep sober, perhaps you would not fall on people's pavement and hurt your legs." But the facts were proved against him and he was fined six cents and costs. Fifteen years later he and Grant laughed heartily over this incident when the Senator entertained the great General at his home in Detroit And Julia, indignant at the time, would have years of social interchange with the Senator in Washington.

In June 1851, Sackett's Harbor became regimental headquarters, and Grant was ordered back to his original base, where he stayed for a year. The lake now was a sparkling expanse of blue, and life was more comfortable for Julia than on her winter sojourn there. With her new baby to tend, the summer days passed pleasantly and she and Ulysses gave thought to their future. His eight-year enlistment period had come to an end. He had done some desultory studying in Detroit, with his old professorial ambitions in mind. Both of the Grants knew that the life of a quartermaster had little to offer him. His paper work seemed more monotonous than ever at Sackett's Harbor and he made many trips to Watertown. Colonel William Whistler was the commander of the regiment and his vivacious daughter, Louise, was not popular with either of the Grants. She had been much discussed in Detroit for waving a dagger at a youth who had made some innocuous remarks in her presence. Now she arranged for the regimental band to serenade her in the evenings, and the officers' wives looked on with some amusement. This daily rite became sheer torture to Ulysses, who was inordinately resistant to music and particularly to military bands. In desperation he sometimes left Julia and the baby to go off to the village for a quiet game of chess behind closed doors, where the sound of the drums could not follow him.

Life took another twist for him at this time. Shortly after he learned that his wife was going to have a second baby he went to Sackett's Harbor Presbyterian Church and joined the Independent Order of Odd Fellows and the Sons of Temperance. During these early years at army posts Julia, the good Methodist, would also attend Presbyterian and Episcopal churches, depending on which was available. The important thing to her was to go to a house of worship every Sunday. Ulysses would sit beside her adoringly, listening to her sweet voice raised in the old-fashioned hymns.

The temperance drive of the moment was focused in the Presbyterian Church. It was fashionable at this time to take the pledge, but it required some courage for an officer to wear the white sash, lapel badge and other insignia in a garrison town of that era, where heavy drinking was a daily rite. Grant attended the weekly meetings with Julia's hearty approval. She hung his parchment proudly in their home. He went the whole way, marching in parades, and holding office in the organization, which then claimed a membership of 148,000 throughout the country.

He was twenty-nine years old, restless, and obviously being used below his capacity. Only Julia saw great things ahead of him. Her sunny disposition helped him through hours of discouragement. It was clear to his army friends that she was both an inspiration and a comfort to the moody captain. She had already developed a deep understanding of his capacities and basic needs. Years later his close friend and secretary, Adam Badeau, would sum up what she had discovered in the earliest days of their marriage: "I found him a man like other men, with feelings as profound as those of the most passionate, but with a power of concealing them almost without example. His reserve, however, was natural in part, as well as in part the result of intention. At times there was a positive inability to reveal emotion, a sort of Inarticulate undemonstrativeness as far as possible from stolidity. He had few affections, but these were intense; he did not hate many, but he could be implacable. . . ."

Julia had found the key to the inner spring of emotion in Ulysses. He had powerful family impulses and small Fred was a never-ending source of delight. Both parents laughed and applauded when he "took turns with the visiting officers in feats of agility, such as jumping from the piazza," his mother observed. "Every one measured Fred's leaps, and to his great delight he jumped his length every time — he could not do less."

When the regiment was ordered to the Pacific in the summer of 1852, Grant faced a decision about his future. They would soon have a second child and there was a certain security about the army. After talking things over with Julia he decided to go West, while she went to Bethel for the birth of the baby. It was arranged that she should join him at the earliest possible moment. Mrs. Gore, Mrs. Henry D. Wallen and several other close friends were going with their husbands and were even taking children with them, but Julia was in no condition to take so long and perilous a journey, although she would gladly have done so, had Ulysses permitted it.

He bade her farewell in the middle of June and set off for Governors Island, New York, on the first lap of his trip. Julia journeyed to Bethel with two-year-old Fred. There was no time to spare. On July 22, a month after Ulysses left, her second son was born. Hannah, silent as a shadow, officiated this time instead of Mrs. Dent. The boy was named Ulysses S. Grant, 2d, after his father. He would always be known as "Buck" because of his birth in the Buckeye state. Like all of Julia's children, he was handsome and bright from birth, and resembled his father.

On the day he was born, Jesse Grant was in Columbus attending the last Whig State Convention ever held in Ohio, and was helping to write its platform. Ulysses was battling with unexpected disaster in the Isthmus of Panama and Julia wept because he was not with her to welcome their new son.

CHAPTER IV: JULIA'S SIXTY ACRES

ULYSSES WAS AT FORT VANCOUVER on the Columbia River, with Mount Hood towering in the distance and all around him giant spruce trees draped in yellow moss, when Julia's first letter reached him after the birth of her baby. She had traced his infant hand in pencil on the last sheet and Grant was touched to the quick. He showed the sketch to an artillery sergeant named Eckerson, who noted that he "folded the letter quickly and left without speaking a word; but his form shook, and his eyes were wet."

By this time Julia had read with alarm of the misadventures of the Fourth Infantry on its way west. The papers had trumpeted the story. Dr. Tripler had warned against sending the troops through the Isthmus of Panama in the midst of a cholera epidemic and his worst fears had been realized. One third of the men were now buried in the jungle or on a lonely island in the Bay of Panama. Captain Gore had collapsed as he played euchre with Grant and Wallen, and was dead by morning. His widow was now on her way home to her family in Covington, Kentucky, and Julia soon got a clear account from her of Grant's initiative and fortitude as he coped with sudden death, cholera, tainted water, heavy rains, the heat of the jungle and a breakdown in transportation facilities. He had looked after the women and children through a series of misadventures; transporting his men and all the army equipment from rifles to kettles across the Isthmus; helping Dr. Tripler with the sick, and attending to the burial of soldiers who died in their tracks in the steaming jungle when cholera broke out among them. They were buried where they fell, with macaws screeching overhead and monkeys chattering in the palms.

Looking at Fred and small Ulysses, Julia felt that perhaps her husband had been right in insisting that she stay at home. "My dearest, you never could have crossed the Isthmus at this season," he wrote to her. At the time she was restless and unsure of the course she should follow. After a few weeks with Jesse and Hannah she decided to return to White Haven, for she was never quite at ease with the children in her father-in-law's home. Their grandparents loved them, but she felt that they were somehow in the way. Fred was a personality from his earliest years and Hannah's bright eyes took note when Julia did not discipline him. Her disapproval was never voiced, but Julia felt its sting.

There was ample room for the children to play at White Haven, horses for them to ride, Grandmother Dent to give them her warm attention, the Colonel to conduct political debates with Julia. That summer and autumn she made plum jelly and preserved peaches and pears. She put up bushels of tomatoes and pickled the cucumbers of which Ulysses was so fond. She bought linen at fifteen cents a yard and made cool little suits for Fred. She sang to the children and moved about the house in muslin delaine, tending the new baby and aching to hear from the absent soldier. When winter came she went to the opera once or twice with the O'Fallons but with her new responsibilities she rarely visited the city. Her friends drove out to call instead. They were reading Shady Side and Life in a Country Parsonage that winter. With the coming of spring Lola Montez arrived in St. Louis and stirred up a storm of comment.

Julia continued to ride but missed Ulysses now on her evening gallops. The woods seemed faded without him. She attended parties along the Gravois Road and kept up her active church work. Her sisters and brothers were scattered now, except for Emma. The emphasis was all on her children. Julia was a devoted and absorbed mother and in her letters to Ulysses she noted each small advance they made — the new word learned, Fred's passion for horses, the baby's beguiling tricks. She sent him a lock of little Buck's hair, entwined with a strand of her own.

A lonely, difficult period followed for Grant in the barracks his old friend Rufus Ingalls had installed at Fort Vancouver. The nearest settlement was Portland, Oregon, then no more than a street of frame houses and log cabins. The surrounding lakes were a deep jade and still as marble. The kingly salmon of the Columbia River was their daily fare. Elk, deer and blue grouse haunted the woods, and even an occasional bear. Grant did not hunt, or fish, or carouse with women like some of his fellow officers but he quickly found himself a fast horse and took long rides in the woods.

Mrs. Delia B. Sheffield, a sergeant's wife who kept house for the officers at the barracks, observed his loneliness and his longing for his wife and children as he played euchre, brag and loo, sat gazing over the river by the hour, or retired to his room when the parties became boisterous or a dance was under way. "Oftentimes, while reading letters from his wife, his eyes would fill with tears, he would look up with a start and say, 'Mrs.

Sheffield, I have the dearest little wife in the world, and I want to resign from the Army and live with my family.'"

She watched him with his trousers tucked in his boots, "sowing oats broadcast from a sheet tied about his neck and shoulders" in one of many attempts he made to augment his army income and raise enough money to have his family join him. Crops failed. A scheme to sell ice, and then livestock, in San Francisco came to nothing. On June 15, 1853, he wrote to Julia, thanking her for the baby's lock of hair and urging her to send him more news of the children, "I am very well dear Julia but to write more about myself, as you so often request me to do, I do not know how."

It was some time before Julia learned that he had been appointed to a full captaincy to fill the place of William W. S. Bliss, Zachary Taylor's handsome son-in-law, who had died of yellow fever. At the same time he was ordered to Fort Humboldt to take command of a company in the redwood region, 250 miles north of San Francisco. This meant a small advance in pay. But his hopes of having his family join him had dwindled by this time and he thought constantly now of resigning from the army.

At Fort Humboldt he came face to face with Colonel Robert C. Buchanan, who had snubbed him at Jefferson Barracks. Old fires came to life again. His quartermaster's duties had at least been absorbing. Now as a field officer he had more time on his hands. Again he was confronted with a boring routine for which he had little taste. He visited San Francisco, which was having its early boom, a pasteboard city with a strange assortment of men and women walking the streets, all feverishly talking gold. One of his first moves was to journey to Knight's Ferry on the Stanislaus River to see Julia's brother, Louis, who was running the ferry boat at that point. They talked together about home and the woman who was rarely out of Ulysses' thoughts. Another winter passed with little hope of reunion.

Mail came to Fort Humboldt even more slowly than to Fort Vancouver. Grant watched hungrily for letters from Julia, but the only communication with San Francisco was by water, and mail took from ten days to six weeks. The officers galloped madly to Eureka, a picturesque village three miles from the fort, when a schooner came in. The settlement had a mill and a score of houses and here they spent much of their free time. Indians lounged about the mill

By this time Julia was getting uneasy. She knew that things were not going well with Ulysses. He had made several applications for leave but without result. He felt he must get home and see her. On February 6, 1854, he wrote that the mail had come in but, to his dismay, there was no letter from her, nor any reply to his application for orders to go home. "The state of suspense that I am in is scarcely bearable," he added. "I think that I have been away from my family quite long enough and sometimes I feel as though I could almost go home nolens volens."

The next two months were painful ones for Grant and their history is still obscure. On April 11, 1854, he wrote two letters on the same day. One was a formal acceptance of his captaincy. The other was a brief letter of resignation from the army. The news was perhaps more startling to his army colleagues than it was to the Dents at White Haven, who had been hearing for weeks of his intense desire to get out of the army and home to Julia. The accepted story at the post was that Grant had come into sudden collision with Buchanan and had been offered his choice of resigning or of facing charges involving intemperance. The official records in no way support the ultimatum theory and William Conant Church, Grant's old West Point mathematics professor, has pointed out that the "Army is as prone to gossip as a New England sewing-society; and the story of his experiences at Fort Humboldt was spread abroad in an exaggerated form, subjecting him to unjust suspicions and false charges. . . ."

Mrs. Eunice Tripler left a pointed comment on the matter. Her husband was augmenting his meager pay at the time with some private practice in San Francisco. He was seeing Grant, Joseph Hooker and E. D. Townsend, all men who would figure significantly in the Civil War. "Grant," wrote Mrs. Tripler, "was in my husband's care and Dr. Tripler was entirely frank and open in dealing with his case. He, at least, resigned from the Army and came East."

Probably Julia alone would ever know the truth of the matter, but her indignation was intense as stories spread in army circles and were whispered in St. Louis. Emma took note of the situation and wrote with some bitterness that the break had come solely through Grant's longing to join his family and the indifference of the War Department to his repeated requests for leave. The Dents felt that other men less entitled to furloughs were getting them every day. "It is not true," Emma pointed out, "that the Captain's personal habits at that time led him into such difficulties that he was asked to resign."

Julia's last word from Ulysses was an unusually curt note from Fort Humboldt, written on May 2, shortly after the crisis, in which he told her not to write to him again at that address because he would be on his way home. She could catch him in New York. He might have to stay in California for a few more weeks to arrange his affairs and he planned to visit her brother on his way home, "My love to all at home," he finished. "Kiss our little boys for their Pa. Love to you dear Julia. Your affectionate husbd. Ulys."

Quiet and sturdy, making no defence of himself, but remarking that "whoever hears of me in ten years, will hear of a well-to-do old Missouri farmer," he left Fort Humboldt Every step that followed was used historically to his disadvantage. He was pictured as sitting in dejection in a cheap room in the "What Cheer House," a miners' hotel in San Francisco, without funds to take him home. There army friends found him and gave him money, which he shared with soldiers worse off than himself on his way back. When he reached New York he used the last of his funds for a trip to Sackett's Harbor to collect a loan of $1,600 from the former sutler of his regiment, but without success. On his return to New York he appealed to Simon Bolivar Buckner, who vouched for his hotel bill until money arrived from his father. Buckner, doing commissary and recruiting work at this time, remembered Sam well from West Point and the Mexican War. This loan was promptly repaid. On his return home Grant had two land warrants, each negotiable in New York for $180. Finally Jesse came to the rescue and he was able to travel to St. Louis.

His son's resignation from the army was a body blow to the elder Grant. He had had some time to think about it and had already been pulling strings in Washington to undo this final act. On June 1, 1854, without consulting Julia, he wrote to Jefferson Davis, Secretary of War: "I think after spending so much time to qualify himself for the army and spending so many years in the servis he will be poorly qualified for the pursuits of private life. ... I will remark that he has not seen his family for over two years & has a son nearly two years old he has never seen. I suppose in his great anxiety to see his family he has been induced to quit the servis."

Jesse proposed a six-month leave of absence as an alternative, or a shift to the recruiting service. In a chilly response, dated June 28, Davis wrote that the acceptance was complete and could not be reconsidered, and that Captain Grant "had assigned no reasons why he desired to quit the service and the motives which influenced him are not known to the Department."

These two men would hear of each other again in a significant way and their widows would find mutual consolation in their old age in comparing notes on the historical injustices done their husbands. But at the moment Julia was deeply concerned over all these rapid developments. She was relieved that Ulysses was coming home at last. At the same time she was much stirred up by the tales that reached her from different sources. She was well aware that his taste ran more to farming than to soldiering, but she did not wish to make any move that might hamper his career. She had listened enough to Jesse to know that he would act as the spirit moved him, regardless of consequences. None had boasted so much or so often about Ulysses, the soldier, as his father.

There was no patriotic necessity for staying in the army at that particular moment. The country was not at war. The Indians were the only immediate problem, and coping with them involved frontier service. Some of the most scintillant West Point figures had turned to other pursuits, and a few were now professors, fulfilling the ambition once harbored by Grant. It would take the Civil War to bring them all back into action. But Ulysses, who cared greatly for Julia's good opinion, was not returning to her with pride at this particular point in his career. He was keenly aware that he was thirty-two years of age and had made no headway in any direction.

Late in the summer of 1854 he arrived home with the worn look of a man who had suffered. This time he arrived at White Haven by buggy, not riding a horse. He flung the reins over the dashboard and jumped out when he saw two small boys playing on the front porch. As he walked up the path toward them the Negro girl who was watching Fred and Buck thought that they seemed alarmed. A second glance persuaded her that the bearded stranger was Captain Grant. She went indoors to spread the news.

Julia rushed out to meet him, and together they embraced each other and the children. The boys stared in bewilderment but Fred, aged four, soon realized that his father had come home. He had grown beyond recognition in the two years that Ulysses had been away, and Buck's was a small new face to behold. Grant must have seen his own image in the square forehead, the thoughtful eyes, the firm chin. They were friendly children and it did not take them long to warm to their father as he tossed them about and teased them.

Julia had been preparing herself for his return. Not knowing when he might come, she had dressed each day most becomingly, her summer muslins crisped and flounced around her short, trim figure. She was now twenty-eight. She had lost some of the girlish look she had had up to the age of twenty-five, but she was still slim, and swift in her movements. Her sense of humor was as keen as ever. She laughed softly and often at the family jokes and worked up many herself. Actually she had changed very little. The real change was in Grant. All the Dents noticed the lines of worry on his face, the tired look in his eyes. But he bore himself with dignity and reserve. He might seem shabby to outsiders but to Julia he looked a king. Her family made him welcome, although her father's comments beforehand had been as sharp as Jesse's. Most of the younger Dents were scattered now and only Emma was permanently at home to observe and take notes. George was married to Mary Isabella Shurlds, daughter of the cashier of the Bank of the State of Missouri, and was working as a broker in St. Louis. John had gone south. Nellie, the family belle, had married Dr. Alexander Sharp.

Starved for affection, Grant had a happy reunion with his family until the immediate cares of his situation came to the surface. He stayed at first at White Haven, weathering the cool looks of Colonel Dent and offering to help him around the farm in any way he could. Emma noted how content he was to be with the children and Julia again, but she also saw that "he was a man whose whole nature demanded work." One ordeal lay ahead of him. He still had to visit Jesse Grant, and Julia decided to accompany him on his trip home late in September.

By this time the elder Grants had moved to Covington, Kentucky. Some thought that Jesse had fled from the gibes in Bethel over the son from whom he had expected so much. Others argued more rationally that the move had been made for the sake of his daughters, who were of marriageable age and would have more social life in the new community. Besides, Cincinnati was across the river, and Julia and his grandchildren could more easily make the boat trip from St. Louis. The elder Grants enjoyed seeing Ulysses' sons.

Hannah, acquiescent as always, placidly remarked that Lyss should not have had anything to do with the army in the first place. Jesse was grim and unsympathetic. This was not like their honeymoon, with everyone trying to do them honor. The elder Grant was going into semiretirement at the time. He was sixty years old and had amassed a fortune of $100,000, which would soon grow to $150,000, an ample sum for these days. He had amicably dissolved his thirteen-year-old partnership with E. A. Collins, celebrating the event with a humorous poem in the local paper. Simpson, who was now twenty-eight, and Orvil, a bright youth of eighteen, had demonstrated their capacity to carry on the business. When Grant was in

Mexico and still in favor with his father, Jesse had considered the Galena retail store which was their outlet in Illinois as a suitable spot for him, should he wish to go into business on his return home. Now his other sons had taken hold there, to his satisfaction, and they planned to expand their activities in Illinois. Jesse would still keep a supervisory interest in the Ohio end of the business and would foster expansion. The tan-yards fed the retail outlets,

Ulysses' prospects were discussed from all angles. Finally, driving a hard bargain, Jesse proposed giving him a berth in Galena, provided he left Julia and the children at Covington or St. Louis. This was a condition that outraged both of the Grants. They would not consider it. Jesse was unyielding and they left with a deep sense of resentment. The elder Grant thought that Julia lived on too lavish a scale and he could not forget that she had three slaves — Eliza, Dan, and Julia Ann, who was known in the family as Black Julia. Colonel Dent had given each of his daughters slaves at birth, just as he gave them land when they married. The current of antislavery feeling ran strong in 1854 with the passing of the Kansas-Nebraska Act in May. A new star had risen in Stephen A. Douglas, although in the North he was accused of weakly yielding to the South in the hope of winning the Presidency. The compromise measures were now forgotten, and the nation was on its way to war. Kansas was in an uproar as adherents of both sides took squatters' rights and fought it out.

It was late in November before Julia and Ulysses returned to St. Louis. The visit to the Grant home had been a strain and Julia was glad to have Ulysses to herself again, away from Jesse's biting comments. As a result of the conferences at White Haven and Covington she and Ulysses came to a decision about the future. They had little choice at the moment. Ulysses had always said he wished to farm, and Julia channeled his course at this point by urging him to cultivate the sixty acres of uncleared land her father had given her as a wedding present. Jesse had promised him a thousand dollars to stock it, and with this assurance they settled down at White Haven to a winter of hard work.

It was not an ideal situation for the young Grants. In spite of Mrs. Dent's smooth handling of the joint household, her husband could not hide his hostility. This was not the fate he had envisioned for Julia. At the same time Ulysses disliked his state of dependency, although he never failed in courtesy and consideration toward his wife's family. But it was clear to various observers that he felt uncomfortable under this arrangement.

Colonel Dent's implacable enemy, Dr. Taussig, mayor of Carondolet from 1850 to 1863, was one of the first to spot the trouble. He would never enter White Haven because of his old feud with the Colonel, and their divergent politics, but he often met Julia and attended her children when she brought them in to stay at the home of William D. Barnard.

She had gone to school with Eliza Margaret Perry Shurlds, who was now Mrs. Barnard and the sister-in-law of her brother George. Whenever she could, Julia liked to visit her old school friend and let the children play in the garden amid the wooden and cast-iron stags, deer and hunting dogs, while she and Eliza chatted about fashions, children, husbands and politics. Barnard was a successful wholesale druggist, spare and handsome. He was fond of hunting and high living, and his jovial manner endeared him to both of the Grants. His warehouse was burned down before the Civil War and he never recovered financially. When Grant became President he made him Bank Examiner for Missouri. Eliza and Julia were lifelong friends, as well as relatives by marriage.

Whatever he might think of Colonel Dent and Grant, Dr. Taussig admired Julia and Eliza. "Both Mrs. Grant and Mrs. Barnard were charming, cultivated ladies, devoted to their husbands and children," he wrote. Taking note of discord in the Dent home he added: "A family physician gets to hear much that is kept from the public, and the, to say the least, dependent position which Grant occupied in the house of his father-in-law, was frequently commented upon in my presence. That he chafed under this condition of things was evident from his desire to obtain a position that would make him more independent."

At this time Dr. Taussig often observed Grant sitting on a log in front of the blacksmith shop that faced his office — "a serious, dignified looking man, with a slouched hat, high boots and trousers tucked in, smoking a clay pipe and waiting for his horses to be shod." He was of the opinion that had Grant had a "snug office, with sufficient income to live comfortably with his wife and children, independent of his father-in-law, it is at least a debatable question whether, at the outbreak of the war, he would have shaken off his easy-going indolence and volunteered into the service." But Grant's army friend, Horace Porter, at the dedication of his hero's tomb many years later, more nearly expressed Julia's view of things: "He was made for great things, not for little things."

She and her mother alone perceived his potentialities in those early days, long before the challenge of war made him a hero. She had faith in him every inch of the way. Knowing him better than any living person, she sometimes voiced her belief that Ulysses was destined for big things, and Mary Robinson took note of her sitting in a large rocking chair one day, discussing the financial embarrassment of her husband with some of the Dent relatives.

"But we will not always be in this condition," she suddenly exclaimed. "Wait until Dudy becomes President."

The others all laughed and thought it a great joke that their impoverished farmer's name should be linked to the White House. But Mary found this quite in key with Julia's view of her husband as a whole. She had often watched Julia come to his defense when his critics pushed hard. She believed that both of the Grants were inclined to look at the bright side of things. "He loved his wife and children, and was the kindest and most indulgent father I ever saw," Mary commented.

She had watched Julia from birth. She knew all her virtues and also her faults, which were chiefly those of an impulsive nature. From childhood she had been inclined to speak with great impetuosity and without much thought. She was so warm-hearted that her emotions obscured her judgment at times. Mary found Grant just the opposite. He always took thought before he spoke. He had temperate judgment and was as quiet at home as in public. He could lose his temper, like other men, but Mary had never heard him swear. However, he liked to chew tobacco and to smoke his pipe, and she was in league with Julia to hide the pipe whenever possible. Sometimes his wife would throw it out altogether and he would look at her with reproachful eyes and buy himself another. Mary never saw him get angry with Julia. On the rare occasions in their married life when he did, he treated her to sustained silence, a severe punishment for his spontaneous wife, who could not bear to be cut off from friendly communication. In general, he stood firm under petty irritations, ignored any quick bursts of temper on her part, and broke up her displeasure by the simple but effective device of teasing her.

Mary Robinson quietly observed the rising tide of discontent at White Haven. She knew that neighbors and relatives gossiped about the former West Point officer who slouched about in rustic attire and whose wife no longer shared in the brisk social life of the growing city. But the neighboring fanners also wore stout country clothes as they went about their work. Only a few were affluent, and Grant's ways would have passed unnoticed but for the bright glow in which he later moved, and the temptation to dramatize the contrast. His descendants do not view this period as one of uncommon stress or hardship, but regard it as an illustration of the sturdy spirit of Julia and Ulysses. Mary Robinson, who was on the spot, had a sound appreciation of this side of the picture. Through all their troubles she was conscious chiefly of the deep love that existed between the Grants; of the charm of their family life, and the delight they took in their handsome children. They were all at their best when they were together.

CHAPTER V: HARDSCRABBLE

ON THE FOURTH OF JULY, 1855, Julia bore her third child and only daughter. The infant was named Ellen for her grandmother but all through life she was known as Nellie. One day she would be a White House bride and the papers from coast to coast would picture her being married under a wedding bell of flowers. Even at birth an air of celebration surrounded Nellie. She became her father's favorite and year after year as she was growing up he fostered the family jest that the salutes and fireworks were in honor of her birthday.

Nellie was born at Wish-ton-Wish, a picturesque cottage in a grove of oaks, three miles from White Haven. Louis Dent had asked the Grants to take over his property and care for it when he left for California. They were relieved to move away from the disapproving looks and sharp comments of Colonel Dent, who still doted on Julia but could see no virtue in Ulysses. Fred and Buck ran wild in the woods around the cottage with the Indian name that meant whippoorwill. They studied their small blue-eyed sister with wonder, as they did the blue cranes, the plover and quail that crossed their line of vision.

Now that they were completely on their own Julia was forced to give careful thought to what she spent, but basic living was cheap. Firewood was abundant. Vegetables were easily raised. Bacon was plentiful on the farm. The children ate well and flourished, and Julia cut up her old dresses to make pantaloons for her fast-growing sons. By this time they were planning a house of their own. Ulysses was at work clearing Julia's acres and hauling cordwood into town to augment the family income. Knowing the White Haven land from birth, she helped him to select a site in a grove of young oaks a hundred feet back from the road. Here they put together the home that Ulysses, in a moment of ironic amusement, named Hardscrabble. Today it is known as the Grant log cabin and stands as Ulysses built it, although some miles away from its original site.

At one stage in its history it was moved to Old Orchard. Next it was shown at the St. Louis World's Fair. Now it may be seen on the Anheuser-Busch estate, close to Julia's old home, White Haven. The farm's 281 acres are devoted largely to animal husbandry and its carriage collection is unique. An ox-cart such as Grant used on his farm stands by the door of Hardscrabble. Lilac bushes bloom there in the spring. Gravois Creek still ripples over its white pebbles close to the cabin and sometimes floods its banks as it did when Julia and Ulysses were courting. Emma always viewed the cabin as her sister's creation, although Grant sweated to build it.

Julia, who liked to sketch, drew the design, knowing that she must make the best of things. Actually, she preferred the comfort and spaciousness of Wish-ton-Wish, but Hardscrabble was a gesture of independence by Ulysses that she strongly supported. Colonel Dent was willing enough to give Julia aid at any time, but Grant was determined to build a home of his own and to free himself entirely from any dependency on the Dent clan. His forest clearing and tedious wood-selling operations were part of a persistent campaign in this direction, and Emma noted that, although Julia had never before lived on so simple a scale, they had "plenty to eat and plenty to wear and no dependence upon their relatives or others."

John W. Emerson, a lawyer whose brother-in-law John F. Long, lived in the Gravois settlement, watched the Grants during this impoverished period and concluded that "no man enjoyed a sweeter domestic felicity — his supreme happiness centered in his home."

Julia and small Fred watched the progress of Hardscrabble with unflagging interest. They often followed Ulysses to the woods as he helped to fell the trees. He hauled stones for the cellar, logs for the walls and shingles which he split himself. He hewed the timber square and notched the ends to make the corners fit. Fred liked to watch him swing his axe and it heartened his father to catch occasional glimpses of Julia and the boys as he worked. In later years, surveying the ground where the trees had been cleared, he observed; "I moistened the ground around these stumps with many a drop of sweat, but they were happy days after all."

Finally the neighbors gathered for the "raisin" and brought their slaves to help. The boys ran back and forth, watching each stage with interest. Julia, in shawl and bonnet, chattered to the men as they worked. I. P. Sappington, later famous for his anti-fever pills with a quinine base for ague, was one of the helpers and he observed Colonel Dent seated on a small white horse giving orders. Charles Weber, a local cabinetmaker, made the window frames, sashes and doors by hand. Ulysses gave it the finishing touches inside. Then it was Julia's turn. She furnished its four good-sized rooms and central hall with skill and taste.

Soon she had a garden, and flowers bloomed both outdoors and inside. Visitors recalled her presiding in her home, her dark hair always neatly dressed, her linsey-woolsey and poplin gowns practical but becoming, a light jest often on her lips. Violets, jessamine, roses, clematis followed one another in succession in the china vases that graced her rooms. Julia took time to arrange her flowers. There was always a moment for beauty. Visitors noted that she brought sophisticated touches to her cabin in the woods. By this time she was a well-trained farmer's wife, taking the keenest interest in all of Ulysses' plantings. She invariably lent him her sympathy and support when things went wrong. In her declining years she recalled him planting okra seed and, "growing impatient to have it grow up, he dug up some of the little hills with his pocket-knife to see why they did not sprout." At last they decided to steep some okra seed in hot water and try a second planting. This time tiny leaves appeared "and many a delicious dish of chicken gumbo" came from this source.

"They were happy days in the log house," Julia observed after she had sampled the White House. Nellie was little more than a baby when Grant taught her to ride on the saddle with him. She had a dreamy little face with her father's grave eyes — a smoky blue — and dark, straight hair. He liked to wrestle with his growing boys and to tease Julia, who acted as umpire in these matches. Fred was an imaginative and daring boy and Buck had the quiet, composed look and manner of his father and Hannah.

Their chief delight was to sit in a circle on the floor around the blazing log fire at night and listen to his tales. Outsiders might think him a man of silence and reserve, but with Julia and the children he was eloquent. He talked most often of Mexico, and to Fred the Civil War tales that came later never seemed as vivid as the charge on Chapultepec, or his father being served bear meat at an Indian blockhouse in the Far West, or the streets of San Francisco, sprawling and wild, with miners in old flannel shirts trading gold dust for goods.

There was less of St. Louis and more of the rural life now for Julia. She was so busy with her children that a trip to town became an event. The opera flourished. The theaters grew in number, and often there was excellent music. But she maintained a social pace of her own and kept the green shoots of friendship alive. She and Ulysses went to neighborhood gatherings and church affairs. The merry days of picnics and sleighing parties with young officers were now succeeded by the same sort of expeditions on a simpler scale for their boys and little Nellie. The Grants no longer had a carriage. Their favorite way of conveying the children about was to take one apiece behind them on horseback. When Julia wished to go to a quilting Ulysses escorted her and the boys in this fashion, then galloped off. by himself. At the autumn shooting matches he sometimes carried off a quarter of beef, although he was not rated a crack shot by his neighbors.

Both Julia and Ulysses found time for acts of mercy. Their generous impulses all through life led them to share with others, whatever their own need. It was useless for Julia to protest her husband's improvident gestures when they had so little themselves, for her own instincts matched his in this respect. A sick child, a family dispute, a neighbor in need, a widow whose home had been burned, a farmer's cart stuck in the mud, all stirred the Grants to sympathetic action. Julia took the children to church as a regular rite, but the inconvenience was great, and when a movement was started to have a church built nearby, Grant subscribed at once, with the comment: "I am very glad to; we ought to have a comfortable place for preaching. I don't attend as much as I should, but Julia and the children do. We ought also to have a Sabbath-school in the neighborhood."

But if Julia rarely rode for pleasure any longer, and Ulysses drove a heavy team instead of a high pacer, they were still alive to the beauties of the changing seasons, to the fine Missouri landscape around them, to the growth of their children and the depth of their own love — a shield against the disappointments and humiliation that Ulysses suffered away from his own home.

His wood-hauling operations and rough attire caused talk in city circles where the gold-braided soldier was remembered. He worked first with one team, then with two, hauling wood ten miles and selling it for four dollars a cord. When Fred reached the age of seven he learned to handle one of the heavy teams, as his father had done in his boyhood. Even the disapproving Jesse paid tribute to his son's industry in the long run, acknowledging that "during all this time he worked like a slave no man ever worked harder."

Sometimes Ulysses went to Jefferson Barracks to discharge a load, and this encouraged the local talk that he was not doing well. Tales from Fort Humboldt had followed him there. After he became a national hero men who had known him during this difficult time dredged up odd bits of information about Grant. He often stopped in at the Planters Hotel where old West Pointers and prosperous businessmen were apt to stay on their visits to the fast-growing city. "I can see him now, sitting in an arm-chair, smoking an El Sol cigar and waiting with an air of extreme patience and resignation. But waiting for what? Did he himself know?" wrote Francis Grierson. "'Plain, unassuming Mr. Grant,' he was usually called."

The smartly uniformed officers who saw him at the hotel took note of his rundown appearance, although Sam Grant had never been one to polish his boots or worry about his buttons. Few traces of the sensitive-looking young cadet were visible in the strong, bearded man who now wore an old blue army overcoat, a battered hat, and long heavy boots with his pantaloons tucked into them. The guests stared a little when he came in to dine with army friends.

On one of his trips to St. Louis with wood he came face to face with General William S. Harney, handsomely uniformed and soon to leave on an expedition against the Indians.

He drew in his horse, Grant stopped his team, and the pair smiled into each other's eyes.

"Why, Grant, what in blazes are you doing?" exclaimed Harney.

The Captain, sitting comfortably atop his load of wood with his ax and his whipstock at his side, shifted one muddy boot across the other and drawled:

"Well, General, I am hauling wood."

The thing was so obvious and Grant so naive that General Harney and his staff roared with laughter. They shook his hand and joined with him and finally Carried him off to dine with them at the Planters Hotel.

On another occasion, Henry Coppee, a West Point friend who was now a professor at the University of Pennsylvania and later would write a book about the General, remembered with pleasure that Grant "in his farmer rig, whip in hand, came to see me at the hotel." Several other old West Point friends were present, including General D. C. Buell, and they all proposed a drink. Grant said, "I will go in and look at you, for I never drink anything." Coppee reported that the other officers, who saw him frequently afterward, told him that Grant drank nothing but water at that time.

One of the most difficult encounters of all was with Longstreet, tall, jovial "Pete" who had meant so much to Julia and Ulysses. He had been at Texas posts but was playing brag with some other officers at the Planters Hotel when he encountered Grant. They had a game together and next day Ulysses was back, this time with a five-dollar gold piece which he put in Longstreet's hand, saying it was a debt of honor from their Texas days.

Pete would not take it, insisting that Sam was out of the service and needed it more than he did.

"You must take it," said Grant earnestly. "I cannot live with anything in my possession which is not mine."

Knowing his character of old, and seeing the determination in his face, Longstreet took it "in order to save him mortification." They were not to meet again until the terms of surrender between North and South were drawn up.

When W. T. Sherman ran into Grant in St. Louis he, too, was out of the army and was staying with his wife's family. His comment was revealing, for he was having difficulties of his own. He had come to the conclusion that "West Point and the Regular Army were not good schools for farmers, bankers, merchants and mechanics."

When he returned at night to Hardscrabble, Ulysses would tell Julia of these encounters with his old army friends. Only she knew how deeply he was wounded at times by the kind but careless gestures of those who had known him in the past. She encouraged him to bring his friends to the farm. There they found him hard at work in the fields, a fanner who obviously knew what he was doing. They always received a warm welcome from his wife, and saw his three handsome children at play. All could see that Grant was happy in his home life, even if nothing else seemed to go well with him at this time.

In the winter of 1856-1857 Julia was in a state of great anxiety. Her mother was at the point of death over Christmas and Ulysses, in deep water, was asking his father for a five-hundred-dollar loan at ten percent interest. He had been laboring under disadvantages, he wrote to Jesse three days after Christmas, but now that he had his own house he hoped to do better. He needed seed but lacked the money to buy it. He had twenty-five acres of wheat at the time and his family practically lived off the land. But his plan was to raise potatoes, corn, cabbage, beets, cucumbers and melons, and take a wagon into market regularly with produce. His letter ended on a cheerful note: "Every day I like farming better and I do not doubt that money is to be made at it."

Julia was at White Haven constantly in the next few days and her mother died on January 14, 1857, after a month's illness. Her wise outlook had influenced them all and her daughter would always be grateful to her for her trust in Ulysses. None had thought more kindly of him than his mother-in-law, except Julia herself, and they had all been impressed by her premonitions that he would go far in the world. She had smoothed over many of the rough spots when Colonel Dent deplored his son-in-law's ineptitude as a businessman.

Jesse ignored Ulysses' appeal and on February 7, in real need of implements as well as seed, and with spring approaching, he wrote again, saying it would be his final appeal. He was not seeking charity but a loan, he pointed out. "I do this because, when I was in Ky. you voluntarily offered to give me a thousand dollars, to commence with, and because there is no one else to whom I could, with the same propriety, apply," he wrote.

He was then making less than fifty dollars a month with his firewood. He was clearing ten to twelve more acres of land that winter and hoped to get three hundred cords of wood from it, but without ready cash, he could scarcely go on farming, he informed Jesse. He now foresaw that he might have to do what Julia's father had suggested — sell the farm and invest elsewhere. For two years he had had to neglect the land while he went off to town with his wood "to buy any little necessaries, sugar, coffee, etc." How frugally Julia managed may be gauged from his next statement:

My expenses for my family have been nothing scarcely for the last two years. Fifty dollars, I believe, would pay all that I have laid out for their clothing. I have worked hard and got but little and expect to go in the same way until I am perfectly independent; and then too most likely.

Although naturally optimistic, Julia was in low water at this time. She had a heavy cold in the early spring. She was sorrowing over the death of her mother. Her father, lost without Ellen, was being difficult and demanding. There is no record of Jesse having sent Ulysses money at this time, but Grant did some planting and by August he and Julia were looking forward cheerfully to a potato crop of 1,500 bushels and to the sweet potatoes, melons and cabbage that they hoped to market. They had decided to keep their oats and corn for family use and sell the rest. Julia was even planning a little trip. She had not been ten miles from home, except to go in to St. Louis, since her visit to Covington three years earlier when Ulysses came back from the West.

But 1857 was a year of disaster. Farm prices dropped at crop time as panic seized the country. Many went bankrupt and business as a whole took a downward swoop. Ulysses made weary trips into town and saw how others suffered. By Christmas he felt desperate. Julia would be having another baby in February. He must find some trifles for the children and a few necessities for her. He took his gold hunting watch and gold chain into the shop run by Louis H. Freleigh and pawned them for twenty-two dollars.

Their fourth child was born in February 1858, and was named Jesse Root Grant after his paternal grandfather. By March Ulysses wrote to his sister Mary that the baby was growing rapidly and was healthy. He was considered the best-looking at birth among the four. "I don't think, however, there is much difference, in that respect, between them," he added.

Nellie, nearly three, was now talking plainly. Fred, aged eight, was driving one of the teams, Ulysses wrote with pride, and he hoped he would soon be going to school and learning to read. The nearest school was a mile and a half away and this was too far to send him in winter weather. They had discussed letting him go to Covington that summer but Julia would not permit him to travel alone with Jesse Grant, who was so absent-minded that he might walk off the cars at Cincinnati and not remember for an hour that he had a child with him. "I have no such fears," Ulysses assured his sister.

He rarely wrote home without inviting some of the Grants to come and visit them. "The whole family here are great for planning visits but poor in the execution of their plans," he noted. Although Julia was an irregular letter writer, she always backed up her husband's invitations with warmth and was interested in all that happened at Covington. But she knew there was little use inviting Hannah to visit them. Hannah did not leave her home, and all the Grants were reluctant to warm their hands at a slave-tended hearth.

By this time Julia and Ulysses were back at White Haven and had rooms to spare for family visitors. Genial invitations went out in all directions. Lonely without his wife, Colonel Dent had turned over the management of his place to the Grants and he and Emma had moved in to St. Louis to live. Hardscrabble and Julia's sixty acres were leased and Ulysses was now responsible for the management of a much larger property. He had two hundred acres of ploughed land to oversee and two hundred and fifty acres of pasture land to fence. Julia surveyed it all with family pride — twenty acres of potatoes, twenty of corn, twenty-five of oats, fifty of wheat, twenty-five of meadow, as well as clover, Hungarian grass and other crops.

But the summer of 1858 brought fresh disaster to her family. Fred became dangerously ill with typhoid fever. He was convalescent by

September but was deaf for some time afterward. Nellie and one of her children, who had come to visit them, also were stricken, and seven of the Negroes. A cold summer delayed the crops and early frost nipped them. Grant was not successful in his first year of stewardship, partly because he was again beset by the ague and fever that had plagued him in his boyhood. Julia, who felt ill herself, was worried about his condition. He was stiff and full of pains and could scarcely drag himself around. She saw that he could not carry on with such heavy outdoor work.

After long discussions they decided that the time had come for Ulysses to give up farming and go into his father's business. He took up his quill on October 1, 1858, and wrote: "I do not want any place for permanent stipulated pay, but want the prospect of one day doing business for myself. There is a pleasure in knowing that one's income depends somewhat upon his own exertions and business capacity...."

A few weeks later G. B. Bailey, of Georgetown, encountered Jesse Grant on the street and promptly wrote to an old West Point classmate: "The old gentleman who by the way is the greatest brag I have ever met with, informed me he would have to take U. S. and his family home and make him over again, as he had no business qualifications whatever — had failed in everything — all his other boys were good business men, etc., etc. The truth is that U. S. is the only one of the family that has any soul in him."

But Jesse was not responsive now to any plea of his son's, and Ulysses went doggedly on that winter — in Julia's estimation much too ill to be doing manual work. She suffered as she watched him come and go, his shoulders more stooped than ever, his hands now horny from labor, his eyes dark with fatigue. His shaking fits were alarming.

Grant's own comment on this period is simple and informing: "I managed to reef along very well until 1858 when I was attacked by fever and ague ... It lasted for over a year, and while it did not keep me in the house, it did interfere greatly with the amount of work I was able to perform. In the fall of 1858 I sold out my stock, crops and farming utensils at auction, and gave up farming."

Julia was convinced by this time that there was no other course to follow and she discussed with her father the possibility of work for Ulysses in town. As a result of her quiet inquiries and Colonel Dent's promptings Ulysses went into partnership on January 1, 1859, with her cousin, Harry Boggs. He ran a small real estate, loan and rent collection business on Pine Street, and was persuaded that Ulysses might bring in business through his army connections. St. Louis was expanding fast and real estate agents flourished, as new homes were built to meet the needs of a population that now reached 180,000. Steamship and railroad companies were building up massive business interests in St. Louis at this time.

Boggs & Grant had desk room with the law firm of McClellan, Hillyer and Moody in an old French mansion. Louisa Boggs, once a close friend of Julia's, gave Ulysses a bare little room with bedstead, washbowl, and chair in their home on South Fifteenth Street, and every Saturday, regardless of snow or rain, he journeyed out to White Haven to spend the week-end with his family. Julia had decided to stay with the children in the country for the winter until Ulysses got a foothold.

She soon saw that things were not going well with him in town. He was still plagued by rheumatism and ague, and on winter days his shaking was sometimes so severe that the law partners had to help him get to the omnibus. He did not have the heart to dun people for rents when he saw that they were unable to pay, and sometimes he turned out his own pockets to help them, particularly if the debtor chanced to be an old army man. Little fresh business came in. The field had become highly competitive with so many real estate firms opening, and this was not the sort of race that stirred Ulysses to action. But his concern for his family kept him going, and each trip home to Julia and the children refreshed him, in spite of the effort he made to get there.

A growing chill developed between the Boggs family and the Grants as business floundered and the hot fires of the pre-Civil War days raged around them. Louisa and Harry Boggs had strong Southern sympathies. So did a large part of the population of St. Louis. Ulysses had many friendly debates on the subject with the law partners in his office. William S. Hillyer, who soon would be a valued aide with him on the battlefield, was a talkative young lawyer from Kentucky, whose sympathies were Republican, or Know Nothing, at the moment. Josiah G. McClellan, a Virginian, was a Democrat and all three argued over political issues.

McClellan decided Grant was "not calculated" for business of that sort although an "honester, more generous man never lived." John Emerson sometimes found him bent over his desk, his hat pulled down to his eyes and the newspapers dangling limply from his rheumatic fingers. The papers were filled with signs and portents of political disunion at home. They also had vivid accounts of the Italian campaign, which he read in detail. As Julia well knew, he would still rather relive the Mexican campaign than collect overdue rents from men who had shared in it.

When spring came she and the children moved in to town and settled in a small frame house that Grant had rented at Seventh and Lynch Streets. It was down by the river, far from the fashionable area that she had once known so well, and out of the orbit of the O'Fallon hospitality, although John and Caroline remained her faithful friends. The rent was only $25 a month, but it was two miles away from Ulysses' office and he was often late for work. In extenuation he sometimes mentioned the fact that his wife had four children to attend to, and that breakfast had been late.

Along the street the wife of William A. Moffett observed the vigorous Grant children at play. One day her brother, Samuel Clemens, would be known as Mark Twain and would be responsible for the publication of Grant's Memoirs. But Moffett, a commission merchant, observed that although Grant was genial when he came to his office he did not seem to wish to enlarge his social circle. And for once Julia was not her usual expansive self. She was hard pressed to manage the children and it hurt her to see Ulysses so tired and beaten. When a business friend of Grant's urged his wife to call on Julia she went but snobbishly reported back: "Why did you send me there? The house is shabbily furnished, and they must be very poor."

Her husband assured her that Grant was an estimable gentleman. After that she came to know Julia well and was much attached to her. The gestures of family hospitality went on. Grant assured his sisters that they had one spare room and a bed in the boys' room and would welcome any of the family from Covington. Julia thought of visiting them that summer but with "four children she could not go without a servant, and she was afraid that landing so often as she would have to do in free states, she might have some trouble."

That March Ulysses had freed William, his only slave, the document reading "and I do hereby manumit, emancipate & set free said William from slavery for ever." Emma wrote that he was "opposed to human slavery as an institution." He could not be Jesse Grant's son and regard the issue with neutrality, but up to that time he had not taken an emphatic stand, and Julia obviously had been brought up in the plantation tradition. Their slaves had given the Dents much trouble in the Gravois region. Most of the surrounding farmers employed white help and Colonel Dent's slaves were a subject of discussion as feeling grew stronger on this whole issue.

Before leaving for the West Fred had fought it out with fisticuffs with one of the Sigerson brothers, powerful neighbors who worked a nursery farm nearby and had white help.

In 1856 Grant had tied his horse to a tree on election day and voted for James Buchanan. It was the first vote he had ever cast and he did it not in approval of the Pennsylvanian but because he distrusted John C. Fremont. He reasoned that with a Democrat elected by the unanimous vote of the slave states, "there could be no pretext for secession for four years." Commenting on this move in later years he said he had hoped at that time that "the passions of the people would subside . . . and the catastrophe be averted altogether."

But the slave issue confronted Grant again when he applied in the middle of August for the post of County Engineer. Here he could use his West Point training and his practical army experience in dealing with roads and bridges. "I do not want to fly from one thing to another," he wrote to his father five days after he made the application, "nor would I, but I am compelled to make a living from the start, for which I am willing to give all my time and all my energy."

A professorship at Washington University in St. Louis had fallen through. His old West Point friend, Joseph J. Reynolds, taught engineering there. Now the post of County Engineer with a salary of $1,500 a year was vacant. He feared the appointment would be made strictly on a political basis, but he had recommendations signed by thirty-four of the most noted citizens of St. Louis. Half-laughingly he told Julia one day that he was going to a French fortune teller to learn his fate. Usually she was the one who dealt in such interviews, and it was the measure of Grant's anxiety about the opening that he should have paid this visit.

Julia and Mary Robinson were tacking down carpets when he came back and announced that he would miss getting the post by a narrow margin but would soon be leaving the city to engage in a mercantile business.

"Something will happen very soon and then I will begin to rise in the world," he observed, in jesting reproduction of the fortune teller's predictions.

Julia was displeased with this crystal ball report. "Nonsense!" she exclaimed. "You will be elected, Dudy, for everyone says you cannot be beaten."

The two Democratic Commissioners voted for him. The Free Soilers were against him and, much as he admired Julia, Dr. Taussig cast the deciding vote against Grant. The doctor's comment on his decision was frank: "The Dents, at least the old gentleman, were known to be pro-slavery Democrats, and, to use the harsh language of that period, outspoken rebels. Grant lived with them, and though nothing was known of his political views, the shadow of their disloyalty necessarily fell on him. We felt bound, foreseeing events to come, to surround ourselves with officers whose loyalty to the Union was unquestioned."

The result was dismaying to Julia, knowing the basis of his defeat. The summer of 1859 ended with Ulysses at a low ebb. She talked things over with Louisa, who felt that he "had no exalted opinion of himself at any time, but in those days he was almost in despair." There was not enough business to sustain two families, and the partnership, which had never rested on a written agreement, was dissolved by mutual consent in September. Grant felt that it might have prospered had he been able to wait for the business to grow.

At this time they traded Hardscrabble and Julia's land for a more comfortable house at Ninth and Barton Streets. It had a steep slanting roof and a shade tree, and it seemed more like a home to Julia as she and Auntie Robinson worked to make it comfortable. Ulysses received a three-thousand-dollar note to cover the difference in the exchange of property. The deal involved a deed of trust on Hardscrabble to meet an overdue mortgage on the Barton Street house. But the title to the city property was not true, and again he was cheated. This deal led to many complications and litigation, and it was not until 1867 that the Grants had full ownership of Hardscrabble again.

With some cash now available and the boys settled in a good school in St. Louis, they found living a little easier. Fred and Buck liked their city school so well that their father was able to write to Jesse that "they never think of asking to stay at home." The younger Jesse was now a handsome little roustabout of a year and a half. Ulysses at this time landed a post at the Custom House, but with his usual bad luck lost it within two months' time, when the collector who had appointed him died.

This was another blow that affected them deeply, although Julia did not ask questions when he came home at night but greeted him in a calm and understanding way. It was strange for her to spend Christmas and the New Year, which had once been so gay for her in St. Louis, in their new obscurity — her husband out of work and with nothing much in prospect. Some of the officers still called to see them. Julia's old friends did not forsake her, and the children were remembered at Christmas. But nothing was as it had been except their devotion to each other.

Far into the night they discussed the future. Grant was still full of plans and kept a steady balance in the midst of discouragement. Julia was practical and came up with many suggestions. A deal to send goods by freight over the Sante Fe railway had fallen through. Should he go to Colorado to set up in business with a friend? Should he start a hardware business in St. Louis? These were possibilities they considered. Devoted as he was to Julia, Colonel Dent was coldly unsympathetic at this time and ridiculed Ulysses, to the deep grief of his daughter.

Meanwhile, John Brown's raid had shaken the country, and lines of demarcation were clearly drawn in St. Louis, with Julia caught in the crossfire between the two families. She had long resisted the thought of leaving her native region and moving north. But now she made her choice. The time had come for them to swallow their pride and again seek a place for Ulysses in his father's tanning business. Julia accepted this decision without question. They turned the key in their Barton Street front door and set off with their four children for Galena. It was the first step in a momentous journey for the Grants.

CHAPTER VI: GALENA

JULIA STEPPED OFF the Itasca at the Galena landing with her four children on an April day in 1860. Ulysses came next, carrying a chair under each arm. Only the levee loungers noted the bearded square-set man with the blue-caped army overcoat, and the neat figure of his bonneted wife. Six years later a great crowd would cheer him in the same surroundings. But at the moment the six Grants suggested a family of modest means, thriftily dressed, headed for a new home in the hilly city of 14,000 inhabitants.

Colonel Dent had prepared Julia for Galena. Early in the century, when the trek to the lead mines brought thousands of settlers into the region, he furnished supplies for the military post there. Now Galena was on the decline after a long period of prosperity. The clock had slowed down in 1855 when the railroad took over and river traffic dwindled. Dubuque now flourished as the western terminus of the Illinois Central Railroad. Thus the oldest city in Illinois, built up by miners, traders, explorers and gamblers at a time when Chicago was no more than a swampy village, was losing much of its trade, although none of its frontier qualities. It still had a number of wholesale firms catering to the surrounding states. There were grist mills, iron foundries, mines, lumber yards, lime kilns and breweries in the valley.

Julia took interested note of the crooked streets and grilled balconies, the steep steps up the hillside and the terraced effect of the homes. Galena had the look of an Alpine village, with houses clinging to its slopes like chalets. Both Dolly Madison and Mrs. Alexander Hamilton had been early visitors, and all the talk at the moment was of two rising men — Abraham Lincoln and Stephen A. Douglas. From the wharf the Grants walked up past the new De Soto House, where Lincoln had spoken from the balcony in 1856.

They were welcomed by Simpson, whose sunken cheeks and high flush proclaimed his rapid decline. Their new home was a two-story brick cottage on Hill Street, high on a bluff. They had to climb two hundred feet of wooden steps to get up to it from Main Street. Three trees putting forth April shoots of green stood in front of the house and a picket fence fronted on the sloping street. It had a flat front with faded gray shutters and was wholly unpretentious, inside and out. The rent was $125 a year and Simpson lived with them, to share expenses. Ulysses had come to an understanding with his father about his place in the firm. Jesse had turned him over to Simpson and Orvil, who offered him $800 a year, with the prospect of a partnership in the business. Actually, he drew $1,500 in the first year but soon paid back the balance when he went in the army.

The Grants dealt in saddlery, morocco linings, shoe findings and sundry leather goods. Their domestic leather was tanned in the oak woods of Ohio, but the hides were bought in Galena, and this became one of Ulysses' tasks. He was bill clerk, and collection agent. In addition he sold stock, weighed leather, did office work and generally made himself useful on the premises. Julia was happy to see that his brothers made no attempt to order him around but treated him with respect as an older man of judgment and worldly experience.

She had her hands full at home and mingled little with the people of Galena in this first year, although she was to make many friends there after the war. For the first time in her life she was without slaves. But Julia had learned long ago to manage well. Now, with the occasional help of a girl named Maggie Cavanaugh, she ran her household smoothly in Galena. Their furnishings were sparse, and they had few possessions at this time.

Neighbors observed Julia going up and down the steps with little Nellie, or walking out on the bluff in the late afternoon to meet her husband coming home from work. His wide-brimmed hat and long army coat attracted attention, and some noted that his clothes bore evidence of careful brushing and mending. If Julia seemed aloof it was because she had so much to do and could not live in the hospitable manner to which she had long been accustomed. Her husband and his brothers always welcomed her to the family store when she came downtown to shop. She soon became accustomed to the cobblestones of Perry Street, to the long flight of steps, to the twists and turns of Main Street, to the imposing facade of the De Soto House.

By this time she was not a novice at worldly observation. She had watched the busy flow of traders through St. Louis for a number of years, but had never seen so motley a crowd as sauntered along the streets of Galena, Anything from a Paris gown to a miner's overalls was on view at the hotel, with its two hundred rooms and lofty ceilings. Gamblers and ladies of the night passed back and forth in the crooked streets and the accents suggested a geographical range from Maine to Georgia, from Stockholm to Zurich. Galena still had the raffish air of a boom town, but it also had pillared mansions, modest homes, and a solid core of substantial citizens.

The town had its own fascination for the children. The boys liked to go down to the landing to watch the Mississippi boats come in. Draymen, porters and runners caused a stir as the passengers disembarked, and the arrivals in themselves were a lively sight. The Indian stockade that had housed the prisoners of the Black Hawk War of 1832 was another favorite spot with the boys. Julia posted her letters to St. Louis from the new post office built by engineer Ely S. Parker, a handsome and highly literate Seneca Indian destined to serve as military secretary to her husband. On Sundays she led her entire family to the First Methodist Church, a brick building where the Grant pew may be seen today, next door to the Galena Historical Museum which houses Thomas Nast's life-sized oil painting: "Peace in Union."

Fred soon became a personality in Galena. He objected greatly to Julia's furbishing instincts. One of the family jests was his resistance to any form of dressing up. He had long protested his mother's habit of putting her boys into waists buttoned to short trousers, and in Galena he thought it iniquitous that he could not go barefoot like the other boys on the hill and wear a shirt with a single suspender. It reminded him of the time that his mother had dared to put him in long pantaloons to have his picture taken in St. Louis. He had planted his hands firmly on the offending trousers and had told her that she must cut them off at the knees at once. Julia, standing side face to the camera, was firm, and Fred's scowl afforded his father much amusement.

In Galena, as elsewhere, she kept the children scrubbed and immaculate, taking particular delight in Nellie's flounces and the long curls that Buck still wore. Otherwise the Grant home was free and easy. The children made as much noise as they liked without reproof, and Julia was generous with jokes and cookies.

"Mister, do you want to fight?" Fred would ask, when his father came home from the store.

"I am a person of peace; but I will not be hectored by a person of your size," Grant would reply.

Jesse could not recall a "single unkind, unfair, or unjust thing" done to him by either parent and "their loving acts would cover every day of our association." The currents of understanding flowed steadily in the Grant home, regardless of setting. Fred thought he was the favorite because he was the eldest; Buck because he bore his father's name; Nellie because she was the only girl; and Jesse because he was the youngest. But so much affection was spread among them that none felt the pinch of favoritism.

Young Lewis Rowley, son of William R. Rowley, clerk of the Circuit Court who later became Provost Marshal on Grant's staff, was in and out of the Grant home. He was Fred's closest friend and in after years recalled how Captain Grant "used to sit and read to Mrs. Grant, or read by himself and smoke a clay pipe." Ulysses came to know Rowley when he went to the court house to measure, cut and tack leather to a desk chair. He was later one of the group of twelve generals and high-ranking officers from Galena to figure in the annals of the Civil War, largely through close links with Grant, who worked so obscurely among them.

But Jesse complained that Ulysses made no effort to widen his acquaintance while there. He thought it a curious fact that "citizens of our town would stop in front of our store, within six feet of the windows, and look in to see which of the Grants it was that was absent when he suddenly became famous." Augustus L. Chetlain, whose fine old homestead stood on ground bought from the government in 1836 for four dollars an acre, noted that "he led a quiet life and seemed little inclined to make the acquaintance of his fellow-citizens, but was highly esteemed by all who knew him."

Grant climbed the hill for dinner at noon every day and to those who noticed him at all he seemed "as diligent as a clock." He was working hard to clear off some of the debts he had left behind him in St. Louis, as well as to maintain his family in comfort. By August he wrote to a friend that he was making headway in Galena and hoped in a few years "to be entirely above the frowns of the world, pecuniarily." And by Christmas he wrote to his father: "I hope to be a partner soon." That winter Julia saw him off on a trip through the Northwest, to collect bills and make sales in Wisconsin, Minnesota and Iowa. He was gradually taking over the ailing Simpson's work. Back in the Galena store, Ulysses sometimes made mistakes, but always in favor of the customer. He was not at heart a salesman and he did not know the stock. Moreover, he was invariably responsive to a hard luck story when it came to collecting bills. The Grant store, like the others on Main Street, was a focus for political discussion as war seemed near at hand. Orvil was a rabid Republican and was almost as loud and explosive as his father. Ulysses stayed in the background, rarely expressing an opinion.

Sometimes neighbors came in during the evening to play euchre or else Grant met them in a room above the store. Orvil and his wife frequently spent the evening with them. Julia's own closest friend in Galena at this time was Mrs. L. S. Felt, the wife of a local merchant. Her daughter, Kitty Felt, would become a protegee in her White House days. When the card players were settled for the evening and Julia had put the children to bed and heard their prayers, if no women friends were present she would seat herself by the china lamp and knit, glancing affectionately at Ulysses from time to time as he smoked and put down his cards in silence. As time went on her circle enlarged and she did some modest entertaining.

In a simple frame cottage along the street from the Grants, the wife of John Aaron Rawlins was dying of consumption. This self-educated lawyer was destined to become a significant figure in Julia's life. He was thirty years old, a lean, blazing-eyed zealot of Scotch-Irish extraction whose father had joined the gold rush in 1849, while his son supported the family by burning charcoal, tending the pits during the night watches, and hauling it to the furnaces and smelting works. With a flair for political debate and intense ambition he finally left the pits, settled in Galena and became one of its leading lawyers. His manners were rough, his speech often profane, but his vigorous personality impressed itself on the Grants.

Both families had a magnificent view from their cottages on the bluff. Julia, studying the wide vista of valley and encircling hills, must have longed at times to go galloping toward the woods. But there was no horseback riding for the Grants in Galena. A hired carriage on rare occasions was the best they could do. The children shared in the excitement of the torchlight processions and fireworks as the presidential campaign swept Lincoln toward the White House. Galena was divided into two camps — the Lincoln and the Douglas supporters. Both men were well known in the community. The Douglas Club elected Grant captain but he refused, saying he wished to attend to business and not get into politics.

The wives took sides. Julia was more prone to voice her views than Ulysses. The romantic Douglas and the tall, strange son of Illinois were live figures in the homes of Galena. The news from Washington was ominous and Julia heard from her father that St. Louis was buzzing with talk of secession. She and Ulysses were watching the political scene with close attention at this time. Grant now viewed the vacillating Buchanan, for whom he had voted, as "a granny of an Executive." He feared some "foolish policy" that would give the seceding states the support and sympathy of the southern states that did not go out.

Galena, like the rest of the country, blazed with excitement on the April day that Fort Sumter was fired on and the Civil War began. All its residents turned out into the streets. Stores were closed and flags flashed into view at every turn. The Wide-Awakes marched with their brass bands. The De Soto lobby was packed with chattering men and women. Housewives talked over their back fences, knowing what it would mean to them. Julia must have realized at once that Ulysses, with his West Point background and war experience, would figure somewhere in the picture. She came from a military family and did not question the necessity.

"I thought I had done with soldiering," said Grant, but he had only just begun. Like many others, he believed that the war would be over in ninety days. Indeed, it took Shiloh to waken him out of this dream. But neither he nor Julia agreed with those who said that there was much bluster about the Southerners but not much fight. He expressed the opinion to Rowley: "If they once get at it they will make a strong fight."

When Lincoln's call for volunteers reached Galena, posters appeared overnight announcing a citizens' meeting. Business came to a standstill and party differences were forgotten for the most part. The courthouse was packed. When the city's mayor suggested compromise two men who would always stand close to the Grants made stern protests. Elihu B. Washburne, a congressman originally from Maine, thin-lipped, tall and smooth-shaven, declared: "Any man who will stir up party prejudice at such a time as this is a traitor to his country." Rawlins, with blazing eyes in n ashen face, made an eloquent speech that stirred his audience to wild applause as he finished: "We will stand by the flag of our country and appeal to the God of Battles for support."

On his way home Ulysses told Orvil that he thought he would go into service. He repeated his intention to Julia, who showed no surprise. When a second meeting was held for recruiting purposes Grant was appointed chairman. The quiet man who was rarely seen with his hat off but was known to have West Point experience, rose from a pine bench and moved forward in embarrassment, his head tilted to one side, his face flushed. He talked quietly, without any bluster or extravagance. Later he could not tell Julia anything he had said. It had all slipped from his mind, but others recalled his promise: "I am in for the war and shall stay until this wicked rebellion is crushed at the cannon's mouth." Washburne, to whom he still was a stranger, expressed surprise that Galena could not find a presiding officer for such an occasion without calling in an outsider.

"I never went into our leather store after that meeting, to put up a package or do other business," said Grant. And Julia was face to face with a new way of life. Ulysses had a long talk with her that night, and they both discussed her father. Next day he wrote Colonel Dent a letter showing firmly where he stood. It was in a sense a challenge to the stubborn Democrat and must have caused Julia some concern:

The times are indeed startling; but now is the time, particularly in the border slave states for men to prove their love of country. I know it is hard for men to apparently work with the Republican party but now all party distinctions should be lost sight of, and every true patriot be for maintaining the integrity of the glorious old Stars and Stripes, the Constitution and the Union. The North is responding to the President's call in such a manner that the Confederates may truly quake. I tell you there is no mistaking the feelings of the people . . . No impartial man can conceal from himself the fact that in all these troubles the Southerners have been the aggressors, — and the administration has stood . . . more on the defensive than she would dare to have done, but for her consciousness of strength and the certainty of right prevailing in the end. ... In all this I can but see the doom of Slavery.

Grant added that Julia and the children were well and that Fred Dent, who was married by this time to Helen Louise Lynd, had a new son whose "novel name" he could not remember. At the same time he wrote with equal frankness to his own father, pointing out that "we are now in the midst of trying times when every one must be for or against his country, and show his colors too, by his every act." He noted that since he had been educated for such an emergency at the expense of the Government its claim on him was superior to any motive of self-interest. He asked for his father's approval or advice, and added: "There are but two parties now, traitors and patriots, and I want hereafter to be ranked with the latter, and I trust, the stronger party."

Having thus declared himself all round, Grant settled down to making himself useful. He had declined the captaincy of the company that had been raised because he hoped to command a regiment. But he agreed to help in any way he could. The Grant home on the hill now became a lively center, with the boys running errands for their parents. Julia was involved at once, for the women of Galena proposed to make uniforms for the first company. They approached Ulysses for precise details on how they should be fashioned. They bought the material; found tailors to cut up the garments, and then they sewed them. Julia, accomplished with her needle and well used to the details of army uniform, became the backbone of this activity. Meanwhile, Grant took the volunteers, divided them into squads, and superintended their drill. By this time Washburne had spotted him as an old West Pointer and a veteran of the Mexican War. They came to know each other better. He took Grant with him to Springfield where the company Grant had trained was assigned to a regiment.

"History supplies few, if any, examples of equally sudden, brilliant, and enduring fame," James G. Wilson later wrote of Grant and his emergence at this time. But no one seemed to be in haste to seek his services in the beginning. He had one disappointment after another and Julia read his letters with dismay. No appointment was forthcoming at Springfield for her able captain. She could not understand it.

He had a room with Captain Chetlain and took his meals at the Chenery House. But he felt lost in the confusing rush of men seeking office. He saw "so much pulling and hauling for favors that I determined never to ask for anything, and never have, not even a colonelcy," he wrote home. Captain John Pope was the military hero of the hour in Illinois and Grant had left Galena with a "slender purse and a lank carpet bag." He was the forgotten soldier. Julia was expecting him back at the end of April when she learned that Governor Richard Yates of Illinois had appointed him assistant adjutant-general of the state. She knew that his military training could now be used to good account, but in actual fact the next few weeks were dim ones for Grant, with men all around him receiving good appointments while he handled blanks and army forms. His own comment was that the "only place I ever found in my life to put a paper so as to find it again was either a side coat-pocket or the hands of a clerk or secretary more careful than myself." However, in this subordinate capacity he helped to muster in the sixteen regiments which formed the state's quota.

"There is no disposition to compromise now," he wrote to his sister Mary from Springfield on April 29, suggesting at the same time that it might be prudent for the Grants to lock up and leave Covington "until the present excitement subsides." If his father were younger and Simpson were strong, he would not advise such a course, he wrote. On the contrary, he would like to see "every Union man in the border slave states remain firm at his post," the equal of an armed volunteer in defense of his country. Ulysses had already written to his father urging him to move; otherwise he might be placed in an awkward position and a dangerous one pecuniarily, although he "would never stultify his opinion for the sake of a little security."

Both families were in an agitated state at this time although Julia and Ulysses took things calmly. Colonel Dent believed that his son-in-law could easily get a high command if he were to join the Confederate Army as Robert E. Lee, Joseph E. Johnston and others were doing. Meanwhile, Ulysses' aunt, Mrs. Rachel Tompkins, who had a large plantation in Virginia and was an ardent secessionist, was having a furious correspondence with the Grants, writing: "If you are with the accursed Lincolnites, the ties of consanguinity shall be forever severed."

Julia was dismayed by some of the letters reaching her from St. Louis at this time. When Ulysses came home on leave late in May they talked over the situation at length and arrived at a firm decision. She caught the full measure of his disgust with the political jockeying he had witnessed on the state level. Now he proposed to offer himself for national service. He moved about the house like a restless ghost, feeling all the time "as if a duty were being neglected that was paramount to any other duty I ever owed," he wrote to Jesse.

Finally he sat down on May 24th and addressed a letter to Adjutant General Lorenzo Thomas, stating his experience and offering his services. "I feel myself competent to command a Regiment if the President in his judgement should see fit to entrust one to me," wrote Ulysses S. Grant with humility. He never received an answer. Years later he learned that the letter "had not been destroyed, but it had not been regularly filed away." He admitted in private to some hesitancy about suggesting the rank of colonel, but he had seen nearly every colonel mustered in from the State of Illinois, and some from Indiana, "and felt that if they could command a regiment properly, and with credit, I could also." Julia had no doubt of this. Before he left for camp she showed him plainly how much she approved his course, and he wrote to his father: "Julia takes a very sensible view of the present difficulties. She would be sorry to have me go, but thinks the circumstances may warrant it and will not throw a single obstacle in the way."

Julia was never disposed to put obstacles in the way of Ulysses, and she always took a straight and practical view of a situation as it arose. Her father and Emma might pull sternly in the other direction, but she stood firm as a rock. She was wholeheartedly with her husband from the start and her loyalty was not questioned in the years to come, although she kept silent when the South was attacked. But at the moment she again saw her Captain rejected. After cooling his heels for a reasonable length of time and hearing nothing from Washington he asked for a week's leave to visit his parents in Covington. His real motive was to see General George B. McClellan, whose headquarters were across the river in Cincinnati. He had known him at West Point, in the Mexican War and at Fort Vancouver. He called twice at his office, without result, and returned to Springfield. On his way back he received a telegram from Governor Yates offering him the colonelcy of the 21st Regiment. "It was the most glorious day of my life when I signed it," the Governor commented later. But the appointment was a fluke. Grant was taking the place of a young colonel so unpopular that his troops would not have him. And the second call to arms had come from Lincoln.

Julia at this time was nursing little Jesse, who had been quite ill during these weeks of uncertainty. She was run off her feet, marketing, cooking, cleaning, looking after the children and doing her war work. Women everywhere were stirred to fresh and unfamiliar activity by the rush of events, and the departure of their men from their homes. They were sewing flags and uniforms. They were saying good-bys but Grant did not feel that the separation would be for long. "A few decisive victories in some of the southern ports will send the secession army howling, and the leaders in the rebellion will flee the country," he wrote to his father. "All the states will then be loyal for a generation to come."

Julia was not so sure. She watched the papers anxiously for news of Ulysses' regiment. He had subscribed to the St. Louis Democrat for her, writing that it carried more army news than any of the other papers and had a regular correspondent with one of the regiments of his brigade. He stayed at Springfield until July 3, getting the men into shape at Camp Yates. He had found them in a demoralized condition. They lacked tents, uniforms and were wholly undisciplined. He arrived on the scene himself in the civilian attire he had worn when he left Julia. The men were not impressed until he went into action and handled them sternly. Then they saw that he was a formidable soldier. He took a hurried trip home for supplies. Collins, his father's old partner, endorsed his note for $300 and he bought a horse and uniform. He had a long talk with Washburne in his library, revealing some of his own inner strength and engendering confidence in the congressman.

Fred had been plaguing Julia to let him join Father and when he said good-by to her for the last time before going into action, kissing her tenderly as he always did when they were parting, his eleven-year-old son walked away by his side. But Jesse later recalled that after a few battles had been fought "when father left mother and me for a battle front, his going aroused no more emotion in me than when he left us each morning for the leather store in Galena."

When orders came to move to Quincy early in July Ulysses wrote to Julia that he was sending Fred home. He assumed that she would be in a state of great anxiety over her small son heading toward danger. But Julia was unafraid. She wrote back immediately, urging him to let Fred go with him. But Fred was already on his way up the Mississippi bound for Dubuque. He took the train from there to Galena, and arrived home, disgusted to be an errand boy again instead of a soldier.

Ulysses had first proposed sending Julia and the children to Covington to board while he was away, but on second thought he wished them to stay in Galena. "The people of Galena have always shown the greatest friendship for me and I would prefer keeping my home there," he wrote to his sister Mary, at the same time reiterating his never answered request that she go and stay with Julia. The breach with Colonel Dent at this point was so wide that he did not wish to have his family stay with his father-in-law in St. Louis. His letter to the old gentleman had stirred up a storm. The colonel could not understand his allegiance to the Federal cause. Grant went to St. Louis to talk things out with him. He stayed with W. D. Barnard and together they drove over to Wish-ton-Wish.

Mary Robinson had never seen Colonel Dent so angry about anything. He pointed out that Grant could easily become a brigadier general were he to join the Confederate Army. Grant stood flushed and resistant. He told his father-in-law that he would not consider such a command unless it were won by the sword. Colonel Dent tried all his powers of persuasion to swing him to the Confederate side, then ended the interview with the observation: "Send Julia and the children here. As you make your bed so you must lie."

Ulysses did not have long to wait for the title Colonel Dent had proposed for him, but it came from the Union side. Early in August, while he was stationed in Mexico, Missouri, to Julia's great delight he was commissioned a brigadier general. He read of the appointment first in a St.

Louis paper. She learned of it in the same way. His father had already written asking if he did not wish to return to the regular army. He said he did not, adding: "I want to bring my children up to useful employment, and in the army the chance is poor."

As he rose in the service he was plagued by requests of all kinds for favors and appointments. Some of them reached him through Julia, who also was subjected to these appeals. When his father suggested a saddlery contract he wrote to him: "I cannot take an active part in securing contracts, ... it is necessary both to my efficiency, to the public good and my own reputation that I should keep clear of Government contracts."

When his father's old partner, Collins, suggested certain staff appointments Grant asked Julia to inform him that he had only two lieutenancies to give away, and they would go to field officers. He wrote quite sharply to Jesse in October that he had not asked for his own position, but now that he had it he intended to perform the duties as rigidly as he knew how, without looking for places for others. "I want always to be in a condition to do my duty without partiality, favor or affection," he informed his father firmly.

But Jesse would not keep quiet. He was proud of Ulysses again, now that he was back in good standing with the army. He boasted loudly of his son's military popularity and skill. He criticized other generals. He read Ulysses' letters aloud to those who would listen. He picked up every attack he saw in the press and made much of it. He passed on his views without thought, in spite of repeated warnings from Grant and Julia. Both were dismayed by such indiscretion. The reverberations got back to headquarters, and Julia heard them in Galena. Grant particularly asked his father not to read to others a letter in which he said that the officers with great unanimity had requested to be attached to his command when he was appointed brigadier general. "I very much dislike speaking of myself," he observed.

Julia now had trouble keeping up with her husband's military moves, but he wrote with regularity and always most affectionately. She was relieved when he settled in Ironton, Missouri, and found that although General William J. Hardee had been reported ready to attack with 8,000 troops, only small scouting parties were detected by the pickets. Meanwhile, he found Ironton "one of the most delightful places I have ever been in." He was encamped in a house close to a spring of cold sparkling water, and was writing to her in the shadow of a magnificent oak tree. But he had little time for correspondence, he informed her. He was usually busy until midnight or later. He had hoped to return to Galena for a brief visit, and to get some things he needed. He was without sword, sash or the appropriate uniform for his new rank and he saw no chance of getting them. "Tell Jess he must be a good boy and learn to read," Ulysses continued. "I hope mother & Simp will stay with you all summer and I don't believe but what he would do better in the Winter there than in Covington. If I can draw my pay regularly I will supply you liberally," but first he had to send $300 to the store to pay off a debt.

Julia relaxed when she knew that he was so well settled in Ironton. But she heard of him soon in Jefferson City, which was packed with fugitive families. By the end of August he was at Cape Girardeau in Missouri and was again urging Julia not to leave Galena. Jesse Grant wished them all to move to Covington but neither Ulysses nor Julia favored this plan. The occupation of Paducah was the next excitement in the Grant home. Julia read all the details to Fred from the paper and waited for word from Ulysses. Before leaving the city he had promised the citizens protection and had left troops to guard them. There was much discussion about his handling of this situation. His next letters came from Cairo and he was considering having Julia, Fred and Jess visit him there but finally decided this move would be unwise. "I hardly think it would be prudent at this time," he wrote to his sister Mary on September 11. "Hearing artillery within a few miles it might embarrass my movements to have them about. I am afraid they would make poor soldiers."

But Julia was to prove herself a good soldier before long. However, at the moment she was grieving over her favorite brother-in-law, Simpson. She had just written to warn Ulysses that he had arrived in St. Paul on his way home and was close to death when the final word came. Grant received both messages together. Simpson had been ill for so long that they all took the news philosophically and Grant commented: "But few families of the same number have gone so many years without the loss of a single member."

By this time he had taken possession of the Kentucky bank opposite Cairo. Julia discussed all this with Fred, who now wanted to know every day what Father was doing. They were beginning to understand that he would be away from home for a long time. Grant no longer thought that the war would soon be over. On September 11 he noted that "this war is formidable and I regret to say cannot end so soon as I anticipated at first."

On November 7 he fought and lost his first battle of the Civil War. Grant did not view it as total defeat. He believed that the national troops "acquired a confidence in themselves at Belmont that did not desert them through the war." But the engagement was severely criticized in the North as being barren of results, an unnecessary battle. It was an independent and spontaneous foray by Grant and brought heavy repercussions.

On the day after the battle Ulysses wrote Julia one of his most informative war letters. He had a copy made to be sent to his father. He explained that the object of the engagement was to prevent the enemy from sending a force into Missouri to cut off troops he had sent there for a special purpose. His men had taken a great many prisoners and burned everything possible before starting back, having accomplished all that they went for, and even more, he wrote. They had fought their way from tree to tree through the woods to Belmont, about two and a half miles, the enemy contesting every foot of the way. General John A. McClernand "who, by the way, acted with great coolness and courage throughout, and proved that he is a soldier as well as a statesman," had his horse shot from under him. So did Ulysses.

"We found the Confederates well armed and brave," Grant added. "There was no hasty retreating or running away. Taking into account the object of the expedition, the victory was most complete. It has given me a confidence in the officers and men of this command that will enable me to lead them in any future engagement without fear of the result."

After Belmont Julia joined Grant in Cairo. It was her first foray into army territory, but not by any means her last, and she studied his surroundings and associates with the greatest interest. A number of wives made their appearance in camp at this early stage of the war, but none was to become so regular and important a visitor as Julia. She was quiet and inconspicuous in all her movements but her boys whipped up a merry din around the General.

Toward the end of November she moved on to St. Louis, with the intention of returning in two weeks should Ulysses still be at Cairo. "It costs nothing for her to go there, and it may be the last opportunity she will have of visiting her father," Grant wrote to Jesse on November 27, knowing that the war was entering a serious phase. He hoped she would also spend a week or two in Covington with his family before returning to Galena.

Julia found St. Louis a changed city. Her father, as she expected, was much wrought up and disapproving. She was stung by his blunt allusions to Grant's Union allegiance. Many of her old friends had swung to the Southern side. She felt a certain loneliness among them, although the gashes of war were not yet wide open, the deaths had not yet spread terror. However, she had a strong taste of what it meant to be on the enemy side. The sympathies of Louisa and Harry Boggs, for instance, were unmistakable. Longstreet and many of her old army friends were now Confederate soldiers. Julia moved tactfully in her father's sphere, her thoughts all centered now on Ulysses and the battles that she knew must come. At the moment he was worried about his command. General Fremont had been superseded by General Henry W. Halleck to head the Department of Missouri. Halleck promptly divided the territory into districts and Grant fell heir to the District of Cairo and a river region, an important command. By the middle of December Julia and the children were back with him. She had made up her mind not to go to Covington as long as Ulysses remained at Cairo, and he anticipated being there for some time. But serious trouble had blown up for Grant during Julia's absence in St. Louis. Rumors of intemperance in camp had reached Washburne in Washington and he had written asking Rawlins for the truth of the matter. Charges had been made by William J. Kountz, superintendent of River Transportation under McClellan, a disgruntled officer who had been hauled up for irregularities in the quartermaster's department. In the end they were set down to malice, and Rawlins wrote to Washburne at length on December 30, 1861, reporting that he had found Grant a "strict temperance man" when he reached Cairo, and was told by those who knew him well that this had been his habit for the past five or six years. Even at a festive luncheon on the cars, with some railroad friends present, he noticed that Grant had not taken more than a half glass of champagne. Rawlins wrote:

If there is any man in the service who has discharged his duties faithfully and fearlessly, who has ever been at his post and guarded the interest confided to him with the utmost vigilance, General Grant has done it. Not only his reports, but all his orders of an important character are written by himself, and I venture here the statement there is not an officer in the Army who discharges the duties of his command so nearly without the intervention of aides, or assistants, as does General Grant. ... I love him as a father; I respect him because I have studied him well, and the more I know him the more I respect and love him. ...

Wholly unaware of the secret interchange between Rawlins and Washburne, Julia stayed close to her husband during this period. She had had little to do with Rawlins up to this time but she quickly detected the influence he had with Ulysses and she studied him with interest. He was a zealot on the subject of temperance, his father having been a drunkard. He was known to have said that he would rather see a friend take a glass of poison than a glass of whiskey. Rawlins got rid of several members of Grant's personal staff whom he considered "roystering [sic], good-hearted, good-natured, hard-drinking fellows." The General, preoccupied with countless tasks, was apt to take a lenient view of their behavior in their free time.

The officers had already begun to notice Julia around camp, and particularly General Rawlins, the self-appointed guardian of her husband's well-being. He became her ally in many respects, although he was never wholly persuaded that there was any place for a woman at army headquarters. However, Julia consoled him in his suffering over the death of his wife from tuberculosis, and she fitted so smoothly into the military pattern that even the implacable Rawlins could find no fault with her.

CHAPTER VII: THE GENERAL'S WIFE IN JEOPARDY

IN THE SPRING OF 1862 Julia watched the emergence of Ulysses from obscurity into the limelight. The capture of Fort Donelson in February, followed by the battle of Shiloh in April, brought acclaim first, then sudden censure. It was clear that a new figure of importance had moved into view in the struggle between North and South. Fort Donelson was a substantial coup; Shiloh a two-day struggle that many in the North considered as much of a disaster as a victory. For Julia these weeks were dimmed with the bitter attacks on her husband that followed both engagements, and the official blackout from which he suffered. She waited and watched in Covington until she was able to join him in July.

Grant had sent his family home late in January, as he was about to open the Tennessee River campaign. Julia knew that big events were coming, although it was not his custom to discuss army plans with her. It was understood that Fred, Buck and Nellie should attend school in Covington while she remained flexible with little Jesse — ready to join her husband at a moment's notice if the opportunity arose.

When she reached Cincinnati on a Sunday morning she hired a Negro hackman to take them over the river to Jesse Grant's house in Covington. After leaving his fares at their destination the driver was arrested by the city marshal as he boarded the float leading to the boat. He was indicted under the act prohibiting Negroes from entering the state without a pass. Jesse, who bailed him out, had much to say about the absurdity of such treatment for a man trying to help the wife of a General fighting for his country.

The children immediately took possession of the Grant home, small images of Ulysses and his brothers in Hannah's eyes. The boys were startlingly like their father. Before Julia arrived Grant had written to his sister Mary warning her what to expect. She would like little Jesse the best of all his children "although he is the worst." He predicted that this four-year-old would whip his Aunt Mary the day he arrived. Buck, on the other hand, was "the best child I ever saw and is smart." Although never actually sick, he had the air of a delicate boy.

Hannah, sunk in the deep gulf of silence that usually enveloped her, moved about the Covington house in black, with snowy linen collars and ruched cap, watching Jesse's antics with unsmiling stillness. Julia finally drew her out with her friendly approaches. They had quiet talks about Ulysses as Jesse read news of him from the papers. Hannah had much less anxiety about him now than during the Mexican War, when her hair had turned white. "She seemed to feel throughout the Rebellion, that he had been raised up for the particular purpose of that war, and that the same power that had raised him up, would protect him," her husband, who alone understood Hannah's depths, commented years later.

They all felt the greatest confidence in him as a soldier. After the capture of Fort Henry and before he had taken Fort Donelson Ulysses had written to Mary that "your plain brother . . . has as yet no reason to feel himself unequal to the task, and fully believes that he will carry on a successful campaign against our rebel enemy. I do not speak boastfully but utter a presentiment. The scare and fright of the rebels up here Is beyond conception." With a sudden flash of humor he added: "G. J. Pillow commands at Fort Donelson. I hope to give him a tug before you receive this."

Julia had faith in all such presentiments and she shared Hannah's confidence in her husband's fate. It gave her calm and assurance during the most difficult days of the war, although she was hurt and shaken in the weeks that followed her arrival at Covington. The first news of the fall of Fort Donelson brought rejoicing in the Jesse Grant home, as it did throughout the North. Grant had emerged as an important General and the first of his classic wartime phrases was being quoted. His answer to General Buckner's request for compromise had its own finality: "No terms except an unconditional and immediate surrender can be accepted. I propose to move immediately upon your works."

Grant was appointed a major general, and young Fred was elated. Julia went proudly about her business and Jesse had fresh ammunition for boasting. They all shared one view of events from the papers; another from Ulysses' letters. Eight days after the fall of Fort Donelson, writing to Julia in great haste as a boat was leaving, he observed: "Secesh is now about on its last legs in Tennessee." He hoped to push on as rapidly as possible "to save hard fighting," and added: "These terrible battles are very good things to read about to persons who lost no friends but I am decidedly in favor of having as little of it as possible." He ended with the usual family chitchat:

"Tell me all about the children. I want to see rascal Jess already. Tell Mary she must write to me often. Kiss the children for me and the same for yourself."

Two days later he wrote again to Julia, saying he was just starting off for Nashville to consult General Buell. He would return at once and would wait until some further action took place.

Since my promotion some change may take place in my command but I do not know. I want however to remain in the field and be actively employed. But I shall never ask a favor or change. Whatever is ordered I will do independently and as well as I know how. If a command inferior to my rank is given me it shall make no difference in my zeal. In spite of enemies I have so far progressed satisfactorily to myself and the country and in reviewing the past can see but few changes that could have bettered the result. Perhaps I have done a little too much of the office duties and thereby lost time that might have been better employed in inspecting and reviewing troops.

"I want to hear from you," Ulysses added. Julia, as usual, had been laggardly about writing. He had not had a line from her since she left Cairo. His clothing had arrived, except for his saddle cover. This item cost thirty dollars and he would be compelled to buy another if it were lost. Did Julia know anything about it? Then, with an unusual carping note for even-tempered Ulysses, he observed that the Gazette "gets off whole numbers without mentioning my name" and it and the Cincinnati Commercial for some inexplicable reason "have always apparently been my enemies." This did not disturb him, however, but he was anxious to get a letter from his father to see what his criticism was. "I write to you so often that you must be satisfied with short letters," he finished, signing himself "Ulys."

But the visit to Nashville was an ill-fated move. It brought on a storm that blew up to whirlwind proportions. Grant was accused of leaving his command without permission; of failing to maintain proper order in camp after the fall of Fort Donelson; of not communicating with General Halleck or answering his daily messages. By the first week of March Julia was stunned to learn that Ulysses was under suspension and that Major General Charles F. Smith would command the expedition on which her husband had set his heart and expected as a matter of course.

The impression that Grant was missing from his post quickly spread. The inferences drawn were obvious. The rumors crystallized in Washington. An investigation was ordered and Grant wrote to General Halleck asking to be relieved of his command. He explained each step he had taken and added that he believed an attempt was being made by "enemies between you and myself to impair his usefulness. His explanations were accepted and by the middle of March he was officially cleared by General Halleck, who found that Grant's purpose in going to Nashville was to serve the public interest; that the disorders in camp were in violation of his instructions; and that the failure in communication was partly due to an interruption in telegraphic service. His fellow officers believed that the missing messages sent by Halleck and Grant were intercepted by a rebel operator who deserted, taking them with him.

Grant, whose headquarters had been moved from Fort Donelson to Fort Henry, was reinstated in his command. He established new headquarters at Savanna, Tennessee. But his punishment did not end there. With the keen eye of an experienced quartermaster he had touched the interests of some powerful contractors in St. Louis. Old enmities, jealousy and distrust came to the surface. All this was intensely damaging to Grant, and his fellow officers thought that it later colored the thinking of Stanton, McClellan and others in high command, until his overwhelming coup at Vicksburg silenced all criticism.

As Henry Coppée saw it, Grant was "sturdy, strong and cool" under these attacks. Meanwhile, Julia was coping with Jesse Grant's excitable protests at Covington. They were allies in their concern over Ulysses but not in their method of dealing with matters. Julia, reading to little Nellie, would hear the Cincinnati papers being fiercely rustled and Jesse, with Hannah's keen eyes focused in his direction, would take up his quill and get off a jeremiad. Julia's own impulses were all to protest the attacks, too, but she knew how her husband felt about such interference, and watched the process with some dismay.

Finally, Jesse wrote to one of his son's most trusted aides for a report on the true state of affairs. When letters arrived in defense and explanation he gamely but indiscreetly had one published. Grant was angry. Jesse felt that it had "a salutary effect on public sentiment in this part of the country; but as soon as General Grant learned of it he telegraphed me not to publish any more," Jesse related. Julia found ample reassurance — if she needed any — in Grant's own letter of defense to her, written on March 29, two weeks after he had been cleared. It took direct note of the attacks made upon him. Always sensitive to Julia's good opinion he wrote that "all the slanders you have seen against me originated away from where I was. The only foundation was from the fact that I was ordered under command of Maj. Gen. Smith."

He carefully explained that he had been sending General Halleck reports ever day, and sometimes two and three times in a single day. But neither man had heard from the other, because of the telegraphic blackout. His troops were astonished and disappointed when he was told to remain behind, Grant assured Julia. When he rejoined them they showed "heartfelt joy." But the papers took up the issue and the "New York Tribune particularly, was willing to hear of no solution not unfavorable to me." The General continued:

Such men as Kountz busied themselves very much. I never allowed a word of contradiction to go out from my Head Quarters, thinking this the best course. I know, though I do not like to speak of myself, that Genl. Halleck would regard this army badly off if I was retired. Not but what there are Generals with it abundantly able to command but because it would have inexperienced officers senior in rank. You must not fear but what I will come out triumphant. I am pulling no wires, as political generals do, to advance myself. I have no future ambitions. My object is to carry on my part of this war successfully and I am perfectly willing that others may make all the glory they can out of it. Give my love to all at home. Kiss the children for me.

Ulys.

When he wrote this letter Grant was recovering from a severe attack of dysentery that had lasted for weeks, he informed Julia. General Rawlins and most of the staff had suffered similarly. He had also been having his old chills and fevers, the malarial tendency that had pursued him for years. Fresh troops kept arriving and he expected soon to have a large army. Julia might expect a "big fight" soon, and it might well be the last in the West. "This is all the time supposing that we will be successful which never do doubt for a single moment," he assured her.

With Julia and the children in Covington, and the papers highlighting Grant's victory and the abuse that followed it, Colonel Dent was more hostile than ever to his son-in-law. Dr. Taussig, driving with John F. Long, met him at a cross-roads near White Haven. They drew up their horses. As usual, Taussig and Dent glared at each other without speaking, but Long made a friendly comment on the fall of Fort Donelson.

"Don't talk to me about this Federal son-in-law of mine," Colonel Dent exclaimed, "There shall always be a plate on my table for Julia, but none for him."

The furor following the capture of Fort Donelson had scarcely died down when Grant fought and won the battle of Shiloh in the first week of April. There was high excitement in the North when the victory was announced in Congress. Guns were fired in salute. Grant was thanked by the War Department. But the casualties were so heavy that a living core of suffering ran all through the nation, North and South.

The picture changed swiftly for Grant, as at Fort Donelson. When the smoke of battle cleared he was charged with having been taken by surprise, with not having adequate defenses, with mishandling his forces. Rumors spread quickly as trainloads of wounded men carried their own message and families everywhere went into mourning. Grant was severely blamed for the massive loss of life in one of the bloodiest engagements of the war, and his removal was demanded. But Abraham Lincoln reached his own conclusion about his General in the West: "I can't spare this man, he fights," he said.

The battle, fought close to the little log church from which it took its name, would remain a matter of historic debate for a century to come. Julia regarded it in some respects as the most painful engagement of the war. It was for the Grant family. Shiloh was likened to Golgotha and Ulysses to a butcher. This seemed unbearable to Julia, who knew that he could scarcely bring himself to shoot a game bird. "The victory was not to either party until the battle was over," Grant commented temperately, when he finally offered his own account of it in his Memoirs.

Four days after the battle General Halleck, with renewed distrust of Grant, set up headquarters at Pittsburg Landing and assumed command of the troops in the field. The chief of staff now headed the Army of the Ohio, with Buell in command; the Army of the Mississippi with Pope commanding; and the Army of the Tennessee, nominally Grant's command. Grant was named second in command of the whole but actually he was out in the cold. All summer he was slighted and ignored.

This was a difficult period for Julia, since she caught the side waves of censure as she moved about. She felt estranged from her own home and her St. Louis friends. A curtain hung between her and her father that could not be pushed aside while he felt so antagonistic to Ulysses. Emma, married to James F. Casey since February, 1861, and living in Caseyville, Kentucky, was an avowed rebel. Julia was observed wherever she went — the wife of General Grant who drew such press abuse, whose sudden fame had tarnished. Moving between Kentucky and Missouri, where feeling was strongly divided, she could feel the chill winds of disunion. By the end of the war Kentucky had sent 80,000 men from the hill regions to fight in Lincoln's army, and the blue-grass plantation area had given 40,000 to the Confederate cause.

But Hannah showed her accustomed calm, knowing full well that things would turn out right for Ulysses in the end. Julia tried to match her in assurance although it was never so difficult as at this early stage of the war. She soon learned that Ulysses had fought at Shiloh with a severely injured ankle sustained a few days earlier in a fall from his horse. On the second day of the battle a bullet had struck his scabbard and broken it near the hilt of his sword. James G. Wilson believed he had come close at that moment to sharing the fate of Albert Sidney Johnston, the Confederate commander who died on the field of Shiloh.

At the end of April the army commenced its advance on Corinth. This developed into a slow siege which stirred Grant to impatience. He was little more than an observer throughout. "My position was so embarrassing in fact that I made several applications during the siege to be relieved," he commented. The apple and cherry orchards bloomed around him. The countryside was beautiful to behold but men dug trenches, hundreds died of dysentery and Grant performed routine duties that were not his idea of soldiering. He smoked at the campfire at night and talked of the Mexican War, or played whist and twenty-one with other officers. "After the war is over," he confided one night to Richardson, "and I wish it might be over soon — I want to go back to Galena and live. I am saving money from my pay now, and shall be able to educate my children."

By the middle of May concern for his family in Covington moved Grant to write to Washburne that, although he would scorn to be his own defender, "to say that I have not been distressed at these attacks upon me would be false, for I have a father, mother, wife and children who read them, and are distressed by them, and I necessarily share with them in it." It also bothered him, he added, that the men subject to his command should read such charges.

Late in May Corinth was evacuated by the Confederates and the Federal forces took possession in a nearly bloodless victory. Things were no better for Grant. Finally he could stand it no longer. He made up his mind to leave the department altogether. Julia was aware of his discouragement and was apprehensive of the course he might follow. He sought leave to visit St. Louis. General Halleck asked him to stay on unless his business there was pressing. It was not, but he had made up his mind to pull out. He did not attempt to deny this when General Sherman rode up to talk to him, having got wind of his intentions in a casual conversation with Halleck.

Fort Donelson and Shiloh had brought Grant and Sherman close together again and he would be Julia's friend to the day he died. He was much upset over Grant's situation. All the hue and cry against him was wrong, Sherman wrote to his wife, and to her father, Thomas Ewing, he expressed the view that it was "villainous" to attempt to throw blame on Grant. "He is not a brilliant man," he wrote, "but he is a good and brave soldier, tried for years; is sober, ever industrious, and as kind as a child. Yet he has been held up as careless, criminal, a drunkard, a tyrant and everything horrible."

Now Grant sat behind a sapling fence that fronted some tents in the woods, breaking up camp and bundling papers in red tape on a rude plank table. Sherman grieved to see so good a soldier leaving the field. When he asked him why, Grant replied: "Sherman, you know. You know that I am in the way here. I have stood it as long as I can, and can endure it no longer."

The blunt and eloquent Sherman talked long and persuasively. He reminded Grant that he, too, had come under heavy fire and had been considered crazy only a short time earlier, but he felt in "high feather" since Shiloh. He predicted that some accident of fortune would restore Sam to favor. Finally he left him to ponder the question. Soon afterward he received a note from Grant saying that he had made up his mind to stay. It was one of the crucial points of his military career and his family heard with relief of his decision.

Early in July General Halleck was appointed to command all the armies and he took his departure for Washington. Grant remained in command of the district of West Tennessee and Kentucky west of the Cumberland River. This gave him more independence, if not more power. He still did not know if he would hold his command. He busied himself constructing fortifications at Corinth. Confronting his army to the south was General Earl Van Dorn.

Julia now joined him with the children and was with him during part of the time that he considered "the most anxious period of the war." His lines were dangerously extended while the Army of the Tennessee guarded the territory acquired by the fall of Corinth and Memphis. He had not yet been sufficiently reinforced to take the offensive. Guerrillas hovered in every direction. He established his family in a house in Corinth and they remained with him through most of July and August.

On her wartime visits to the field Julia suited her living arrangements to the conditions surrounding her husband. She might dwell in a house, a hotel room, in lodgings, a cabin or sometimes a tent. When the children en masse were with her she usually settled in a house or lodgings. Grant sent for his family only when the army was not in motion, and the summer of 1862 was one of the rare periods when he was not waging an offensive campaign, although he was continually on guard.

All through the war Julia moved from point to point, adapting herself to every new circumstance, trying always to make her movements conform with an opportunity to visit Ulysses, or even to catch a fleeting glimpse of him. The children viewed it all as a great adventure. They had seen none of its bloodier aspects up to this time and they liked the drams and bugles. Father's officers were like knights, and tents were medieval. But Julia was all too conscious of the crowded cars, the trainloads of wounded men, the sad-faced women in black so numerous after Shiloh, the fleeing Negroes who swarmed into camp.

Jesse did not approve of the children being at headquarters, but Julia and Grant both had absolute faith in their young and their sense of self-preservation. When Jesse wrote querulously to Ulysses about this late in July, Grant promptly answered: "Your uneasiness about the influences surrounding the children here is unnecessary. On the contrary it is good. They are not running around camp among all sorts of people, but we are keeping house, on the property of a truly loyal secessionist who has been furnished free lodging and board at Alton, Illinois; here the children see nothing but the greatest propriety."

Julia firmly believed that it was good for Ulysses to have the children within reach. He enjoyed them as Lincoln did his sons. Without any hesitation she bundled them up in warm clothes with strong boots for muddy fields as they set off for the front with their pantaloons and kilts, dresses and pinafores. She and her four children came to be known on the river boats traveling between St. Louis and Cincinnati. Her boys all closely resembled their father and as time went on the whole family was readily recognized in public. "There go Grant's boys," fellow passengers would remark. Julia was always a brisk and amiable mother, wearing her wide hoops and modest bonnets without any show of fashion. She took warm shawls to the field for her own use. But pretty little Nellie was always dressed like a doll, and so she seemed to her father.

Grant gained weight during this period and looked healthier. He put on fifteen pounds between the time he left Cako and August 19, when Julia left him again to visit her father in St. Louis. But she thought that he looked older and more troubled. He acknowledged to his family that he had little hope of getting home before the end of the war, when he would "take a few months of pure and undefiled rest."

Before Julia left they talked over plans for the children. Proof that she was feeling the pinch under Jesse Grant's roof lies in Ulysses' comment to his sister Mary that although Julia was satisfied that Covington was the best place for the children, "there are so many of them that she sometimes feels as if they are not wanted." They had enjoyed their visit "down here in Dixie," he wrote, and were loath to leave but he thought it best for them to go.

Now she was considering sharing a house in St. Louis with Mrs. Hillyer, wife of the genial young lawyer who was on her husband's staff. But after Julia had visited her own home, and another broadside of chatter from Jesse had reached Grant's ears, the General advised her strongly to take the children to Detroit, where she had many friends. He realized how difficult things were for her in both their homes. Neither of them liked Jesse's criticism of the way in which they handled their children. But Julia gave up the thought of Detroit as being too far away from Ulysses. She wished to be within reach in case he needed her. They were always alert to the chance of a meeting, however brief. Emma Dent Casey recalled that General Grant was at White Haven perhaps half a dozen times during the war years, when he came to spend a few days with his wife and children. On these occasions he never discussed his campaigns or any matters concerning his field operations. But he was always optimistic about the outcome.

When Julia left the children in Covington or with the Dents they were on their honor to behave, a custom that the General and Julia considered more effective than punishment. It was the family verdict that both parents had a "high opinion of their character and ability." But the children's erratic schooling gave Julia some concern. Buck was an attentive pupil but Fred's thoughts strayed always toward the battlefield, even before his legs took him there. After Vicksburg he definitely established himself at camp with his father. But in the meantime Julia sometimes let him go on trips by himself, putting him on the river boats and having him met at the other end. Emma remembered him visiting her alone at Caseyville, Kentucky, while his parents were at Cairo. The Caseys adored him. He was bright, entertaining and imaginative.

The Grant physiognomy soon was spotted in town and a squad of eight Confederate cavalrymen rode up to the Casey home and asked if the General's boy was there. Emma assured them that he had gone and added that some gunboats would soon be up the river looking for them. She sent a messenger at once to her husband urging him to get Fred on a coal boat and to send him down the river to Cairo as fast as possible. She also suggested that if possible he communicate with a gunboat for further protection. "Had they found Fred," Emma noted, "they would certainly have dealt his father a hard blow."

Soon after this she and her husband moved farther south to a plantation owned by her brother at Friar's Point, Mississippi. They passed most of the years between 1864 and 1880 in New Orleans, but Emma always took the most vivid interest in Julia and her children. She knew her perhaps better than anyone but Ulysses.

After repeated warnings to his father to hold his tongue, to steer clear of the Cincinnati papers and to stop worrying about what other generals were doing, Ulysses sent him an indignant letter while the garrison at Corinth was being threatened in the middle of September. When Julia got back to Covington Jesse was still smarting from his son's reproaches. At the moment Confederate forces were pursuing a concerted plan for an advance all along the line from the Mississippi to the Atlantic seaboard. Pope had been defeated in Virginia. Lee was invading Maryland. Bragg was aiming for the Ohio River. Grant controlled a vital area. He would have sent his father more particulars, he wrote, but he dared not trust him with them, adding:

I have not an enemy in the world who has done me so much injury as you in your efforts in my defense. I require no defenders and for my sake let me alone. I have heard this from various sources, and persons who have returned to this army and did not know that I had parents living near Cincinnati have said that they found the best feeling existing towards me in every place except there. You are constantly denouncing other general officers and the inference with people generally is that you get your impressions from me. Do nothing to correct what you have already done but for the future keep quiet on this subject.

Grant was again in action in the first week of October, this time commanding the engagements at Corinth. He emerged the victor and Western Tennessee was cleared of invaders for the time being. When Julia joined him briefly in Jackson, both Corinth and Iuka were behind him and he was in good spirits. While there Black Julia, the tiny ginger-colored maid Julia had had from birth, ran away. Grant was relieved. He forbade any attempt to bring her back, and expressed the wish that he could get rid of Julia's two other slaves in the same way. He had often told Auntie Robinson that he "wanted to give his wife's slaves their freedom as soon as he was able."

By November he was in full command of the Department of the Tennessee, with headquarters at Oxford, and was opening up the way for the assault on Vicksburg. But his first setback came at Holly Springs, which he had made his secondary base of supplies. Here Julia came close to being captured by Van Dorn's troops in December 1862. This was her closest brush with the enemy at any stage of the war.

She and Mrs. Hillyer had traveled from La Grange to Holly Springs, on their way to join Grant at Oxford. The railway had just been finished up to this point and a brief meeting was planned. Ulysses had written to Mary on December 15: "I shall only remain, here tomorrow, or next day at farthest; so that Julia will go immediately back to Holly Springs. It is a pleasant place and she may as well stay there as elsewhere." With Julia en route to join him he asked Mary to tell the children to learn their lessons, mind their Grandma and be good children. "I should like very much to see them," he added. "To me they are all obedient and good. I may be partial but they seem to me to be children to be proud of."

He had a big army in front of him as well as bad roads and much mud, Grant wrote. But his plans were completed for weeks to come and he hoped to have them work out smoothly. With the note of confidence he always used with his family, and with them alone, he added: "I shall probably give a good account of myself however notwithstanding all obstacles."

But his plans went seriously astray. On December 20, General Van Dorn appeared at Holly Springs in a whirlwind attack, captured the garrison of 1,500 men and took munitions, food and forage. Warehouses and stores were burned. This was one of the surprises of the war to Grant and a real humiliation. The culprit was Colonel Robert C. Murphy, of the 8th Wisconsin regiment, an "elegant, conventional gentleman, fond of song and story," in the words of Sylvanus Cadwallader, a newspaper correspondent at Grant's camp. He had already displeased his superior officers by mismanaging the evacuation of stores from Iuka in September and had failed to destroy those that were left. General William S. Rosecrans had disciplined him but Grant had excused him on the grounds of inexperience.

On the afternoon preceding the raid Colonel T. Lyle Dickey had ridden in with news of Van Dorn's approach. Grant had at once alerted the commanders at Holly Springs, Davis Mills, Bolivar and Middleburg. But Murphy went off to bed that night without making a move to defend his base. Most of his men were asleep when the enemy troops rode in. Dr. J. G. Deupree, a Huguenot from Mississippi who was a member of the invading party that night, recalled in 1901 that Mrs. Grant was in town right through the raid but was not molested. However, her descendants remember her telling them that she left Holly Springs the day before the raid and reached Oxford shortly after Colonel Dickey had ridden in and alerted her husband. According to their recollections, she found Ulysses busy sending warnings to the various posts.

Holly Springs was overrun with a large floating population when Julia arrived there and took up quarters in the mansion of Harvey W. Walters, whose family was secessionist in sympathy. She intended to return as soon as she had seen Ulysses. She was treated with courtesy but aloofness. Soldiers, army sutlers and speculators were moving about, giving the place an air of animation in spite of the icy weather that had followed a great rainstorm on the 18th. The muddy roads were freezing hard and it was bright and cold as Julia took note of the supplies her husband had assembled for a stiff drive toward Vicksburg. The town, was like a Gargantuan warehouse, with bales of cotton piled in the Court House and public square. A long train of boxcars stood near the depot, loaded with rations and clothing ready to be sent to the field. Warehouses were stacked with supplies. Holly Springs seemed so safe and the place was so attractive that many of the officers had settled their families there for the time being.

But within a matter of hours guns and sabers created their own explosive and metallic uproar; flaming torches sizzled in the freezing air; tents, homes and warehouses were on fire; whiskey ran in the gutters from emptied casks; the Negroes rushed about in confusion and Holly Springs had the look of an inferno. The Union men who emerged from their tents and offered resistance were quickly overwhelmed. Van Dorn's soldiers burned and plundered for hours after seizing the depot. Colonel Deupree recalled seeing "women in dreaming robes, and with dishevelled hair floating in the morning breeze, clapping their hands with joy and shouting encouragement to the raiders; a mass of frantic, frightened human beings, presented in the frosty morning hours a motley picture, at once ludicrous and sublime."

Julia's horses were seized and her carriage was burned, but the Walters family protected her personal belongings, and Deupree noted that u in consideration of the courtesy shown his wife, General Grant gave this house a safe-guard and a guarantee during the remainder of the war against search or trespass or devastation by Federal parties." The depot changed hands several times but in 1901 the house still stood — "a monument of Grant's appreciation of Southern chivalry," according to Deupree.

Jesse, the four-year-old child who was with Julia at the time, grew up to believe that he and his mother fled from the raiders but he may have confused this with another occasion because of his youth. In his book about his father he wrote: "I can see the dim, shadowy interior of that empty boxcar, with mother sitting quietly upon a chair, while I huddled fearfully upon a hastily improvised bed upon the floor as an engine drew rapidly away. And then I must have fallen asleep, for I remember no more."

The General's wife would have been a rare catch for Van Dorn. As things were, she apparently was with Grant when word reached the large house he occupied in Oxford that Holly Springs had been taken. He sent out support at once but Van Dorn's men were already riding off with from two to six pistols, and one or more carbines and sabers apiece, as well as ammunition, blankets and clothing. Holly Springs was in chaos.

The population showed its Southern sympathies in the most emphatic way. Grant was asked how he expected to feed and arm his men now that all the depot supplies were gone. But he had already made plans to have them live off the surrounding country. Murphy was dismissed. The General was forced to abandon his main line of attack on Vicksburg for the time being, and all hope of joining forces with Sherman dissolved when his fellow General failed at the Yazoo River. Sherman knew nothing of the Holly Springs debacle when he was meeting his own disaster. Both officers were foiled in their concerted plan for Grant to advance to the rear of

Vicksburg by land, while Sherman proceeded down the Mississippi to attack by way of the river, aided by gunboats.

With railroad communication disrupted Grant moved his men by dirt road to Memphis. Julia, little Jesse and Grandfather Grant, who had joined his son at Oxford from Holly Springs and, like Julia, had come unexpectedly close to capture, traveled on the same train as John Eaton, a Sanitary Commission official who had charge of the Army of Contrabands. The Grants took rooms in the Gayoso House, although official headquarters were established in a local bank building. The population was openly hostile and a large number of soldiers lay ill in the hospitals.

Ulysses was much upset by the Holly Springs disaster and Julia decided to stay on with him, ministering to him when he was stricken with one of his severe headaches. Eaton, who had to consult him about problems involving the Negroes, called to see him at the hotel and found him "with his head and neck all swathed in hot poultices, which his wife was applying in order to relieve the violent sick headache from which he was suffering and to which he was subject."

A woman member of the western branch of the Sanitary Commission, who called on the Grants at this time, talked to Julia in the ladies' parlor. She found her much concerned about her husband. The medical director had just seen him and had told him he could not go any farther unless he took stimulants, but Grant was resisting the idea. The Sanitary Commission worker quoted Julia as saying: "And I cannot persuade him to do so; he says he will not die, and he will not touch a drop upon any consideration."

Julia was greatly plagued by misunderstandings about her husband's habits. He suffered recurrently from the headaches that today are known as migraine. They usually prostrated him completely, strong though he was, and just before the surrender of Robert E. Lee he was suffering from one of these attacks. His grandson, Ulysses S. Grant, 3rd, inherited the same tendency. The family consistently maintained that reports of intemperance were apt to spring from confusion over these undeniable headaches. Julia had devised her own way of dealing with them. She usually had him rest in a darkened room, giving him a mustard foot bath and a dose of medicine. She had experimented considerably with compresses but she learned that these headaches ran their own course. They were devastating while they lasted but when they left him he was completely well and plunged at once into hard work. All of his staff were aware of this susceptibility.

Although Julia could not ignore the charges of intemperance that flew back and forth at different times in her husband's career she kept silent, but her sister Emma spoke for her years later:

During all the time I knew Grant, between his return from California in 1854 to the fall of Vicksburg, I never saw him intoxicated. I never saw him under the influence of liquor. If he ever was it was not known to the members of his immediate family. Charges that he was a heavy drinker were made in those days, and have been made since. General Grant never gave them any notice. Mrs. Grant also ignored them, though she felt deeply cut by the injustice of them . . . I will content myself with saying again, that if General Grant was ever a victim of the liquor habit it was a condition which he happily concealed from those nearest his heart, closest in their association with him, and who loved him best.

Taking the stand she did, Julia might not have appreciated the observations of Sylvanus Cadwallader, complimentary though they were to her. She had been dead for fifty-three years when the journal he compiled long after his war years with Grant was dug up and published. In it he wrote:

Rawlins' ablest coadjutor in restraining Gen. Grant from drinking was the latter's excellent wife, Julia Dent Grant. Everything seemed absolutely safe when she was present. Her quiet firm control of her husband seemed marvelous. . . . When the army had a period of repose and inaction ... it was noticed that Mrs. Grant and family invariably visited headquarters for a few weeks, when "all went merry as a marriage bell."

Julia first met Cadwallader in Jackson. He had been assigned by the Chicago Times to interview her husband. During the Vicksburg campaign he corresponded for the New York Herald. He soon became a privileged person around camp. He messed with the staff and his tent was always pitched close to Grant's. He sent off his dispatches in the official pouch and stayed aloof from the other correspondents. He was a persistent, combative reporter who had ample opportunity to observe Julia and her General, and he left some graphic notes on them. He found Grant "pure in speech and heart," honest, and with few blemishes of character other than those "incident to our common humanity." Instead of seriously damaging him in the estimation of right-minded men, his faults tended only "to emphasize his virtues, which were many and strongly pronounced," in the opinion of Cadwallader.

Another camp correspondent, Albert D. Richardson, who would leave a record of these years, wrote that "during the entire conflict he probably consumed less than any other officer" who tasted liquor at all. Some regarded him as a periodical drinker who was a zealous abstainer the rest of the time. Others insisted that he drank nothing at all, even refusing a glass of champagne at a banquet. All of his associates agreed with Richardson that he "was never under its sway to the direct or indirect detriment of the service for a single moment." This undoubtedly was one of Julia's problems, since so much was made of it in the early days of the war and on more than one occasion President Lincoln was urged to remove him.

By this time she was familiar with all the men who circled around her husband. Richardson and Horace Porter, Rawlins, Sherman and Cadwallader all had firsthand views of the General's wife and left their impressions of her. Porter considered her a "woman of much general intelligence, and exceedingly well informed upon all public matters." He commented on her amiability, her cheerful disposition, and her cordiality of manner. He recalled that she was "soon upon terms of intimacy with all the members of the staff, and was quick to win the respect and esteem of every one at headquarters." Richardson thought she had a "sprightly mind, and a most sterling, lovable character . . . amiable in disposition, comely in person, well-bred and attractive in manners."

The officers around Grant soon knew his family well and were impressed with his love for his children and for Julia. It was an aspect of the impassive General's nature that they came to respect. His wife's presence at camp was rarely mentioned, so that the public did not know how often, she was within range of Grant during the war years. Actually, she joined him at Cairo, Corinth, La Grange, Oxford, Jackson, Memphis, Nashville, Vicksburg and City Point, with meetings at some intermediate points. He was as silent with her as he was with others about the vital moves he was making, but she was always alert to what was going on and was quickly aware of attacks made on her husband. The dabblers in cotton, the contractors whom he frustrated, were ever ready to stir up fresh and damaging tales about him.

When in camp Julia knew without delay what the correspondents had to say. She watched them with a wary eye. There were twenty to thirty of them at headquarters by this time and they came and went. She knew them individually and had read many of their dispatches — often hostile to her husband. Sherman openly flouted and insulted them and wanted them expelled from camp but only once did Grant protest, saying to Richardson: "Your paper has made many false statements about me, and I presume will continue to do so. Go on in that way if you like, but it is hard treatment for a man trying to do his duty in the field. I am willing to be judged by my acts, but not to have them misrepresented or falsified."

Sometimes Julia greeted visitors from home points and was always cordial to the officers' wives and relatives. At times they were surprised to find her there, but she was invariably unobstrusive and helpful. Washburne visited Grant in camp and Augustus L. Chetlain, serving under him as lieutenant colonel, wrote back to Galena: "This man is the pure gold." The General was gradually establishing himself as a personality and a fighter.

Julia brought many friendly touches into camp. She visited officers and soldiers on the sick list. She was interested in their family affairs and chatted sympathetically with them about their wives and children. Upon occasion she pinned stars on officers and her thimble was always in use. She sewed on hundreds of buttons, including many on her husband's uniform, to take the place of those appropriated by souvenir hunters. She was a familiar sight, seated on a rustic bench or camp chair under a tent-fly, out of the sun, which hurt her eyes, fanning herself and showing the most alert interest in everything that was going on. She was always ready with a warm greeting for the passerby.

At times Julia consulted the cook, not only about her husband's tastes in food, but those of other men in camp, particularly any she knew to be ailing, Occasionally she took her meals with the mess, chatting brightly at the long table around which they all sat. The staff took turns catering for a month at a time and Grant usually sat to the right of the officer who happened to be presiding, instead of at the head of the table. The fare most often was beef, canned vegetables, condensed milk, coffee, rice and soft bread when in camp, hardtack when on the road. All meat had to be extra well done for Grant and he avoided mutton and fowl. He liked oysters and clams, and breakfasted sometimes by preference on cucumbers and coffee. He preferred his food plain, without sauces or dressings of any kind, He ate small portions of anything and liked to nibble on fruit, Julia knew that he was particularly fond of corn, pork, beans and buckwheat cakes. Her own tastes ran to hot breads, sweets, gumbo, fritters and the Southern dishes on which she had been reared, but in camp she adapted herself readily to whatever was available. She even tried to hurry over her meals, knowing that Ulysses could not bear to linger at the table, either in peace or war. All through their married life Julia dawdled over her coffee, and he could not speed her up, except in the war days.

Although she was much less punctual in her ways than her husband, and was prone to put things off, in camp she conformed in every way to army discipline and did her best to make things pleasant around him. "They were a perfect Darby and Joan," Porter observed. "They would seek a quiet corner of his quarters of an evening, and sit with her hand in his, manifesting the most ardent devotion; and if a staff-officer came accidentally upon them, they would look as bashful as two young lovers spied upon in the scenes of their courtship."

The children were no less welcome in camp although, like Lincoln's boys, they created some commotion. Both parents were indulgent with Nellie and the boys but Porter noticed that the children were always respectful "and never failed to render strict obedience to their father when he told them seriously what he wanted them to do." However, the staff became quite accustomed to seeing them hanging around Grant's neck while he wrote, making a "terrible mess of his papers, and turning everything in his tent into a toy." He gave them mock examinations on their studies, posing all manner of mathematical problems, and asking them to spell words with half a dozen syllables. Julia often joined in these quizzes, and Grant would play the same game with her. He liked to work up a high-powered description of an imaginary campaign, naming impossible numbers of troops, scrambling the geography, and outlining a plan of "marvellously complicated movements in a manner that was often exceedingly droll."

Julia sometimes joined the circle around the campfire at night. She liked to sing and to listen to songs. The General enjoyed a joke on these occasions and talked most readily of West Point or the Mexican War. His tent was slightly larger than those of his staff members. It had an inner division to give Mrs. Grant some privacy when she was visiting camp. Officers came and went. Conferences were held. Plans were discussed and Grant was often busy over papers until two o'clock in the morning.

His attitude to Julia was reflected in his chivalry to other women during the war. When he caught a straggler who had stopped at a house and assaulted a woman he sprang from his horse, seized a musket from the hands of a soldier, and struck the sinner over the head with it, sending him sprawling to the ground. He had a particular horror of such crimes, Porter noted, and showed no mercy for the guilty.

"No family could have been happier in their relations; there was never a selfish act committed or an ill-natured word uttered by any member of the household, and their daily life was altogether beautiful in its charming simplicity and its deep affection," said Porter, in a rare tribute to the Grants.

When they were separated Ulysses always wrote to Julia on the night before he went into battle. His letters were frequent, even during a campaign, and "no pressure of official duties was ever permitted to interrupt this correspondence." Watching him bent over a rough plank table in camp with a guttering candle beside him, the officers closest to him usually knew when he was composing a letter to Julia. Everyone understood how much he loved her. When the pressure was great the letters were brief. When he had time he wrote at length. Porter could only guess at their contents while the war was on but long afterward Julia told him that they always had words of cheer and comfort, "expressed an abiding faith in victory, and never failed to dwell upon . . . the great sufferings that would have to be endured by the wounded."

Her granddaughter, Princess Cantacuzene, remembered "surprisingly quiet pages" scribbled in haste before the General went into battle. There were no complaints, but many allusions to the children's progress and education, to family affairs, to the chance of a meeting. They were expressive of the General's strong family feeling.

At this time he was forty years old. His appearance had changed since the outbreak of war and a troubled, anxious look seemed permanently engraved on his face. His hair and beard, neatly trimmed after the first year, were a chestnut brown with a tawny hint. His fellow officers observed the small wart on his right cheek. They remembered him best as being florid. But his son Fred pointed out at a later date that in one respect he had not changed. He still flushed easily although never showing emotion in any other way. In the field he was weather-beaten and his face sometimes seemed crimson and mottled, although his complexion in reality was as fair and delicate as of old. His eyes were almost startlingly blue but during this period Julia could detect the anxious look in them and the lines that were gradually furrowing his brow.

Grant was far from being one of the more resplendent generals. His coat was seldom buttoned up to the throat. He often came into camp spattered with mud from head to foot. He rarely carried a sword and particularly disliked one on a horse, saying that it hurt his leg. He never marched in time to a band, and all tunes were alike to him. But his endurance was proverbial. He could outride his staff, go without food or sleep longer than the youngest; show indifference to heat, cold, fatigue or exposure, and sleep under a tree in the rain, as he did after Shiloh when he could not endure the anguished cries of the wounded being operated on in the improvised log cabin hospital where he had taken shelter.

By the summer of 1862 Julia was thirty-six. She was now slightly heavier in build, less light of foot, and she did not gallop on horseback with her old zest. On special occasions she dressed her hair with a waterfall of curls, although for the most part she wore it simply parted in the middle with a chignon, as she had done in her early twenties. She moved with an air of authority and had a firm, brisk walk.

This was a period of growth and development for Julia one of sadness and anxiety, too, as men died by the thousand in her husband's command, and friends on both sides went down in battle. Her sympathies deepened with this close-up view of the wounds, necessities and horror of war. She was at the heart of the picture, if only an observer. She learned a great deal that she never discussed, even with her intimates. In spite of her impulsive nature Julia functioned with tact and understanding through it all. Except for some captious observations by Rawlins there were no tales of her giving offense in her unlikely surroundings, or of embarrassing her husband in any way by being at his side. Instead, the picture emerges of a warm and stable family relationship, miraculously sustained through the years of war.

CHAPTER VIII: THE GUNS OF VICKSBURG

JULIA STOOD ON THE DECK of a transport on the Mississippi on an April night in 1863, an observer of one of the more spectacular engagements of the Civil War. Admiral David Porter's ironclads were running the batteries at Vicksburg. "The reverberations of artillery, the howling of rifle shots, and the constant bursting of shells made the scene one of the most terrific ever witnessed in warfare," wrote Charles A. Dana, who stood close to Grant and his wife.

Julia caught the look of strain on Ulysses' face that Dana also observed as spasmodic flashes illumined the scene around them. Much was at stake for him. He had ordered this bold maneuver as part of a master plan to move his army south of Vicksburg and open his siege. Sherman and other army leaders had told him it was madness to run the batteries. Now "Gump" sat in a yawl on the river, watching Porter's ships steam past Vicksburg under fire. It was the culmination of weeks of planning by Grant, of bitter disappointments and various ingenious efforts to get his army out of the mud and into action.

His own transport was out on the river as close to the batteries as it was wise to go, but he evidently considered it safe to have his family with him, and Julia was eager to watch the spectacle. With her shawl wrapped tight around her, and one hand occasionally reaching out toward Ulysses when the shells crashed, she was unafraid. But Jesse cowered with each explosion and clung to Dana until his father ordered him sent below deck.

The little group had watched the ghostlike advance of the ironclads, steamers, and barges loaded with army supplies, as they moved out in a solid black mass from Milliken's Bend. The vessels were guided by lanterns hung astern and not visible to the enemy. Then in a moment a battery between Vicksburg and Warrenton rattled into action. The upper batteries opened fire and all along the line there were detonations. Rockets exploded. Geysers of water shot up and glittered in flashes of light as shells landed in the river.

The gunboats ran close to the bluffs and opened fire, but with little effect. They were hit time and again. A ten-inch shell pierced the boiler of the Henry Clay and it went up with a tremendous bang. Julia watched horror-stricken as fire spread to the barges in tow and ran up a curtain of flame. Meanwhile, the Confederates lighted bonfires and fired houses on the east side of the bluff to illumine the ships in the river. "The sight was magnificent, but terrible," Grant commented.

The small fleet pushed on and soon was out of range. The blazing beacons on the bluffs subsided. The batteries were silenced. No lives were lost although Dana had counted 525 discharges during the bombardment. Again Grant had done the daring, the imaginative thing. By the end of April his men were on the same side of the river as Vicksburg, and transports were bringing in their supplies.

It was Julia's most memorable glimpse of warfare, although she watched the preliminary arrangements and aftermath of several engagements. She had come from Memphis early in April, bringing the children with her. Fred's desperate entreaties to be taken out of school in Covington in order to join his father had finally been heeded. In spite of protests by Hannah and Jesse, Julia decided that it would be good for his father to have the boy with him.

They all sailed up the Mississippi and joined Grant at Young's Point, where he was quartered on a steamer tied up at the levee. From then on Fred campaigned with his father. He strutted around camp wearing a sword attached to a yellow sash. He rode the smart little Indian pony sent on for him from Illinois. He shared the soldiers' mess and had a cot in his father's tent. In after years he recalled the General pacing up and down in the tent, poring over maps, planning strategy, or writing out his clear and concise orders.

"Fred never knew what it was to be afraid," his father said of him in his later years. "My son accompanied me throughout the campaign and siege, and caused no anxiety to me or to his mother, who was at home. He looked out for himself, and was in every battle of the campaign."

Grant took pride in the hardihood of his boys and indeed of his entire family. The only vanity Fred ever observed in him was his emphasis on their endurance. Julia matched him in this. She had plenty of physical stamina and showed no alarm when danger threatened. But during the siege of Vicksburg she lost all track of her oldest son. She returned to St. Louis with the other children and in time heard that Fred had been nicked in the thigh with a musket ball at Black River Bridge, and that Ulysses, under fire at Port Gibson, had smoked quietly and observed to Governor

Richard Yates of Illinois: "Governor, it's too late to dodge after the ball has passed."

All through May, while Grant was fighting the battles of Port Gibson, Raymond and Champion Hill, Fred was tagging along. His father tried to separate himself from his son until Grand Gulf was taken. He left him sound asleep on a steamer at Bruinsburg but when Fred wakened and found his father gone he started off on foot after him. Dana, also left by the wayside, caught up with the boy as he tramped along in the general direction of Port Gibson. They gypsied together, foraging as they went, and finally rode into camp on two enormous old white horses. The General laughed heartily at the grotesque picture they presented. After that, Fred moved with the army.

It was fast moving, too. Twenty days after he began his campaign Grant had marched more than two hundred miles and beaten two armies in five battles. When he reached Grand Gulf he had been without baggage for a week, had never changed his clothes, or had a tent over his head, or a meal to eat except such as he could forage by the wayside. None of this was surprising to Julia.

But at last he was quartered on a bluff five miles from Vicksburg, with a clear brook running close by and a strip of trees for shade. Chaplain John Eaton, general superintendent of Contrabands who consulted him constantly at this time about the handling of the Negroes, found him giving out orders from a rough board seat attached to tree trunks. He wore an old brown linen duster and slouch hat and paid no attention to the roar of artillery or the intermittent sputter of muskets.

Grant made a number of inspection trips. Early in June an abortive expedition up the Yazoo River to visit a detachment of troops near Satartia left historic echoes. Many years later Cadwallader wrote a graphic account, not published until 1954, of an alleged three-day spree on shipboard and a John Gilpin ride through the woods. Charles A. Dana, who was on the scene, and various other historians have contradicted him. Whatever the facts of the case Rawlins sent him one of his cautioning letters at this time, adding: "If my suspicions are unfounded, let my friendship for you and my zeal for my country be my excuse for this letter."

Grant took all Rawlins' warnings and threats in good part and approved his iron vigilance around the camp, however much the other officers rebelled. Even Cadwallader was forced to concede that "no officer or civilian ever saw any open drinking at Gen. Grant's headquarters from Cairo to Appomattox."

Julia was in St. Louis when Vicksburg fell. Gettysburg had held the headlines for several days until the great fortress of the South fell into Union hands on July 4. She was serenaded at the Planters House, where Ulysses had once been discounted by his old West Point friends. Her husband's name was ringing through the streets and there were shouts for Mrs. Grant. At last she appeared at a window, on the arm of General William E. Strong. Toward the end of her life Julia recalled that this was one of her proudest moments. She had many.

No one knew better than she how desperately her husband had wished for this victory; how he had stood alone in his decision and the boldness of his strategy; how Jefferson Davis had called Vicksburg the Gibraltar of America; how Lincoln had been uneasy because things were moving so slowly on the Mississippi. Now she read of the hillside encounter, near a stunted oak tree, of the austere Pennsylvanian, General John Pemberton, and her own sturdy Ulysses; of the Confederate soldiers marching in gray lines out of the garrison they had defended so long and so valiantly, and stacking their arms for their conquerors. Grant and Pemberton at Vicksburg. Soon it would be Grant and Lee at Appomattox. But Grant expressed the view in later years that the "fate of the Confederacy was sealed when Vicksburg fell." It was a massive capture of men and materiel.

Church bells pealed throughout the North. The State House bell rang in Philadelphia, A hundred guns boomed in Burlington. Illuminations were general in hamlets and cities. Even Colonel Dent was heard to concede, according to his daughter Emma, that if Vicksburg had to fall, he was glad the surrender had been made to Grant. The victor was appointed a major general in the regular army and Lincoln sent him a personal note of thanks, conceding that he had been mistaken when he misjudged Grant's campaign plans and put forward suggestions of his own. He wrote to the General on July 13, 1863: "I do not remember that you and I ever met personally. I write this now as a grateful acknowledgment for the almost inestimable service you have done the country ... I now wish to make the personal acknowledgment that you were right, and I was wrong."

Fred rode into Vicksburg with his father on July 6 and Julia prepared to join him with the other children. Jesse later recalled a "joyous start and, next, a confusion of crashing noise, and mother striving to dress me, bewildered and cross, in the darkness." Although the Union forces by this time were in control of the Mississippi from St. Louis to Vicksburg, their steamboat was shelled from the shore, wrote Jesse.

When their carriage drew up at headquarters Jesse rushed to the Shetland pony that his father had provided for him. One of the soldiers had made a miniature saddle and bridle for Rebbie, who would live until 1883 and become a much loved Grant horse. Like Fred, Jesse now rode out with his father on some of his inspection tours — sometimes on Rebbie; again seated behind the General, clinging to his belt and thundering along on a buckskin horse known as Mankiller.

In the South General S. Cooper took Julia's arrival at Vicksburg as a sign that "General Grant would make that place his headquarters for some time" and telegraphed General Joseph E. Johnston to that effect. From time to time Julia's movements appeared in official army orders. Stanton sometimes sent Grant messages about her whereabouts and welfare when she was moving from place to place. The General usually made careful arrangements for her journeyings. He sent small craft up the rivers to meet her. He welcomed her himself at stations when he could; if not, he sent emissaries. Her brother, Brigadier General Frederick Dent, who was on his staff, often acted for him in this capacity. Another favorite with Julia was the genial, dark-bearded Major General James B. McPherson, much beloved around Grant's headquarters.

Dana observed that Grant was neither elated nor made vain by his victory. He occupied himself consolidating his conquest and reorganizing his command. Julia was on hand to watch the humane moves that her husband made after his victory, and even to share in some of the incidents. When he gave a Southern woman who was trapped in Vicksburg a permit to go home she bundled it up with $4,000 in Confederate money. Furniture seized by an overzealous officer to embellish the Grant headquarters was promptly returned. Plundered goods were restored to a widow. A wounded young Confederate officer was cared for when he was discovered hiding in a house taken for military purposes. When Mrs. W. W. Lord, fresh from weeks of agony with her four children and husband in one of the caves of Vicksburg, called to ask that she and her family be sent to New Orleans with the soldiers as prisoners of war, she observed: "Gen. Grant . . . behaved throughout our interview as a brave soldier and gentleman should, admired the heroism and self sacrifice of our army and people as much as I could ask, and as for the women of the South, he said they could not be conquered."

Julia could scarcely be unaware of the deep enmity of the women of the South. General Sherman observed just after the fall of Vicksburg that "no one who sees them and hears them but must feel the intensity of their hate . . . begging with one breath for the soldiers' rations and in another praying that the Almighty or Joe Johnston will come and kill us, the despoilers of their homes and all that is sacred."

Vicksburg had a battered look and Julia was alive to the sufferings and hunger endured by such women as Mrs. Lord. A chunk of earth had fallen and nearly killed one of her daughters during a sharp explosion. They had not undressed for weeks but they had niches for flowers, a closet for food, books, and an arbor over their dining table. One cave a hundred feet in length had four apartments, with carpets, tables and chairs.

The houses of Vicksburg were riddled with shell holes. Porches were piled with cannon balls that had fallen in the yards. Gate posts were topped with unexploded 13-inch shells. Barricades and rifle pits were still in view when Julia arrived. Dust lay over everything. The Grants were quartered in a spacious house belonging to Mrs. Lum, a well-off widow. It had been General Pemberton's headquarters, and the family still occupied a small part of it. Julia regarded it as the most stable spot she had found since the start of the war. There were shade trees nearby and pasture for the horses. The figs were ripening. Hedge roses bloomed abundantly, and almost as soon as she arrived she drove over with Ulysses to call on General Sherman who was established at Big Black, eighteen miles from Vicksburg, in the "handsomest camp" he had throughout the war.

Julia appreciated the cynical wit, the literate conversation and keen responses of Sherman. Above all, she liked him because of his unswerving loyalty to her husband. Like Ulyss, he often teased her, for it was a family joke that Mrs. Grant, a tower of strength in emergencies, could be scatterbrained over trifles. She now called Ulysses "Victor" when they were alone or with intimate friends, and she basked in the approval directed at her husband. Earlier that year he had been savagely attacked in the press, and the Mississippi drive had seemed like a swamp operation until the campaign solidified into brilliant consummation. Now gifts were showered on the General. Rawlins frowned on them and advised refusal. He stood as the family watchdog and found the Grant approach to life too genial. His letters show that he had some reservations about Julia's visits to camp. He dreaded banquets unless he was there to see that Grant's wine glass was turned down like his own. He deplored the General's liking for the theater when on official missions. He was ever vigilant for a display of the relaxed spirit, and feared that applause might go to the General's head.

But at Vicksburg the zealot fell in love and Julia subtly promoted a match for Rawlins, whose wife had died of tuberculosis two years earlier. She bolstered his growing interest in Mary Emma Hurlbut, a Connecticut girl who had moved south to work as a governess for the Lum family. Grant was skeptical at first, but soon saw that Julia was right about Rawlins.

A great banquet was given for the General at the Gayoso Hotel in Memphis and he then went on to New Orleans to confer with Major General Nathanial P. Banks. Rawlins did not approve of this trip. Julia had decided not to go along, since it was strictly military business. But crowds flocked to see him at the St. Charles Hotel. Others watched this invasion from the North with hostile feeling. The city was decorated and Grant was serenaded.

"Deservedly popular he finds friends wherever he goes . . . may his shadow never grow less," commented Adjutant General Lorenzo Thomas, of Delaware, after following him through a series of festivities and a military review held in the suburb of Carrollton. General Banks gave Ulysses a blooded bay from Virginia to ride and Grant dashed along the lines to his position under a massive live oak tree, a plain figure in undress uniform, surrounded by officers brilliantly appareled.

On his way back to the city his horse was startled by a locomotive whistle. It dashed into a carry-all. Grant held his place in the saddle, but when the horse fell it rolled over on him. Some time later he wakened in the Carrollton Hotel with several doctors bending over him. His body was swollen up to the armpit and the "pain was almost beyond endurance," commented the Spartan General, who nearly lost his life on this occasion.

He was helpless for days, then was taken by litter to the steamer that conveyed him back to Vicksburg and Julia. It took him weeks to recover and he used crutches for two months. The usual rumors spread concerning the fall of so brilliant a rider. Julia nursed him devotedly in the big house on the bluff and the children were a constant delight to him. Little Nellie came in and sat at his bedside. It had been a long time since he had had much opportunity to study her small, sweet face. Fred and Buck hung around with the soldiers, but came whooping in to see Father. Jesse, then as always, was a "toy, a delight," to Grant. Julia came and went, making him comfortable, telling him jokes.

The war seemed distant for the moment but its echoes soon reached Grant's sick room as Sherman came to him for decisions. Messages, gifts, honors and applause still rained on the Grant family. Julia cared only because it meant that Ulysses at last was recognized. He now had a commanding place in the public eye. Success had silenced criticism. He was the soldier's soldier, liked by the man in the field. By this time he also had strong appeal for the man in the street. His way of getting about without fuss, his silent operations, his lack of burnish and polish had their own appeal at a time when more flamboyant Union generals had toppled one by one. It was noted that he could be tough and exacting, but he was also just, and human in his weaknesses.

Chickamauga ended this interlude of peace. Grant broke camp at Vicksburg early in September. He and Edwin M. Stanton, Secretary of War, met for the first time in a railroad car in Indianapolis and traveled together to Louisville, but without mutual sympathy. He gave Grant his orders for full command of the Military Division of the Mississippi, Grant had always believed in the concentration of the western armies under a single head. Now he had a free hand, with Chattanooga as his focus.

Meanwhile, Julia did her best to comfort Mrs. Sherman. Like Grant, General Sherman had brought his wife and four children to stay with him at camp but they all fell ill. Willy, his oldest son, aged nine, died of typhoid at the Gayoso Hotel early in October while his father was hurrying his troops to support General William S. Rosecrans after his defeat at Chickamauga. He blamed himself bitterly for inviting his family into the unhealthy Vicksburg area during the hot weather, and on October 8, 1863, wrote to his wife Ellen: "Why was I not killed at Vicksburg, and left Willy to grow up to care for you?"

Julia and Mrs. Sherman were good friends, although they were women of disparate interests. Ellen was a devout Catholic who spent much time on prayer and good works. She was unworldly but highly cultivated and she knew the official pattern well, for she was the daughter of Thomas Ewing, a lawyer who had served in the cabinets of John Tyler and William Henry Harrison.

Julia soon moved on to visit her husband's relatives in Bantam, Georgetown, and other points in Ohio. A young cousin named William W. Smith, who had gone south to join the General at Chattanooga returned with letters and a package for her from Grant. The youth told thrilling tales of the campaign in the mountains. Julia found it hard to forgive Major

General George H. Thomas for the chilly reception he gave her husband on his arrival at Chattanooga to direct operations. Grant was near collapse from the mountainous journey. He was chilled to the bone, soaking wet and was still suffering from his leg injury. He had to be carried part of the way. But General Thomas made no move to offer him hospitality until Grant's aides drew attention to his sufferings. Then he played the part of host with more spirit.

The tables now were turned. Grant was in supreme command, where Thomas had virtually superseded him during the Shiloh-Corinth campaign. But Grant tactfully chose him over Rosecrans. Julia had her own pet officers and her tastes usually coincided with those of her husband, although there were exceptions. She was apt to display more personal feeling than the General, but Badeau observed that she could not influence him to any extent against his better judgment. "Mrs. Grant never dreamed of influencing his military decisions or his political ones," Badeau wrote, "except in regard to individuals . . . like all women, she was full of personal feeling, but it was feeling about and for her husband." She did not "overstep the line which both perceived, though possibly neither ever indicated it to the other."

Soon Julia was getting letters from Chattanooga as Grant mapped out another of his great campaigns — this time in the mountains, a drama of Valkyrian proportions. Bragg occupied the heights of Lookout Mountain and Missionary Ridge and threatened to shell Chattanooga. The army lacked food, clothes and equipment and the base of supplies was Nashville, a hundred miles away.

Young Smith told Julia of riding with Grant through magnificent scenery within range of enemy guns; of watching the enemy rifle pits being stormed; of viewing the valley dotted with thousands of white tents and soldiers' huts; of Generals Sherman, David Hunter and Grant bending over their maps by the campfires; of the soldiers gathering around to stare at the celebrated generals, and Grant patting the heads of the children in a house where they stayed; of his quiet delight in Lincoln's message: "God bless you all."

"The spectacle was great beyond anything that has been or is likely to be on this continent," Grant wrote to Washburne on December 2, 1863, describing the grand panorama and his fifteen-mile line. "It is the first battlefield I have ever seen where a plan could be followed and from one place the whole field be within one view . . ."

Again the papers rang with the superior generalship of General Grant, this time with comparatively little loss of life. After Missionary Ridge Grant's fame became worldwide. Comparisons were drawn with Napoleon, a general whom he never admired. He was in the curious position of being a military leader who did not like war; who threw in his men in hordes, then followed victory with merciful terms.

Julia heard the echoes in far-off Ohio, among his family and friends. As usual, she made preparations to join him, now that the fighting was over. Rawlins had been worrying about him again in November. Early in December Grant went to Nashville to inspect the arrangements for handling supplies and there Julia joined him. She traveled in many strange trains during the war, sometimes in boxcars and with long waits in lonely spots. She jounced about in ambulances and spring wagons. She had long ago learned to ford a river and was never dismayed by mud. She had picked up food at eating tents and roadside "stalls." But she never could accustom herself to the sight of the wounded by the wayside, of the dead lying in the fields, of the amputation cases that had become so common by the summer of 1863, of the corpses of animals and the ruined crops.

She had a new impression of the havoc of war on this trip South. Nashville, once a flower-decked city, had an air of ruin and desolation. Mansions were wrecked along the way. Fences were down. Factories and bridges were in ruins. Convalescent troops limped around at large camps and soldiers were in tents by the wayside. Farther south the railroad bridges were strongly guarded. The women looked at her with sad eyes, but few knew that she was Mrs. Grant. Julia was fatalistic. She had absorbed her husband's view that massive numbers must be used to shorten the struggle but she shuddered under the impact of each fresh engagement.

Julia went over the scene of the battle and felt exalted with the magnificence of her surroundings when she reached Chattanooga, with Lookout Mountain veiled in mist and the Tennessee River washing its base, a silvery thread winding through wintry landscape, then losing itself suddenly in deep gorges. Grant felt better but Rawlins was coughing desperately. The campaign had tired Rawlins but just before Christmas he went north to Danbury, Connecticut, and married Emma Hurlbut. He was back at Nashville early in January, with his bride, and his children by his first wife, for a brief interlude before shipping them all off to his parents' home in Galena.

But by this time the Grants were at the bedside of Fred in Louisa Boggs' home in St. Louis. He was critically ill with pneumonia on top of a long siege of dysentery that had reduced him to a skeleton. Like Willy Sherman and the other Sherman children, he had developed intestinal trouble at Vicksburg and had been ailing for some time. The rigors of the battlefield had been too much for the spirited boy.

Julia was the first to be called away from Nashville. Late in January she decided that the time had come to summon Ulysses. Fred was thought to be dying. Only an extremity would have induced her to make this move. She had taken care of each family problem as it arose and had never added to Ulysses' worries by enlarging on family difficulties, Ulysses responded at once but was ordered by Stanton to retain direct command of all his forces and communicate both with them and with the government. An expert telegrapher accompanied him to St. Louis.

Grant noted that he hardly expected to find Fred alive on his arrival. He was just recovering from one of his own migraine headaches at the time. But while he was en route Fred passed the crisis in pneumonia and when his father entered the room his tired eyes lit up with swift recognition. The small soldier was winning his own battle. Julia was not an apprehensive mother. She had developed a great sense of calm in the midst of stress. There had been anxious hours when Fred was out of sight and none knew where he was. But he seemed a small and helpless figure in the high bed and the Grants stood hand in hand watching him. Both were so relieved that Grant was able to relax for a few hours.

He took Julia and other members of the family to see Richelieu at the St. Louis Theater. The party rode downtown in a street car. They occupied a private box and Grant sat well back out of sight but soon was recognized. There were cries of "Grant! Grant! Get up!" at the end of the first act.

The bearded veteran of Chattanooga rose, bowed with some embarrassment and sat down abruptly. Julia Dent, well known in St. Louis, smiled contentedly over this recognition. There were many familiar faces in the theater, and memories for her of happy occasions before and after she married Ulysses; then of dim days when they were impoverished and forgotten. All had good will for her, and some remembered how faithfully she had defended Grant. His old friend, Colonel O'Fallon, arranged a banquet at the Lindell House, with Generals Rosecrans, John M. Schofield and other ranking officers present. Best of all, in Julia's estimation, her father was there, looking inscrutable as the band played "Hail to the Chief" when Grant walked in to storms of applause.

Julia, with Caroline O'Fallon and Louisa Boggs, watched from an adjoining parlor. It was not an affair for women, but she could observe that the men who had ignored her husband in his days of obscurity were present cheering him now. Leading citizens who had thought that Grant the West Pointer had wasted his opportunities were already talking of him as a presidential candidate.

General Schofield, sitting at Grant's right, noticed that he did not touch the wines. The General explained: "Sometimes I can drink freely without any unpleasant effect; at others I cannot take even a single glass of light wine." He rose and bowed in response to toasts and told Schofield he found it impossible to utter a word when on his feet. But out on the balcony after dinner, when there were cries for a speech, he made a brief statement: "Gentlemen: making speeches is not my business. I never did it in my life, and never will. I thank you, however, for your attendance here."

Grant returned to his post and Julia stayed on with Fred, nourishing him back to health. The papers now openly hinted at Grant as a presidential possibility. But Julia had seen this in her crystal ball many years earlier. It was no surprise to her, although Ulysses kept denying it — to his father, to Washburne, to Sherman, to Rawlins, to anyone who brought up the subject. "I never aspired to but one office in my life," he wrote to Jesse from Nashville on February 20, 1864. "I should like to be mayor of Galena — to build a new sidewalk from my house to the depot." But the public response was growing in strength and Rawlins wrote that he grew "dizzy in looking from the eminence he has attained and tremble at the great responsibility about to devolve upon him."

Early in March Grant was summoned to Washington to meet Abraham Lincoln for the first time and to receive public thanks for his victories. Julia was unable to join him on this occasion. Fred, skinny but picking up strength again, accompanied his father. The General, appearing in a shabby uniform and carrying his own bag, was assigned to a small room high up in the Willard when he registered for himself and Fred as U. S. Grant and son, Galena, Ill. Used to the spanking George B. McClellan accouterments, the clerk did not recognize the soldier in the shabby uniform who carried his own bag. But John Sherman soon pounced on the coming man and again he was mobbed, in the dining room and the lobby.

Grant grasped the lapels of his coat, his head was bent slightly forward and his sad blue eyes were upturned to Lincoln when these two significant figures of the Civil War met face to face for the first time. All those around them were struck by the drama of their meeting. The President clasped Grant's hand in both of his with brotherly warmth. Mrs. Lincoln paraded with him and Seward made him stand on a sofa where the cheering guests could view him. He was flushed with embarrassment. "Oh what enthusiasm prevailed," Rawlins wrote to his bride. "The General was certainly last night more than President in the hearts of the immense concourse of ladies attending the White House. It would have filled Mrs. Grant with delight."

Fred stood by his father's side next day while President Lincoln formally commissioned him lieutenant general and Grant read off in a low voice a few brief sentences written with pencil on a half sheet of paper. Mrs. Lincoln invited him to a military dinner with twelve other prominent generals but Grant asked to be excused, as he wished to hurry back to his post.

"I don't see how we can excuse you," said Lincoln. "It would be Hamlet with the Prince left out." But Grant explained that he had had "enough of the show business" and went on his way.

Immediately after his departure he was appointed supreme commander of all the armies and Julia learned that she must now prepare to move East. Her husband returned to Nashville to arrange for the transfer of his command there to General Sherman, and the two Generals went on to meet their wives in Cincinnati. Julia and Ellen Sherman sat in one room in the Burnet Hotel while "Cump" and Ulyss spread out their maps on a table in an adjoining room and discussed the strategy of the future. Grant, heading the Army of the Potomac, would concentrate on Lee. Sherman, supreme in Mississippi, would focus on Joseph E. Johnston.

Julia was pleased at the prospect of going to live in Washington but for once Hannah had some doubts about her son's infallibility. When he went over to Covington from Cincinnati for a quick visit she asked him if he were not afraid to attack Lee.

"Not at all," he assured her. "I know Lee as well as he knows himself. I know all his strong points, and all his weak ones. I intend to attack his weak points, and flank his strong ones."

Jesse had sent a carriage to the wharf to meet the General, but the driver, looking for an imposing figure, had failed to notice the drab soldier in a plain overcoat carrying a carpet bag, and Grant arrived at the gate on foot.

By March 26 he had taken up headquarters at Culpeper Courthouse and Julia, at the Willard Hotel, was having her first glimpse of the muddy, bustling capital. She had stopped off in Philadelphia to buy some clothes for herself and the children. She knew that she would now be on view in the nation's showcase and if Ulysses cared little for appearances Julia was quite the opposite. She carefully selected some gowns of rich material but conservative cut with which to meet the dressy Mrs. Lincoln and the ladies of her court. It was a big plunge for Mrs. Grant to take, although she was rarely at a loss on the social front.

PART TWO

CHAPTER IX: MRS, GRANT MEETS THE LINCOLNS

ABRAHAM LINCOLN failed to catch the name Grant as Julia moved up to him deferentially in the receiving line. She hesitated for a moment, then Adam Badeau, her husband's military secretary, repeated: "Mrs. General Grant, Mr. President."

At once he seized Julia's tiny gloved hand in both of his and beamed on her warmly. "The tall, ungainly man looked down upon his visitor with infinite kindness," Badeau noted, and he led her directly to Mrs. Lincoln. The President's wife studied Julia with close attention and greeted her effusively. After an amiable chat she told Colonel Badeau to show Mrs. Grant the conservatories. As a lover of flowers this seemed a thoughtful touch to Julia.

Badeau, a Huguenot recently introduced into the Grant circle and still walking with a limp from war injuries, thought that the ladies around Mrs. Lincoln were disposed to patronize Julia. But at no time in her life did she lend herself readily to this sort of treatment. Her retiring manner was deceptive, for she was self-assured in a quiet way and understood all the social usages. Those who thought her prosaic and dull, an impression gained largely from her heavy features, were unconscious of her sprightly wit and discerning shrewdness. Any fumbling she might do was due to her shortsightedness and not to ineptitude. Snobs were apt to be disarmed by her candor. It soon was clear to all the women, sophisticated or naive, that Julia was a person of genuine good will, too plain to arouse envy, too devoted to her husband and family to incite gossip, not sharp enough of tongue to stir up controversy. But she was not simple and she could readily detect the machinations that muddied the social current around the Lincolns.

Badeau decided that she handled her first visit to the White House with tact and "asserted herself delicately but skilfully." When the women crowded around her for introductions in the lobby she hurried off to her carriage, saying she would be pleased to receive them at her hotel. She avoided all their attempts to rush her, to engage her to sit in their theater boxes, to put her on display.

But Julia was involved almost at once with the most beautiful and dashing of them all — young Kate Chase, the red-haired and brilliant daughter of Salmon Portland Chase. She had married Senator William Sprague of Rhode Island in 1863, with Lincoln looking on and Mrs. Lincoln sulking at home, having hidden his dress trousers to make him late for Kate's wedding. She was already a dominant figure in the Republican party. Her pride, her Paris clothes, her wealth, her brains, her determination to make her father President, were much discussed. She was at odds with Mrs. Lincoln, drawing all the masculine attention to herself when both were in the same room.

With her Cincinnati connections Julia knew what to expect from Miss Kate, whose early life was based in Ohio, but she was not prepared for Mrs. Sprague's insistence that General Grant should call first on her father. All the dignitaries of the Government had paid courtesy calls on the General who had come out of the West with such uncommon laurels. Kate argued it out with Badeau at a dance but he resisted her authority and advised the General against it. However, whether Julia took a stand or Grant decided the issue was thistledown he called on Chase during an afternoon drive and told Badeau that he paid too much attention to such trifles.

The call was returned at once and the Grants were asked to dinner. Kate soon was seen steering the General around the dance floor and making him look less awkward than he had ever seemed before in a similar situation. She had won her point and Julia and she would have many social encounters in the days to come. She was deferential to Mrs. Grant until the General loomed as a threat to her ambitions for her father.

Wherever Grant showed up there were tornadoes of applause and he was cheered and serenaded to an extent that he found most unwelcome. He had had enough of this on his earlier visit, when he was more or less on exhibition. He was still concerned with one thing only — winning the war. The social picture was remote from his calculations, and at this stage Julia felt aloof from it, too.

"Do you think he will capture Richmond?" a fellow guest asked her at one of the receptions.

"Yes, before he gets through," she answered quietly. "Mr. Grant was always a very obstinate man."

Swift reorganization went on at Culpeper Courthouse and Julia saw little of the General as he laid plans for his campaign against Lee. The "ring of his orders" was music in Rawlins' ears and the arrival of small, vigorous Philip Sheridan to command the cavalry was applauded. March was a rough month of wind and snow in Washington and Julia was glad to see the leaves unfold in April. Early in the month she went to Fort Monroe with Grant. He reviewed Negro troops camped nearby, visited the ruins of Hampton and ran down to Norfolk. Rawlins was impatient on this occasion because she was along.

"If Mrs. Grant had remained in Washington, we would not have mixed with this trip any curiosity or pleasure not strictly in the line of duty," wrote the inexorable Rawlins to his wife. "When a man's wife is with him he can't help bending a little to the desire of pleasing her, even against her protestations."

Julia again showed poor judgment, in Rawlins' estimation, in voting for General McClellan's sword in a contest held at a Sanitary Fair at Palace Garden in New York late in April. Like her husband, Mrs. Grant could no longer move without attention and when she visited the Fair with Mrs. William S. Hillyer, her old St. Louis friend, she found herself at once in a covey of Generals' wives. Mrs. George B. McClellan, Mrs. John C. Fremont and Mrs. Irwin McDowell all were in the trophy room. Julia said she would prefer to move around incognito. When shown the voting stands she observed that McClellan was ahead by 1,620 votes. She took up a pen and cast another vote for him.

"The spectators took a deep breath and felt much easier," the New York Herald reported on April 23, 1864. "The incident created quite a sensation, and was talked of the rest of the day by the visitors." But Rawlins reported to his wife that "the General feels considerably annoyed about the matter."

From this point on the name Grant became a daily, and sometimes a terrifying, sight to the reading public. On April 24 Grant wrote lovingly to Louisa Boggs about Julia and the children and noted that he had a "big contract on hand" that must be finished before he could hope for rest or pleasure. The "contract" went into execution when he crossed the Rapidan early in May and the bloodiest engagements of the war were ushered in. As he set the armies in motion it was noted that his coat was formally buttoned up to his chin. He wore a sword and dressy brown gloves, which were promptly credited to Julia's solicitude. But he soon undid his buttons, took off his sword and abandoned the formal gloves for shabby buckskin.

His headquarters were now the field. On May 11 he wrote to General Halleck: "I am now sending back to Belle Plains all my wagons for a fresh supply of provisions, and ammunition, and propose to fight it out on this line if it takes all summer." The Battle of the Wilderness was followed by Spotsylvania and North Anna. All through May the fields ran red with blood. June brought the Battle of Cold Harbor. In 1884 Grant wrote: "I have always regretted that the last assault at Cold Harbor was ever made." Six thousand Union soldiers died in the span of an hour.

The horrors mounted. The entire country watched the titanic struggle between Grant and Lee — some saw it as the bludgeoning sword against tempered steel. Jeb Stuart went down at Yellow Tavern in a melee of sabers and pistols, and Longstreet was wounded in the Wilderness fighting his old friend Grant. Julia grieved when General McPherson was killed during the summer's savage fighting. By the end of June Sherman, busy with his own campaign against Atlanta, was writing to his wife: "It is enough to make the whole world start at the awful amount of death and destruction that now stalks abroad . . ."

Julia by this time was back in St. Louis and Stanton had notified Grant of her safe arrival. At the end of May Grant was suffering from one of his migraine headaches and Theodore Lyman, an aide to General George G. Meade, watched him applying chloroform to his head. On June 4, with the horrors of Cold Harbor all around him, Grant wrote a tender letter to Nellie that gave no suggestion of his grim surroundings. He praised her for her good writing in a letter she had sent to him. He commented on her appearance at the Sanitary Fair in St. Louis as the Old Woman Who Lived in a Shoe. He predicted that she and Buck would be speaking German by the end of the year and that he would then buy them the "nice old watches he had promised." The General continued:

We have been fighting now for thirty days and have every prospect of still more fighting to do before we get into Richmond. When we do get there I shall go home to see you and Ma, Fred, Buck and Jess. I expect Jess rides little Arkell every day. I think when I go home I will get a little buggy to work Rebel in so that you and Jess can ride about the country during vacation. . . . You must send this letter to Ma to read because I will not write to her today. Kiss Ma, Cousin Louise & all the young ladies for pa. Be a good little girl as you have always been. Study your lessons and you will be contented and happy.

From Papa.

Nellie and little Aline Sheafe Taylor were much observed at the Sanitary Fair, sitting in the old woman's shoe dressed like old ladies, drawing numbers in raffles, exhibiting dolls. Wherever she was, Julia did what she could in the way of war work. She sewed and visited hospitals. She patronized fairs. There were many calls on her time in St. Louis, because of her old connections there. She was sought out by those with Union sympathies, and shunned by many who favored the Confederacy. She boarded with Louisa Boggs, who had long ago forgotten the animosities of the Hardscrabble days. From time to time she went out to Wish-ton-Wish to stay with her father. There was talk of guerrilla raids at this time and Jesse recalled getting home from a ride at his grandfather's place and finding his mother missing. "A hasty search, a few frantic shouts, and two panic-stricken boys were whipping their ponies along the empty road to St. Louis," he wrote. Julia had merely gone into town.

The scene of battle now shifted to the Petersburg front, when Grant and Meade broke camp near Cold Harbor on June 12 and transferred their base to the James River. Early in July Julia moved East with all the children. Her brother Fred was sent by Grant to meet them at City Point, a village on the James River, ten miles from Petersburg. The General relaxed for the first time in many weeks. After the terrible ordeal of May and June Julia and the children were especially welcome.

Horace Porter walked in on them in the headquarters boat on the James and found Grant "engaged in a rough-and-tumble wrestling match with Fred and Buck." He was red in the face and out of breath. The boys had gripped him, and he was on his knees on the floor grappling with them and joining in their laughter "as if he were a boy himself," Porter observed.

When Grant saw that Porter had dispatches in his hand, he got up at once, brushed off his knees and remarked apologetically: "Oh, you know my weaknesses — my children and my horses."

The James was a lively sight, with craft of all kinds moving back and forth on wartime missions. Bugles sounded over the water and flags whipped in the breeze. Lady Bankshire roses bloomed in golden clusters. The children found much to interest them in the river life. They frequently went ashore from the official steamer to visit their father's tent and the headquarters' mess. To Jesse it was always "Father's Army."

Grant had been restless until his family arrived. Jubal Early's raid on the capital in July was a great humiliation that sent him speeding in to Washington to study the capital defenses. At this time Lincoln took note of the fact that Julia often called her husband Mister Grant. When Stanton protested the General's having moved large numbers of troops away from Washington, the President replied:

Now, Mr. Secretary, you know we have been trying to manage this army for nearly three years and you know we haven't done much with it. We sent over the mountains and brought Mr. Grant, as Mrs. Grant calls him, to manage it for us. And now I guess we'd better let Mr. Grant have his own way.

August was blazing hot and many of the officers were ill, including Julia's brother Fred. Rawlins joined his family in Connecticut for three months to recuperate from his exhausting cough but Dana was of the opinion that "there was no escape for him." Grant's one conception of warfare was to advance and his course now was slowed. By the middle of August he was persuaded that the Confederates were down to rock bottom in manpower. But they still showed plenty of life and he came no nearer to the conquest of Richmond. The mine explosion at Petersburg from which much had been expected had fizzled in its ultimate aim. Early in September Atlanta was evacuated by General Hood, a heavy blow to the South. By that time Julia was in Philadelphia looking for a home. She hoped to start the children in good schools, yet keep them all within easy reach of the General. They were drawn to Burlington, New Jersey, through Captain Miner Knowlton, who had taught Grant mathematics at West Point. They settled on a two-story house on Wood Street, with a spacious porch covered with ivy. There were fir trees at the gate, and French windows upstairs and down.

The neighbors decided that Mrs. Grant was a "sensible, plain, good woman" when she settled there with her brother Fred late in September. Almost immediately she received a telegram from Stanton, who recognized Mrs. Grant as an integral part of his military family: "Sheridan fought another great battle yesterday and won a splendid victory." The cavalry commander was striking at Jubal Early in the Shenandoah Valley.

The boys went galloping about on the frisky pony the General had given them after Vicksburg and they were generous in sharing him with their friends. Nellie, in ruffles and long stockings, attended Miss Kingdon's School, and Buck objected to wearing kilts, a Celtic fancy of his mother's that her sons deplored. Both Nellie and Buck attended dancing school and neighbors recalled that Julia often came to the door and called "Ho, Buck," and Buck failed to answer. Fred got into fights with boys of Southern sympathies. Burlington's leading industry was shoes. Before the war there had been much trafficking with the South in footware, and feeling for the Confederacy was strong. But Fred was an object of great interest to the other boys, since it was known that he had been to the battlefields. He was independent and spirited and none could express a view in his hearing that did not uphold the Union. The boys attended a military school and Fred went through the gestures of drilling as if he had never foraged and marched with General Grant himself.

Soon after the re-election of Lincoln a burly stranger in a long overcoat stepped off a special car with a companion officer one night and remarked to two men on the Burlington platform: "They say I live here, but I don't know where."

"Thunder, it's General Grant," said Anthony Smith, the local policeman, staring hard at the bearded figure revealed by lantern light.

He was ceremoniously escorted to the house on Wood Street, answering questions about the army as he walked along. The General knocked at the door. It was long past midnight. Mrs. Grant appeared on the upstairs porch and called softly: "Is that you, Ulyss?"

"Yes," said Grant.

She came hurrying down and let him in with the telegrapher he had brought to handle army dispatches. Word spread like wildfire that Grant was in town. He scarcely had time to finish his breakfast in the morning and light his first cigar when the townspeople swarmed around the house. Julia left the door open and cordially invited them in. Little Sarah Gaunt, who later became Mrs. D. V. Holmes, climbed in the General's lap and kissed him. Six-year-old Thomas Milnor brought him a basket of fruit.

But the General had to hurry off to catch a ten o'clock train. Julia left with him, headed for a shopping trip in New York. As they passed along the street, leading an impromptu parade, Mrs. Charles Kinsey came out on her porch and waved her flag over the General's head with the Barbara Fritchie touch, saying: "General Grant, permit me to have the honor of waving this glorious flag over your honored head."

Grant had not seen New York since his West Point days, and he hoped to keep his visit quiet, but again the secret of his presence leaked out. Private carriages and policemen were at the ferry landing. The Astor House was mobbed. When he dined that night with Governor Reuben E. Fenton guests jumped on chairs and tables to cheer for Grant. The crowds gathered wherever he went. Women in crinolines pushed around Julia as she walked through the aisles of A. T. Stewart's. Invitations poured in on them. Next day Grant managed to walk a few blocks in civilian clothes without being recognized but finally had to seek escape in one of the new street cars.

By this time Julia was feeling far from well but she was determined to go to the opera that night. The Triplers called to see them and she told Mrs. Tripler that the doctor must not come into her bedroom, for he would forbid her to go out, and from force of habit she would obey.

"Things have changed," Mrs. Tripler pointed out. "You can trample on Dr. Tripler if you wish."

"Oh, if Dr. Tripler forbids it, I wouldn't dare to go," responded Julia. But she did, and enjoyed It too. Ulysses liked a good play but he had little zest for opera. Julia's old interest in music was still alive, and his aversion to it had not diminished.

The same mob scenes were repeated in Philadelphia when Grant accompanied his wife back to Burlington. He finally took refuge in Independence Hall. Rawlins, reading the dispatches in the New York Herald about all these doings, was much annoyed. He felt that the General was "entitled to respite and rest" after his labors.

Fred soon took French leave of his school again and set off to join his father. Julia arrived with the other children in December to spend Christmas at City Point, where the General now had a roomy cabin in place of a tent. Mrs. Rawlins was invited to join the party. But Rawlins demurred and wrote to Emma that although he would like to have her there he disapproved of having officers' wives in camp. "It does not look like war to me, to see it heralded throughout the country by the press that the wife of the General and also the wife of his Chief of Staff are at City Point," he wrote.

Emma was bitterly disappointed and Julia thought it ridiculous to take this stand. She scolded Rawlins, who would listen to her more readily than to anyone else. He wrote again to Emma, this time saying that Mrs. Grant thought she must be a very considerate and obedient wife to ask her husband if she should come to visit him and "that she intended having your visit here as a surprise to me and the next time she sees you she intends to give you some instructions as to how to manage me." In the end Julia persuaded Rawlins to bring his wife to City Point and she stayed there until the end of the war.

Fred wanted to go bird shooting during the Christmas holidays but sporting guns were not among the army supplies. However, Grant let him have an infantry musket and he set off in a rowboat with Bill, a Negro servant. They paddled down the river in search of ducks but soon were accosted by naval pickets. They were taken aboard a gunboat as rebel spies. No one believed Fred at first when he announced: "I am Frederick Dent Grant, sir, son of General Ulysses S. Grant, Commander-in-Chief, who will be very angry if I am killed."

Close inspection of the unmistakable Grant features persuaded the pickets that a deplorable mistake had been made. It was late when they got home but Julia was no more concerned than usual over his absence. Grant was much amused. He teased Fred about this scrape and told him he was lucky not to have been hanged at the yardarm as an enemy of the republic, and his body consigned to the waters. Rawlins always referred to Fred as the "Veteran" and shook his troubled head over these escapades.

Jesse, too, had moments of excitement to remember as he grew older. On one occasion he was with his father, President Lincoln and Tad Lincoln when the rebels opened fire at Petersburg. Grant hurried them all into a shelter but both boys wanted to stick their heads out to see what was going on. Jesse thought that "no matter how great the strain and responsibility of his position, it troubled father more to be entirely separated from the family."

After the Christmas holidays the older children were sent back to school. Fred was desperately anxious to stay but Julia told him firmly as they boarded the tug: "Now remember, Fred! Not a word!" Jesse knew that Fred considered him a great baby because he had to stay with his mother, and would be lonely in Burlington without her,

Julia now became a familiar figure at City Point. The cabin stood on a bluff and had a view of the James River. It was part of a little village of log cabins but was distinguishable by the flag in front and the trees nearby. It had a large room with an open fireplace that served as living room, dining room and office.

Behind were two small bedrooms. Julia made these quarters look like home. She picked wild flowers and saw that Grant had his favorite dishes.

They were snug winter quarters, unlike conditions at Valley Forge, and here General Grant was able to a certain extent to replenish his batteries for the final encounter. Once again Julia was on the spot at a crucial moment. Once again she was there to lend the comfort and support to Grant that his lonely nature demanded. The children, when they came, were an additional delight to him.

By this time Washburne had rounded up for Julia her old Galena maid, Maggie Cavanaugh, and she was on her way East to join the children. Julia had written to him just before Christmas: "I am getting to be such an old soldier (since I have such an indifferent cook) that I really fear for the Genl's peace of mind when he comes home (after Richmond is taken) and beg for his sake you will put someone on Maggie's track & have her locked up and carefully shipped to your friend & admirer, Julia D, Grant."

They had notable visitors, and vital conferences were held in the little cabin. Here Grant received daily reports from his subordinates. Here he and Julia followed the course of Sherman's march to the sea. Because of the intimacy of their quarters Julia heard a great deal of the military maneuverings in the closing days of the war. She could not always close her ears but in spite of her candid nature she was as discreet as her silent husband when it came to war secrets.

In January they all put in an anxious night when the Confederate ironclads moved quietly down the James. Grant, Julia and Ingalls sat in the front room of the cabin discussing this emergency. When news came through that the Confederates could not pass the obstructions in the river they both retired, leaving word that Grant should be called if the situation changed.

It did. Soon after one o'clock he was routed out of bed by the news that the enemy vessels had broken through. He was ready in two minutes, drawing his top boots over his drawers, and putting on his overcoat. He lit a cigar, listened to the reports, then wrote out orders in great haste.

Julia appeared, hurriedly dressed, and asked: "Ulyss, will those gunboats shell the bluff?"

Grant could not guarantee what they would do if they got that far. Porter, a witness to the scene, reported that Julia was one of the most composed of those present. She drew her chair a little closer to Grant's and inquired in a mild voice: "Ulyss, what had I better do?"

"The General looked at her for a moment and then replied in a half-serious and half-teasing way, 'Well, the fact is, Julia, you oughtn't to be here.'"

Another officer suggested hitching up an ambulance and driving her far enough back into the country to be beyond reach of the shells.

"Oh, their gunboats are not down here yet," answered the General, "and they must be stopped at all hazards."

But the Confederate boats went aground. The shore batteries were reinforced. Next day the Onondaga went into action. The Confederates withdrew up the river, but made another attack, and again were forced to retire. It was the last foray of the enemy fleet in the James River.

Again Julia was directly involved in enemy operations, this time in a scheme so visionary that Porter wondered how it could have been seriously discussed. General Edward O. C. Ord and General Longstreet, meeting between the lines to discuss the fraternization of pickets, considered the possibility of a friendly conference by Grant and Lee, aided by the good offices of Mrs. Grant and Mrs. Longstreet, who were old friends from their St. Louis days. The women were pictured as crossing enemy lines and acting as mediators. Mrs. Longstreet was summoned to Richmond from Lynchburg for this purpose. It was only a straw in the wind as dissolution set in. Mrs. Longstreet, in the end, was one of the women who sat quietly in St. Paul's on the April day when Jefferson Davis received the message from Lee that Richmond must be evacuated.

Grant's sister Clara died of tuberculosis that March and in writing of her death to his father the General remarked: "The rebellion has lost its vitality." Hood had been whipped in the West. Sherman had delivered Savannah on Christmas day. But Petersburg still held out and the bombardment went on.

President Lincoln made a number of visits to City Point, and Jesse played host to his young son. When Tad refused to ride a small horse named Jeff that had been provided for him, Jesse decided he was "not a confident horseman." Grant quietly interposed: "Jesse will ride Jeff." They galloped off, with Tad on Rebbie. But Jeff bolted and soon both Grant and Lincoln were in pursuit of the boys, whose horses wound up in the corral.

The presidential party was quartered on the River Queen but Lincoln came ashore frequently, walked up the hill, conferred with Grant and was entertained at the headquarters mess. The President liked to visit the wounded and wander about the camp with giant strides. He was even known to pick up an axe and swing it on a log. When Mrs. Lincoln was with them Tad was kept busy running ashore with notes summoning Lincoln back to his wife.

On Mrs. Lincoln's first visit to City Point Mrs. Grant called on her but it was not a happy occasion. The President's wife was in one of her moods and the story spread that when Julia sat beside her on a sofa she said: "How dare you?" In later years Julia explained that she had got up of her own free will when she felt she was crowding Mrs. Lincoln. But Emma Dent Casey often told the story that Julia was outraged because Mrs. Lincoln had expected her to back out of the room and to treat her like royalty.

In any event there were cool relations between the two women from the start. Both Badeau and Porter were witnesses to discordant exchanges between them, which they have left on record. Late in March Lincoln wanted to visit the front. Grant thought it was not safe but when the fighting subsided a special train was made up and Julia and Mrs. Lincoln, jolting along on the road bed which General Porter compared to a corrugated washboard, witnessed the newly dead and the wounded lying along the tracks in the vicinity of Fort Stedman. Gray and blue uniforms were bloodily tangled together in a glimpse of war horrifying to both women.

The railroad took them only part way. Then the men rode on and Julia and Mrs. Lincoln traveled by ambulance, with Badeau for their escort. He chanced to mention the fact that all wives had been ordered to the rear because of active operations except the wife of General Charles Griffin, who had obtained a special permit from the President to stay.

"What do you mean by that, sir?" Mrs. Lincoln exclaimed in a sudden burst of excitement. "Do you mean to say that she saw the President alone? Do you know that I never allow the President to see any woman alone?"

Mrs. Lincoln bounced about with rage, and insisted on being let out of the carriage. "I will ask the President if he saw that woman alone," she exclaimed. She told the driver to stop and when Badeau protested she leaned over and pinioned the coachman's arms. Finally Julia prevailed on her to wait until they had reached their destination. There General Meade came up to greet them and Mrs. Lincoln went off on his arm. She had calmed down by the time she returned. The Secretary of War, and not the President, had given Mrs. Griffin the permit, she informed them haughtily.

Mrs. Griffin, who afterward became the Countess Esterhazy, was, one of the great beauties of Washington. Julia warned Badeau that night to keep quiet about the whole affair. She found it so mortifying and distressing that she would mention it to her husband only, she said. But she released Badeau from his pledge after a more devastating experience on the following day.

A review of General Ord's army was held and Philip Sheridan's cavalry crossed the James River by pontoon. The headquarters party sailed from

City Point in the morning. On landing, Lincoln, Grant and Ord rode on horseback several miles to the reviewing grounds. Mrs. Lincoln and Mrs. Grant again swung their hoops into an ambulance and drove with Porter and Badeau. They met with delays along the way and were late arriving. Meanwhile Lincoln had decided to go ahead with the review. The men had been waiting for a long period. Their dinner hour was overdue. So the bands played. Colors were dipped. The troops presented arms.

Mrs. Ord, a fine horsewoman and acknowledged beauty, was in a quandary as she waited for Mrs. Lincoln and Mrs. Grant to arrive. She asked Captain John S. Barnes, who commanded the Bat, if she should accompany the cavalcade. He did not know what move to make but turned to a staff officer, who remarked: "Of course come along." Mrs. Ord followed the reviewing column and gave every appearance of riding with the President.

They were half way down the line when the ambulance drove up. As soon as Mrs. Ord spotted it she said: "There come Mrs. Lincoln and Mrs. Grant — I think I had better join them." Barnes galloped across the field with her and found Mrs. Lincoln in a passion. "What does the woman mean," she exclaimed, "by riding by the side of the President and ahead of me? Does she suppose that he wants her by the side of him?"

When Mrs. Ord greeted the ambulance party with a friendly smile Mrs. Lincoln "positively insulted her," according to Badeau, "called her vile names in the presence of a crowd of officers, and asked what she meant by following up the President."

Mrs. Ord promptly burst into tears and asked what she had done. Mrs. Lincoln ranted on. Julia, who was fond of Mrs. Ord, defended her vigorously. The anger then was turned on her. "I suppose you think you'll get to the White House yourself, don't you?" Mrs. Lincoln exclaimed.

Badeau noted that Julia remained calm and dignified, remarking quietly that she was quite satisfied with the position she had. It was more than she had ever expected to attain. But Mrs. Lincoln gave her one more dig. "Oh! you had better take it if you can get it. 'Tis very nice."

The men were speechless during this exchange. Both feared that Mrs. Lincoln would jump out of the carriage and start shouting at the cavalcade. Julia was silent and embarrassed. "It was a painful situation, from which the only escape was to retire," Barnes noted. "The review was over, and Mrs. Ord and myself with a few officers rode back to headquarters at City Point."

In his account of the day's events Porter made allowance for the fatigue and annoyance endured by Mrs. Lincoln on the trip. "Mrs. Grant enjoyed the day with great zest," he noted, but both ladies had had their heads severely bumped against the top of the ambulance, and their bonnets flattened down, when a sudden jolt lifted them clear off their seats and tossed them into the air. Mrs. Lincoln had insisted then on getting out but since the mud was hub-deep Julia and Porter persuaded her that the wagon, rough though it was, should remain their ark of refuge.

Like Grant, Mrs. Lincoln suffered from migraine headaches, and her later decline softened the historian's view of the day's events. Even Julia, who was outraged at the time, in the long run made allowances for her irrationality. At dinner that night on the River Queen Mrs. Lincoln berated General Ord and urged his removal. Grant defended him stoutly. Badeau thought that Lincoln bore it as "Christ might have done, with an expression of pain and sadness that cut one to the heart." He called her "Mother" and treated her kindly through it all.

The Grants were their guests that night. The band was brought down to the River Queen and an impromptu dance was held. Lincoln and Grant sat aft conversing. General Sheridan spent the night at City Point. Late in the evening Barnes was summoned to the upper saloon, where he found that the Lincolns quite obviously had been discussing Mrs. Ord. Mr. Lincoln "very gently suggested that he had hardly remarked her presence; but Mrs. Lincoln was not to be pacified, and appealed to me to support her views." Barnes felt he could not umpire the question, but he explained as well as he could the circumstances that had led up to the episode.

Julia, too, liked to pretend that she was jealous of Ulysses when women fluttered around him in camp, as they did then, and later in the White House. But it was nothing more than badinage between them. It had none of the pathological aspects of Mrs. Lincoln's envy. Grant at this time was more sympathetic to Mrs. Lincoln than Julia was. He had only to look at her husband's saddened face, to hear his kind and apologetic references to his sick wife, to appraise the depth of this tragedy.

Mrs. Stanton had told Badeau some time earlier that she would not go to the White House or visit Mrs. Lincoln. But Julia decided to keep the peace if she could. She was not going to let herself be smothered by a female quarrel. Sherman arrived at this juncture, fresh from his victory in the South. Grant had asked several prominent officers to meet him at City Point. Sherman came bounding off the Russia and with long strides reached his old Mend Grant. "Their encounter was more like that of two schoolboys coming together after a vacation than the meeting of the chief actors in a great war tragedy," Porter observed.

"Grant is almost childlike in his love for me," wrote Sherman to his wife. Julia greeted him affectionately at the cabin door and he held them all enthralled with his story of the march through Georgia. Porter thought it sounded like a "grand epic related with Homeric power," while Sherman spoke of himself as the "vandal chief," regarded by the Southerners "just as the Romans did the Goths and the parallel is not unjust."

The two Generals went off to call on Lincoln and Julia prepared refreshments for them. On their return she asked them at once if they had seen Mrs. Lincoln. Grant said that they had not thought to inquire for her. Sherman did not even know she was on the boat. Julia reproached them for being neglectful and Ulysses promised to make amends when they called next day. But again Mary was not on view. Lincoln went to her stateroom, and returned looking inexpressibly sad. He begged them to excuse her, since she was not feeling well.

Meanwhile, Julia was an interested party to discussions between her husband and Sherman.

"Perhaps you don't want me here listening to your secrets?" she remarked.

"Do you think we can trust her, Grant?" asked Sherman.

"I'm not so sure about that," said Ulysses, joining in the fun.

Sherman turned his chair around, folded his arms and solemnly questioned Julia, in the manner of a pedagogue, on the geography of the Carolinas and Virginia. "Mrs. Grant caught the true essence of the humor, and gave replies which were the perfection of drollery," Porter noted. Grant looked on, much amused, and finally Sherman said: "Well, Grant, I think we can trust her." He then escorted her to the officers' mess and took a seat beside her at table.

Julia's next encounter with Mrs. Lincoln was a troubled one, too. Robert Lincoln, now on her husband's staff, had invited the unfortunate Barnes to go with them on an excursion to Point of Rocks. He joined Julia when he saw her sitting alone in the forward cabin. Mrs. Lincoln stood on the uncovered deck, near the pilot house. Julia suggested that Barnes push a large upholstered arm chair through the door so that she could sit down. He bade her good morning politely. But Mrs. Lincoln refused the chair and glared at him.

Barnes went back to the friendly Mrs. Grant "who had witnessed my failure." Soon Mrs. Lincoln beckoned Julia over and they had an animated conversation. On her return Mrs. Grant told him that the President's wife objected to his presence on their boat and had asked her to tell him so. When they reached Point of Rocks the Lincoln party rambled in the woods. Julia stayed behind and helped Barnes get off on the other side of the river, where he found a horse and rode back to City Point. He felt that Lincoln had intended to heal the breach by bringing him on board for that expedition.

However, the River Queen and the Martin came to be known as Mrs. Lincoln's Boat and Mrs. Grant's Boat. The respective skippers had a hard time pleasing the two ladies. Mrs. Lincoln thought that the President's boat should always lie nearest to the dock, and declined to go ashore if she had to cross over the Martin. On several occasions the Grant boat was pushed out into the stream while the Lincoln boat took its place. "Of course, neither Mr. Lincoln nor General Grant took any notice of such trivialities," Barnes observed.

Mrs. Lincoln soon returned to Washington, leaving the President and Tad at City Point. Julia had few strong dislikes but it is reasonably clear that Mary Todd Lincoln was one of them. Possibly Mrs. Elizabeth Keckley, the Negro seamstress who took such intimate notes on Mrs. Lincoln and Mrs. Jefferson Davis as she sewed for them, held the key to Mrs. Grant's feelings for the President's wife. It was no secret that Mary disliked Grant intensely. Mrs. Keckley wrote:

"He is a butcher" she would often say, "and is not fit to be at the head of an army." Lincoln mentioned Grant's victories, which she admitted, but "he loses two men to the enemy's one," she protested. "He has no management, no regard for life." There was further opinion and advice. Then, with a twinkle in the eyes, and a ring of irony in the voice, Lincoln said: "Well, Mother, supposing that we give you command of the army. No doubt you would do much better than any general that has been tried."

The hour of crisis had now arrived and by the end of March Grant prepared for his final swing around the Confederate right. He and his staff moved to the Petersburg front. The General lingered long at the cabin door, kissing Julia repeatedly as he bade her farewell, and then returning to kiss her some more. "She bore the parting bravely, although her pale face and sorrowful look told of the sadness that was in her heart," Porter noted. Lincoln was at the station to bid Grant farewell. At the last moment all the officers raised their hats to him. The salute was returned by the President. "Good-by, gentlemen. God bless you all! Remember, your success is my success," he said. The train moved off and Grant's last campaign had begun. Porter thought he had never been more sanguine of victory. But Julia was both silent and sad that night.

CHAPTER X: RETURN OF THE VICTOR

JULIA WAS ASLEEP in a berth on the headquarters boat on the James River when Grant returned from Appomattox. Word had reached her the evening before that he would be back for dinner and she and Mrs. Rawlins had prepared a festive meal for the warriors. They still lacked details but they knew that Lee had surrendered to Grant and that the war was virtually over. All night long they waited for the General. Julia sang her favorite songs and chatted with Emma Rawlins. Finally she could bear up no longer. Just before dawn, having given up all hope of Ulysses' immediate return, she flung herself fully dressed on a berth and fell into a sound sleep.

When Grant arrived he "went hurriedly aboard the boat, and ran at once up the stairs to Mrs. Grant's stateroom," Porter observed. "She was somewhat chagrined that she had not remained up to receive her husband, now more than ever her 'Victor.'" But she quickly joined the group in the cabin and extended "enthusiastic greetings and congratulations" to all. The dinner was served as breakfast for the famished party.

Julia soon heard every detail of this climactic event in her husband's life. Grant, like Lee, had come out of the encounter with enlarged stature, to live historically as the ruthless warrior who had also displayed the qualities of the courtly knight. Ulysses had little to say about it himself. Jesse took note of the fact that in after years he never discussed the surrender with his family. But the official reports, the staff officers who were present and whom Julia saw immediately afterward, the newspapers, the speech makers, brought every detail into focus. It was living drama, soon absorbed into the stream of American history. The memory was part of Julia's life till the day she died. She would rejoice when Robert Louis Stevenson in his essay on "Gentlemen" cited the faultless instinct with which Grant at Appomattox had taken one perceptive glance at Lee's jeweled sword and then forgotten it.

At the moment it was enough for Julia that the war was over, the North had won, the killing had stopped at last. Ulysses was recovering from one of his blinding headaches when he learned that Lee was ready to surrender. He had tried mustard plasters on his neck and his wrists, and had soaked his feet in hot water and mustard, to no effect. Porter had found him hours later pacing in the yard of the Clifton House in the settlement of Curdsville. He was holding his head between his hands and was in great pain. Toward morning he drank some coffee at General Meade's headquarters along the road, felt a trifle better and sent off a historic message to Lee.

Grant was fully recovered and grave when he reached City Point. He saw no reason for extravagant jubilation. He had been too close to the core of the struggle for that. He hastened back to Washington to countermand orders for supplies and reinforcements and to communicate with the generals still in the field. He had no wish to excite demonstrations by his presence but the Grants were momentarily out of view in the moment of victory. The headquarters boat still floated in the James when Lincoln and then his wife visited Richmond.

Mrs. Lincoln sailed in with Mrs. Keckley, annoyed that the President had not taken her with him on his first visit to the conquered city. She wandered through Mrs. Jefferson Davis's stately reception rooms and saw the porch from which her small son Joe had fallen to his death. By this time Varina Davis was a fugitive traveling along the back roads of Georgia with her small children. One day she and Julia would discuss their war experiences with mutual comprehension.

By April 13 the Grants were both at the Willard in Washington and a great celebration was planned for that evening. Mrs. Lincoln sent Grant a note inviting him to the White House at eight o'clock. Although the President had a severe headache she asked him to drive around with them to view the illumination. But Julia was not mentioned in her note and Grant declined the invitation. Instead, they went to a reception at the Stantons.

At seven o'clock the lights flashed on and, as Julia drove through the streets, she saw one of the unforgettable sights of her lifetime — Washington celebrating the end of the war. The Capitol blazed from dome to portico. The White House looked like marble in the moonlight, although spiked with glitter and hung with flags. A monster fifty-dollar bond pricked out in lights adorned the Treasury. Jay Cooke's banking house across the way signaled "Glory to God" in golden stars. Transparencies flashed against the skyline. Rockets exploded and fireworks shot up over the Potomac. Public buildings, hotels, restaurants, shops, homes, all signaled victory with lights. People swarmed in the streets and bands played the familiar war tunes. The fall of Petersburg and the capture of Richmond had swung the North into one great paean of rejoicing. The names of Lincoln and Grant brought an overwhelming response, and at the Stanton home Julia watched the guests close in on her husband. But she and Ulysses were chiefly concerned with getting back to their children.

Next day they were invited to go to Ford's Theater with the Lincolns to see Laura Keene in Our American Cousins. The Stantons were invited, too, and Mrs. Stanton consulted Julia. "Unless you accept the invitation, I shall refuse," she said. "I will not sit without you in the box with Mrs. Lincoln." But Julia had already made up her mind not to go. She had a good excuse to offer. She must get back to Burlington and the children. Grant was embarrassed when she made her decision, since he had already told the President that they would go. Once again Julia unconsciously was a significant factor in his life. Had they gone with the Lincolns that night the chances are that Grant would have died with the President, for he was on the assassins' list. On the other hand, in later years he was known to express regret that he had not attended the play. He always wondered if the outcome might have been different had he been there. His own stalwart form and a military guard might have made a difference. Another family legend, handed down by Emma Dent Casey, was that Julia had had one of her premonitory dreams of disaster for that night, and when these occurred she was hard to budge. But dreams were in the air. Lincoln had had one, too, presaging his own death.

In the early afternoon Grant shook hands with the President and said good-by, unconscious that it was forever. They had known each other little more than a year, yet between them they had made history. When Ulysses got back to the hotel Julia told of a fanatical-looking man who had sat opposite her and Jesse in the dining room, staring hard and listening to her conversation. Later in the day as they rode to the station a horseman galloped up to their carriage on Pennsylvania Avenue, leaned down and peered inside. Julia was sure he was the man she had spotted in the dining room. Before they reached the depot he returned and did some further scrutinizing.

They traveled to Philadelphia in the private car of John W. Garrett, president of the Baltimore and Ohio Railroad, and before they reached Baltimore a man appeared on the front platform of the car and tried to get in. The conductor locked the door against intruders. Crowds greeted them at Philadelphia. They stopped for a late supper at Bloodgood's Hotel near the Walnut Street wharf, after driving across the city to take a ferry. They had no sooner settled there than a telegram was handed to the General. He read the message and then sat in silence with his head lowered. Porter noted that he gave Julia warning of the news to come but Captain S. H. Beckwith, the telegrapher who was with him, had a slightly different version of what happened next:

We walked into the parlor and the three of us, General and Mrs. Grant and I, sat down upon a sofa in one corner of the room. He read the dispatch and without comment passed it to his wife, who in turn read it and with an exclamation of painful surprise handed it to me. I shall never forget the dumb horror of that moment. My heart seemed to leap into my throat. None of us spoke a word. We simply sat there and wondered. Lincoln was shot.

Other messages from Stanton followed. He directed Beckwith to have a pilot engine precede their train on the way back to Washington. Garrett was notified to clear the road. Grant's life might well be in danger, too. Burlington was only an hour away and the General found he would lose no time if he escorted Julia and Jesse home and then made the connection back to Washington.

"The President died this morning. There are still hopes of Secretary Seward's recovery," Beckwith informed Julia, in telegraphing her that her husband had arrived safely at his destination. The Secretary of State had been attacked in his own home, but eventually recovered. It was a time long remembered by the Grant family, as by the nation as a whole. Grant called it the darkest day in his life. Julia's suspicions of the danger to him were strengthened long afterward when an anonymous letter arrived from a man who thanked God that he had failed in the mission assigned to him to kill Grant.

Julia remained in Burlington with the children through the days of mourning that followed. Grant stood at the head of Lincoln's catafalque in the East Room and figured prominently in the funeral ceremonies. Julia thought with sympathy of the anguished woman in the White House who moaned and sobbed as she sorrowed for her idol. The funeral train moved slowly across the country. Even in the South good things were spoken of Abraham Lincoln. All felt that his judgment would have been merciful. Stanton and Grant drove hard for the capture of John Wilkes Booth and his associates.

But a dark April faded into a flowery May and on the 23rd and 24th Julia and Ellen Sherman sat together in the reviewing stand opposite the White House to watch the great victory parade. The Army of the Potomac marched on the first day and the Army of the Tennessee on the second. Julia's sight was not keen enough for her to identify tattered, blood-stained flags, or distinguish one notable figure from another. But the shouts of the crowd informed her when Meade went by with flowers in his path and garlands on his horse; when John A. Logan, black-haired and smaller than Ulysses, rode past with a flourish; when General George A. Ouster, with scarlet necktie and dangling locks, brought thunderous shouts; when Mother Bickerdyke, a much-beloved Union nurse, came into view riding sidesaddle and gowned in calico. Jesse leaned over the railing and waved his Glengarry at the passing columns in response to shouts of "Grant! Grant! Good-by, old man." Banners flew as infantry, cavalry, artillery and every branch of the service marched past. The muskets looked like a "wall of steel" to Porter. The war tunes, to Julia, seemed to sum up years of anxious waiting. Spring flowers had been fashioned into garlands, and soldiers and cannon were oddly decked with blossoms. The Negro regiments were applauded with genuine emotion.

 Both Sherman and Meade gave Grant a special salute in passing. He had arrived at the reviewing stand on foot to avoid a demonstration. He was now being compared to Napoleon, to Garibaldi, to Alexander. Mrs. Sherman had not seen her husband in eighteen months and the two wives jumped to their feet and waved their handkerchiefs when torrents of applause greeted the appearance of the most controversial General of them all. Sherman's sword flashed before his face. He looked lean, cynical, war-worn, and reckless. He was under fire for the terms he had given General Joseph E. Johnston and Grant had been forced to ease the situation. When he dismounted he shook hands with President Johnson but openly snubbed Stanton. The White House, across from the reviewing stand, seemed still and empty with its great man gone.

 In June Grant was backing a pardon and amnesty for Lee. When the Southern general was threatened with trial for treason he said he would resign rather than fail to honor his pact with his Confederate adversary. From the start he was in favor of fair and considerate treatment of the South. He had written to Julia from Raleigh, North Carolina, on April 25 that the "people who talked of further retaliation and punishment, except of the political leaders, either do not conceive of the suffering endured already or they are heartless and unfeeling."

 The first summer after the war was passed largely in travel, and Julia and the children stayed close to Grant after the years of separation. They traveled all through the North with a military staff, and the tour had some of the aspects of a Roman holiday. Parades, banquets, public receptions followed one another in swift succession. Audiences rose in the General's honor wherever he appeared. Crowds mobbed his carriage. Horses, jeweled swords, medals, honorary degrees, all came his way. The Grants were swamped with invitations and three homes were offered them. Julia, who always stood modestly in the background, became used to armfuls of flowers, to cheers and the band music that Ulyss abhorred. She enjoyed it more than her husband did. In fact, she came to like it, not for herself but for him. "Hail to the Chief" was the family theme song and people turned out even at village stations to have a look at Grant.

In July they were at Saratoga and Julia took delight in the scene around her as she drove past the rangy wooden hotels of Broadway, with cupolas, balconies and cornices half hidden by tall old elms that rustled softly and preserved an air of village simplicity at the worldly spa. Woodbine draped the seventeen columns of the piazza of Congress Hall. Roses rioted in pink and crimson clumps, and flowering shrubs outlined the grounds. The Southern belles with crinolines and bishop sleeves, tulle bonnets and point-lace parasols, who had haunted the spa before the war, were no longer in view. Basques and tiny tilted Watteau bonnets were now in vogue. But the old four-in-hands, with burnished harness and high suspension springs, still went pacing along, and Grant took note of the horses.

From Saratoga they went to Boston. A reception at Faneuil Hall, a visit to Harvard and an honorary degree followed. Julia led them all to the somber pews of the Old South Church. They toured the factories of Lowell and spent some days in Maine, then visited Canada and some of their earlier haunts. They reached Detroit on August 12 and, remembering her early married days there, Julia took pride in the enthusiastic crowds that greeted her soldier. They were entertained by Lewis Cass and Zachariah Chandler. At the Chandlers Mrs. Tripler caught another enlightening glimpse of Julia. Eunice Tripler was wearing one of the low, rounded décolletages of the era but Mrs. Grant was rather primly dressed in a rich but enveloping gown, with long sleeves.

After studying her friend's costume Julia broke loose with one of her teasing challenges to Ulysses, showing that, like Abraham Lincoln, he had definite ideas about his wife's attire. Mrs. Tripler had vivid recollections of this incident:

Mrs. Grant nudged me with her elbow, schoolgirl fashion, as she said to her husband, "Now, General, here is Mrs. Tripler with a low-necked dress. I have a neck, too. But you don't let me wear such a dress." I said, "But you really ought to. Every woman is bound to make the best appearance she can in observance of the proper customs of her time and station." I thought I would help her this much — for I was an older woman than she. General Grant kept silent, uttering no single word — entirely impassive. ... I have reason to think that my words on this occasion had weight, for I understood that at like companies a little later Mrs. Grant wore rather more conventional attire. She certainly did on the next occasion when I met her, which was in 1870 at a reception given by General McDowell at Black Point in San Francisco harbor.

A few days later they were in Galena, where a banner stretched across the street read: "Hail to the Chief who in Triumph Advances," and another on Main Street informed the General that the sidewalk he had wished for had been built. A crowd of ten thousand greeted the Grants and thirty-six girls in white welcomed them to the DeSoto House. Washburne delivered a speech and they drove up the lull to the brick house given them by the townspeople. It stands today, with many of the original Grant possessions. S. W. McMaster, a neighbor, who remembered the shabby leather merchant buying dressed hogs for the firm of Grant & Perkins, observed "tears trickling down his cheeks" as he came out of the house, fresh from seeing what the people had done for him. He had gone to the war obscurely from Galena; now he was home, a world-famous General.

They toured Batavia, Bethel, Georgetown and Ripley, and visited Jesse and Hannah in Covington. Jesse could scarcely contain himself with pride but Hannah showed up in her apron, as calm as ever, and observed: "Well, Ulysses, you've become a great man, haven't you?" Then she went on with her household tasks.

One of their most tumultuous welcomes was in St. Louis, where Julia was almost as much of a personality as Grant. This turned into a romantic pilgrimage for them as autumn swept the countryside, and trees and thickets were veined with scarlet and gold. Wild flowers hoisted the first bright signals of fall close to the Gravois, and goldenrod spurted in ragged clumps at the rail fences and pasture edges. Grapes ripened on the vines and streams were pewter-dark with autumn shadows. Again they could take a country walk and enjoy the golden transparency of the air, as the wind blew in sudden gusts, sweeping the bright-hued leaves into gullies and under the trees.

All this was a refreshing change for Julia and Ulysses, after the horrors and gigantic effort of the past four years, but they found that it was now impossible to escape observation. Still, Grant relaxed, clear of army worries for the moment. "My whole trip has been conducive to health if one judges from corpulency," he wrote to Washburne. "I have got to be afraid to weigh almost Mrs. Grant and children keep pace with me, in enjoyment of travel, if one judges from the difficulty with which they are got up to time in starting from any point where we have spent a day."

On their return Grant traveled to the South on an inspection tour and Julia stopped off in Philadelphia to do winter shopping for herself and the children. She knew that she must be prepared for all manner of occasions. Characteristically she concentrated on fine materials and good laces rather than on style, but she did not forget what Eunice Tripler had advised about her neckline.

They had finally decided where to live. The Union Club members of Philadelphia had given them a completely furnished home valued at $30,000. Their old friends in Galena had presented them with another, which they were to enjoy for years. But the Grants settled in Washington, after trying the Philadelphia arrangement and finding it impractical, since the General had to travel back and forth in order to be with his family. By Christmas, 1865, they were settled in a spacious home at 205 I Street, in a section known as Minnesota Row, and originally identified with Stephen A. Douglas.

That winter they were invited everywhere, and although Julia made no particular impression at first, she was treated with deference and affection. She brought her father on from St. Louis and he spent most of his time in her home from then until the day of his death. He no longer argued so violently with Ulysses, who was now in the curious position of being criticized in the North for the report he had brought back from the South. The radicals all felt that he took too lenient a stand.

At this time President Johnson used Grant as a strong card in his deck. He sought him out on every possible occasion, sending him notes almost daily and dropping in at his office for consultation. He appeared with him in public and went regularly to Julia's receptions. Her relations with his daughters, Mrs. Martha Patterson and Mrs. Mary Johnson Stover, were close and cordial.

The band played "Hail to the Chief" as Julia and Grant walked in for the New Year's reception at the White House in 1866. The ruin and tatters of the last days of the Lincoln administration had been covered up by the Johnson daughters. All the scars and frayed edges were discreetly hidden under fresh linen coverings, and some new satin damask was on display. The walls had been freshly paneled, with gold moldings. The ancient mustiness was sweetened up with an abundance of flowers, and Julia complimented the tall, fair-haired Mrs. Stover as she stood receiving her guests in a black silk dress with a lace collar and natural flowers in her hair.

The reception that followed at the Grant home was jammed. Julia wore a rose silk gown, with long sleeves. A Honiton lace shawl was thrown over her shoulders. Sam Hooper from Boston gave the General a letter signed by himself and forty others, offering him a carefully chosen library of books for his new home. As usual, the most imposing men circled around Kate Chase, who was interested to observe Charles Summer's expression as his young bride, Alice Hooper, in black velvet, with a flexible golden serpent twisted through her hair, flirted lightly with a Prussian attache. The frost was already settling on the recent Sumner marriage as the Senator battled the reconstruction issues and had little time for romance. He was one of those who most strongly disapproved of Grant's report on the South. No love was lost between Grant and Sumner, then or later, and as Kate studied General Grant and talked in her absorbed, intelligent way to Julia, she was aware that another sturdy contender for the Presidency now stood across her father's path.

Hundreds not invited crashed this first reception of the Grants, because of the General's fame. Julia accepted it in good part and was flattered as she tried to expedite a line that took two hours to get from the street to the cloakroom upstairs. After that the General announced through the newspapers that he would be "happy to see his friends." They came in great numbers and if Julia's early receptions were not exclusive, they were popular, friendly and well attended. Grant became a full General in July 1866.

His trip across the country with Andrew Johnson that summer to visit Stephen A. Douglas 5 tomb in Chicago caused much talk. It was a frenzied tour and often the shouts for Grant outdid the shouts for Johnson. The President received as many brickbats as plaudits. Mrs. Patterson, Mrs. David Farragut and Mrs. Gideon Welles were in the party but Julia stayed at home with her children and read about it in the papers. The General became ill in Detroit and called in his old friend and critic Dr. Tripler, whose wife later recalled that, pessimistic as he had once been about Grant's future, "no man anywhere rejoiced more truly than Dr. Tripler at his final triumph."

While Grant was on tour Hannah had her first and last brush with the public. She was brought to the platform against her will at a Fourth of July rally in a grove outside Cincinnati. The applause for the hero's mother was deafening but Hannah felt outraged. The newspaper accounts that followed were "'nough to frighten a modest old woman," Jesse reported. "Since that she can't be got out to any public place. She says she don't want to make a show of herself." By this time Jesse was making $3,100 a year as postmaster at Covington, a billet assigned him by President Johnson.

Washington was socially gay but politically in a state of confusion during the winter of 1867-1868 as Andrew Johnson lashed out on all fronts and the problems of reconstruction seemed at times to be almost as desperate as the problems of war. Julia was much in the forefront. "General and Mrs. Grant were the recipients of much attention," Mrs. John A. Logan noted. "You met them everywhere." The General, now at heavy odds with the President, was often observed walking to army headquarters from his home. "He was a familiar figure trudging along on a stormy day in his army cloak and slouch hat," Ben Perley Poore, a social commentator of tie period, remarked. Children saluted him and he frequently exchanged greetings with Sir Edward Thornton, the British Minister, who also was addicted to using his legs instead of a carriage.

Julia had good training for the White House during these postwar years, as she came to know the diplomatic set and to cope with the complex social cross currents of the capital. The functions did not equal in magnificence the prewar routs but the pace was being speeded up again. She had always liked the theater and during these years she saw Edwin Forrest and Mrs. Scott Siddons in Shakespearean roles. She watched Joe Jefferson play Rip Van Winkle. She heard Fanny Kemble give dramatic readings, little dreaming that her own Nellie would marry into the Kemble family. Washington had all manner of entertainments in the postwar years and she had a chance to see Adelaide Ristori and to hear Adelina Patti. She took in Anna Dickinson's lectures, Ole Bull's concerts, and Charles Dickens, lecturing in Carroll Hall in February 1868. But her special admiration went to Dr. Edwin H. Chapin, the divine who was thrilling the multitudes after the war. Her old evangelical spirit was as strong as ever, and she observed that he was the "most eloquent man" she had ever heard. A good sermon was true refreshment to Julia.

It was not a happy winter for Grant. When Johnson appointed him Acting Secretary of War late in 1867 and ousted Stanton, he took the post with great reluctance and was relieved to turn it back to his old chief five months later when the Senate upheld Stanton under the Tenure-of-Office Act. Meanwhile Sheridan and Daniel E. Sickles had been removed from office, over his outraged protests.

The bitter battle that broke out between Johnson and Grant as Stanton resumed his post and a controversial correspondence ensued between them, became the talk of the day. Charges of treachery were abhorrent to Grant. But Johnson showed "no traces of care on his brow" at his New Year's reception in 1868, although impeachment proceedings were close at hand. Grant, however, gave evidence of concern. Julia could see that he was worried and Sherman wrote to his brother John on January 31, 1868, that although he had been with Grant in the midst of death and slaughter "I never saw him more troubled than since he has been in Washington." Both Sherman and Grant felt confused in their new milieu, neither one at ease among the devious politicians. Both felt they were being used by Johnson to break Stanton. Grant's popularity with the more radical politicians swung with the tide — down when he was with Johnson, up when he fought him, but he kept the affection of the people throughout.

His hold on the public was deep-rooted, and his nomination for the Presidency in 1868 was foreordained. Stanton brought him the news at army headquarters. "There was no shade of exultation or agitation on his face, not a flush on his cheek, nor a flash in his eye," Adam Badeau noted. Julia heard it at I Street and later she invited a few intimate friends to their home to celebrate. Mrs. Logan was one of them. She observed that Colonel Dent stood beside his daughter to watch the man he had long reviled, and "Mrs. Grant was so cordial and unassuming and received her guests with such simplicity of manner that she won all hearts. Every one went away quite as ready to be her champion as that of her husband, their chieftain."

Grant made no attempt to campaign for himself but passed the summer quietly with his family at Galena. The soldiers took great delight in the campaign. Flags, banners, patriotic music, were used in a rousing campaign for the soldier nominee. The Civil War tunes were heard again. Appomattox was a key word. Old charges were revived, too, and Theodore

Tilton, of the Independent, raised the intemperance bogey. But the arrows of a political campaign left Grant unmoved. Julia did not like the revived attacks, however, and had a hard time holding her peace. Young Jesse remarked that the family at this time "would often wax furious over some slanderous tale at which father would only smile patiently."

Sherman found them back paying a brief visit to the old Dent property in the course of the summer and wrote to his wife that they were living "almost as plainly as before the War." Grant had a horse and borrowed buggy, a pair of mules and an ambulance, and he, Sherman, had loaned Buck a horse which he liked greatly.

Although Grant felt that he had little money to spare for farm improvements that summer he and Julia had big dreams for the future of White Haven, some of which they were able to realize when he became President. Both looked forward to a model farm, stocked with blooded horses and cattle. Since the beginning of 1867 the title had been clear, after much litigation. Grant had long ago paid all the debts outstanding when he entered the army. He was now a man of some means as well as fame. He and Washburne had been making investments through Jay Cooke and he had even been able to make a $5,000 loan to his brother Orvil.

By 1873 he would own more than a thousand acres of White Haven land again, the area that Dent had had when Ulysses married Julia. By the end of 1866 he had recaptured more than six hundred acres of the old Dent property, but his plans for orchards and stock grew more ambitious from year to year as he prospered. Julia loved these familiar acres and took a personal interest in every move made at White Haven. She preserved the fiction for her father that the property still was his. His losses had been cushioned by Grant and Julia, who were now urging their superintendent to produce more pork, to breed horses, to try growing Catawba grapes, and to make sure to sprinkle the carpets with camphor before the summer heat set in.

Galena was much in the limelight all that summer through the presence of a presidential candidate in the brick house on the hill. Grant cut himself off as much as possible from the political storm and saw only a selected part of his mail. The party managers could not enlist his aid and although political conferences were held in the DeSoto House he stayed in the background while his friends worked for him and Badeau wrote a campaign pamphlet. But the General's name was enough. He was a popular hero of simple habits with an appealing family around him.

"My time passes very pleasantly and quietly here and I have determined to remain until some time after the October elections," he wrote to Washburne on September 23. "A person would not know there was a stirring canvass going on if it were not for the accounts we read in the papers with great gatherings all over the country."

Julia was enjoying her new Galena house, knowing full well that she might soon be receiving in the nation's foremost dwelling. The General was comfortable in his library with its oak furniture, marble fireplace, and bronze warriors on the mantelpiece. The parlor was mid-Victorian, with marble-topped tables, Brussels lace curtains and much rose and gold brocade. Julia sat on a horsehair sofa from which she could see herself in a large gilt mirror by the light of a ruby-red chandelier, but vanity was not one of her qualities. The family dined around an octagonal oak table, where many jokes were exchanged. Julia had silver perfume bottles on her dressing table and an ornate rocker with crimson brocade in her bedroom. Her kitchen had a brown wood sink and table and she liked to share her recipes with the ladies of the Presbyterian Church. A favorite, composed by Julia herself, and given them for their cookbook, is still on view in Galena:

Slice as large pieces as you can get from a leg of veal; make stuffing of grated bread, butter, a little onion, minced salt, pepper, and spread over the slices. Beat an egg and put over the stuffing; roll each slice up tightly and tie with a thread; stick a few cloves in them, grate bread thickly over them after they are put in the skillet, with butter and onions chopped fine; when done lay them on a dish. Make their gravy and pour over them. Take the threads off and garnish with eggs, boil hard, and serve. To be cut in slices.

Julia gave modest receptions at their home, serving macaroons and ice cream to long lines of visitors. The country rang with the name Grant and Julia's doings were observed with interest. She waited at home on election night while her husband followed the returns in Washburne's pillared house. Badeau had gone with him and he noted that he had known the General to show more interest in a game of cards than on that night "when the Presidency was played for." Between one and two in the morning his companions felt that the moment had come to offer Grant congratulations. They walked up the hill with him to his home and there he quietly greeted Julia, who also had stayed up with friends.

"I am afraid I am elected," he told her, rather sadly.

Then he spoke to a gathering of well-wishers who had assembled at the door. At last the lights on the hill went out and Julia and Ulysses had taken another step along the road to enduring fame.

CHAPTER XI: FIRST LADY

THE GRANTS AND THE DENTS were present IB. force for the inauguration of Ulysses S. Grant as President on a March day in 1869. Hannah alone was missing on her son's great day. Julia sat with her father and waited anxiously for the inaugural address. Nellie left her side suddenly and joined the General, who held her hand until a chair was brought for his fourteen-year-old daughter.

The public knew by this time that Grant would rather fight a battle than make a speech. Julia, studying his compact figure close to the towering magnificence of Chief Justice Chase, had no idea what he was going to say. For days she had been urging him to consult the eloquent Roscoe Conkling about his address. When the moment came Ulysses, meticulously attired under her watchful eye, drew some pages of foolscap from his pocket and without embarrassment followed the text with his customary thin, slow enunciation.

It was a speech economical in words, precise in thought. He would have a policy of his own to recommend on all subjects. He would promote "the greatest good to the greatest number" and a calm approach to the postwar problems "without prejudice, hate or sectional pride." As he finished he turned first to Julia and shook hands with her. "And now, my dear, I hope you're satisfied," he said.

She was. She knew that the sound of Ulysses' voice had not traveled far, but they were good words, and she wished them to be heard. Yet Grant's most quoted phrases did not come from his inaugural speeches. They lay embedded in battlefield orders and in the letter accompanying his acceptance of the nomination in which he wrote: "Let us have peace."

A salute was fired, steam whistles blew, bells pealed, the bands played and the crowds applauded their soldier President. The city was packed with visitors who had come to see Grant assume office. The weather was harsh, the sky overcast as a blizzard threatened, but the flags, uniforms and postwar fashions gave dash and vitality to a dun setting. Andrew Johnson was missing from the scene. Neither man could forgive the other. Grant drove to the Capitol with the dying General Rawlins while Johnson stayed at the White House signing bills.

Immediately after the ceremonies Justice Chase sent Julia the Bible on which her husband had taken the oath, with the hope that it would be a "precious memorial ... to be ever associated in American remembrance with the perfected restoration of peace. . . ." He drew her attention to the fact that Grant's lips had pressed the 121st Psalm.

Instead of settling at once in the White House the Grants returned to I Street, a home to which Julia was devoted and which she was at first reluctant to leave. She made her debut as First Lady at the inaugural ball, wearing heavy white satin trimmed with point lace. Her jewels were pearls and diamonds. The ball, held in the newly finished north wing of the Treasury Building, was a memorable fiasco. No one noticed the fine assortment of marbles or the striking bronze gallery. Everyone noticed the dust in the air from building operations and many fainted. Only a fraction of the crowd ever reached the supper tables. The checking arrangements for wraps were confused. Carriages could not be found and many of the guests trudged home through slushy streets without their coats and hats. Horace Greeley stalked out in a huff, having lost his cherished white beaver. But celebrities clustered around the Grants and Julia stood smiling through it all. Farragut, McDowell, Sherman and other Civil War figures pushed their way through the jam to bow over her small, gloved hand. Julia Ward Howe made stately progress to her goal. In the course of the day's excitement the elder Jesse Grant had a fall, which the President thought would lame him for life.

Julia mapped out with Orville E. Babcock her plans for the renovation and decoration of the White House before leaving the capital for the summer. She settled her family in Long Branch, New Jersey, and made trips with Ulysses to New York, Boston, the White Mountains, Newport, Saratoga and western Pennsylvania. But the cares of state pursued them. They already felt the scorching breath of disapproval over Grant's unconventional Cabinet appointments. The men from Galena loomed up strong on his list. Washburne was his first choice for Secretary of State. When he offered the Treasury Department to A. T. Stewart, the merchant prince, Gideon Welles scornfully observed that "Stewart's silks and laces, scandal says, were potent in the appointment." But Grant insisted that he had consulted no one about his appointments, "not even Mrs. Grant," and he teased Julia about having to hide his waistcoat under his pillow to keep her from getting at his list. Rawlins became Secretary of War, a post that he greatly coveted, although Grant and Julia wished to send him to Arizona instead. The President was at Saratoga when word reached him that his faithful friend was dying. He hurried to his bedside but arrived an hour too late.

Rawlins' death was a deep grief to Julia. She had asked him to live with them at the White House until his family joined him. Emma Rawlins was already infected with tuberculosis and had only two more years to live. Five months after Rawlins' death Stanton, his wartime predecessor, died in a mysterious way. Grant wrote at once to his widow, praising his "ability, integrity, patriotism." Their paths had diverged, but their names would always be linked historically.

"My family are well and I attribute the fact to having sent them out of the White House during the summer," Grant wrote to Washburne at the time of Rawlins' death. They were all glowing with health from the months passed at the seaside. By this time Fred was a cadet at West Point and Buck was entering Harvard that autumn. But the President was faced with his first political emergency as the season ended. Late in September he returned to Washington in great haste to face the gold conspiracy crisis that culminated in Black Friday. Jay Gould and the flamboyant Jim Fisk had tried to corner the gold market. The President promptly released a flood of gold through the Treasury that broke the corner and defeated their aims, but not before some tar had stuck to his own relatives. Abel Rathbone Corbin, an elderly lobbyist and speculator who had married Grant's sister Virginia, had used his White House connection in his strange partnership with Gould and Fisk.

The President was playing croquet with Horace Porter in a little hamlet in western Pennsylvania, the wind-up of the summer, when an urgent letter from Corbin was delivered by special messenger, imploring him not to interfere in the gold crisis. An answer was requested, but the messenger left empty-handed. That evening, however, Julia sat down and wrote a sizzling family letter to her old friend Virginia. Among other things she said: "My husband is annoyed by your husband's speculations. You must close them as quick as you can."

Corbin backed down fast and approached Gould to get out of the deal, since the President was angry. It was agreed that Julia's letter should not be discussed. But Grant moved in fast to checkmate the swindlers. The traders rushed to sell their "phantom gold" and the day went down in history as a Wall Street landmark. Fisk, who had been roaring fantastic bids in the Gold Room, barricaded himself in his office to escape attack. Thousands were ruined. The scandal had wide repercussions and Julia's name got a slight dusting of frost. It was recalled that Grant had been entertained at sea by Fisk and Gould while on his way to the Peace Jubilee in Boston that year, and that he and Julia had occupied a box at the Fifth Avenue Theater with Fisk, Gould and the Corbins.

But in the Congressional investigation that followed the gold panic, the President and Julia were completely exonerated. Corbin's duplicity and the manner in which he had used the family name were made clear. Fisk and Gould continued to operate dangerously in other areas. The Corbins remained on friendly terms with the Grants and the administration had weathered its first scandal. Thus they were again a storm center as in the early days of the war but no scars showed on the social front when Julia took hold with quiet authority in the winter of 1869-1870. Her simplicity of manner made an immediate impression and Alexander K. McClure noted that she entered the White House "an unusually sweet, unaffected, capable woman, and was as unobtrusive and unpretentious as her distinguished husband."

Julia wore a costume of black Lyons silk velvet with Chantilly lace and a satin sash at her New Year's Day reception in 1870. Mrs. Hamilton Fish, wife of the Secretary of State who had speedily succeeded Washburne, was beside her. The appointment of the worldly and statesmanlike Fish with his Knickerbocker tradition was the only one of Grant's choices that everyone approved, except Charles Sumner, who expected the role for himself. It was clear from the start that Mrs. Fish would be Julia's most important ally. They were already good friends. Julia had visited them at Glenclyffe, their magnificent home up the Hudson.

Ben Perley Poore, the social commentator who detected both Doric simplicity and vulgar ostentation in the Grant regime, thought that Mrs. Fish "was born to be a queen." Others described her as the most superb woman of her time. No situation caught her off balance and she was adept at coping with the fused elements in the capital. She put the shy at ease, and was notably kind to the untried and naive in government circles. Like Julia, she was vigorous mentally and physically, and had a good sense of humor, although her long, aquiline features, thoughtful eyes and heavy coronal of graying hair, suggested both hauteur and melancholy. She was of medium height and stately carriage, but did not tower over Julia. Although at first she steered her over the social shoals, the time came when the mistress of the White House showed her own hidden power. Within the next eight years Julia was to become an independent and, at times, an autocratic force. But Mrs. Fish remained her friend as long as she lived and Grant, in begging Fish not to resign after the San Domingo crisis, cited Julia's need of his wife.

Although Mrs. Laura C. Holloway, an author and experienced observer in the capital, found Mrs. Grant's eight years in the White House a period of "great elegance and dignity," her intimate friends knew that she could also be a Mrs. Malaprop. Mrs. Logan, black-haired, intense, a native of Missouri like Julia, a wife who also had camped with her husband during the war, summed up this quality in her friend:

She often failed to remember that Mr. and Mrs. So-and-So had been twice married, were or were not temperance leaders, Protestants, or Catholics, and of such personal tastes or opinions as to make it dangerous to express oneself too frankly. The President at such times would lead her on to her own undoing, and then chuckle over her embarrassment, as one has seen brothers do when teasing their sisters. The absolute harmony of their domestic lives was ideal. The boasted domestic bliss of our ancestors in the early days of the republic furnishes no history of a happier or more devoted pair than the General and Mrs. Grant.

The parading women reporters took note of the lace curtains that had taken the place of Mrs. Lincoln's tatters, the fresh draperies of crimson brocatelle, the chandeliers "blazing like mimic suns," the gilt cornices, frescoed walls and ceilings, and the oil portraits of former Presidents that had been moved from the East Room to the hall. The exterior of the building had been steam-washed. For her private quarters Julia presided over eight rooms on the second floor, with a minimum of plumbing and no closets, a situation that she soon put to rights.

Her first state dinner was rated a success and there was the usual keen interest in the new First Lady. Almost at once she and the President eased some of the burdensome rules of precedence that had been handed down from one administration to another. Julia surrounded herself at receptions with a corps of Cabinet and Senators' wives, as well as with visiting celebrities and relatives. This not only became a popular custom but it was of great help to her, since she could scarcely distinguish one face from another as the guests moved past. A friendly hint from her receiving line saved her on many occasions. It gave her pleasure to have Mrs. Henry T. Blow, who had bought Ulysses' wood in St. Louis, and her three young friends from Galena — Julia Estey, Katherine Felt and Annie Campbell — share in the worldly benefits of her new estate.

As she watched Mrs. Grant receiving in the East Room Mrs. Blow had vivid recollections of her at Hardscrabble, happy and well-adjusted then as now. She was a warm and unassuming hostess in both settings. They all jested a little about these difficult days and the President remarked to Mrs. Blow on one occasion: "Do you recollect when I used to supply your husband with wood, and pile it myself, and measure it too, and go to his office for my pay? Mrs. Blow, those were the happy days; for I was doing the best I could to support my family."

It was clear from the start that the Grants were diverging radically from the established pattern. They dined out at will — the President more often than Julia, who sometimes preferred the company of her children to the Gargantuan feasts and biting chatter of the capital. They paid calls, if they so desired, and settled a number of social forms according to family convenience. Mrs. Mary Clemmer Ames, another correspondent who observed them closely, believed that there was "never so little formality or so much genuine sociability in the day-receptions at the White House." Its stiffness had softened down into a "look of grand comfort." The roof might leak occasionally. A ceiling might fall, as one did in 1872, but the Executive Mansion was "brightened by ever-blooming flowers, and happy children moving about." Observing the Grants together in the conservatory Mrs. Ames decided that the President had a "true and likable side" that no one understood as his wife did.

Julia's reception day was Tuesday until 1875 when she changed it to Saturday. The President received on Thursdays and all were welcome for the traditional open-house days. Those slated to join Julia in the receiving line usually lunched with her beforehand and Grant often strolled in at the tail end of her weekly receptions. It pleased Julia to have him join her on these occasions.

The Grants liked to think that their functions were truly republican in feeling. The idea soon spread that the girl who worked in the printing office and wore alpaca was just as welcome a guest as the Worth-gowned pearl of fashion. Poore observed: "There were ladies from Paris in elegant attire and ladies from the interior in calico; ladies whose cheeks were tinged with rouge, and others whose faces were weather-bronzed by outdoor work; ladies as lovely as Eve, and others as naughty as Mary

Magdalene; ladies in diamonds, and others in dollar jewelry; chambermaids elbowed countesses, and all enjoyed themselves."

The diplomatice corps rolled up in fancily upholstered carriages. The working girls arrived in the new street cars that had taken the place of the wobbling omnibuses of the war era. These much discussed conveyances had jingling bells and a rollicking air, but the windows rattled with chilly blasts, the floors were knee-deep in straw for muddy boots, and the White House passengers huddled in their Indian shawls to keep warm.

Mrs. Emily Edson Briggs, whose pseudonym was Olivia, observed that a "perfect river of human life" poured through the Executive Mansion in the time of the Grants and that the guests usually were packed like sardines in a box. She thought that the President had a far-off look in his eyes at times and had trouble suppressing his yawns, but Julia kept up an animated response to the last moment. Apparently he no longer objected to low decolletage, for Olivia commented on Mrs. Grant's expanse of "comely neck and shoulders."

The first royal guest arrived in January 1870. He chanced to be Prince Arthur, the third son of Queen Victoria. Relations between Great Britain and the United States were delicate at the moment and the young Prince, the guest of the British Minister, Sir Edward Thornton, was observed with close attention. The State dining room was festooned with evergreens and decorated with British and American flags. The twenty-nine-course dinner was an ordeal that Julia survived with grace.

Nearly a year later Grand Duke Alexis, third son of the Czar, was her guest, a dazzling figure in blue with gold epaulets more formidable than those her young lieutenant had worn at White Haven. They chatted together for a long time in the Red Parlor. All through her life Julia had practice in talking to gold-laced officers and she understood every nuance of the military tradition. She wore black silk with point-lace trimmings and bright colored ribbons on this occasion, and young Nellie hovered around in apple green. Prince Arthur and the Grand Duke Alexis were the first of a long line of royal heirs whom she entertained. Before her death Julia had met nearly all the crowned heads and government leaders around the world.

It took her some time to get Ulysses into an evening coat and white tie. He adopted formal dress only when he found he made himself more conspicuous by avoiding it than by donning it, and he still left waistcoat buttons undone. But his intimates thought that he adapted himself surprisingly well to the social usages of the White House. Soon he was reminding Julia that she must make her formal calls if she showed any signs of procrastination, as she sometimes did. He took an interest in the seating arrangements, and chose the wines himself with the greatest care, although his own glass usually was turned down.

One of the first changes Julia made involved the kitchen. She objected strenuously to the quartermaster installed by Ulysses, who viewed the dining room as a super mess where quantity was the important element. She brought in an Italian steward named Melah to fill a role that had been neglected since the days of Dolly Madison. He had catered for the nation's most fashionable hotels, and the White House cuisine became justly famous under his guidance. The table seated thirty-six and dinners were given practically every week. Grant preferred small dinners with a few intimate friends to state functions, but Julia saw to it that a balance was maintained.

Melah liked to serve at least twenty-five dishes at a formal function and he was extra proud of the rice pudding he made for the President. He went in notably for filet of beef, a favorite dish of Grant's, partridge, frozen punch and the elaborate confections of the era. He also catered to Julia's fondness for Southern dishes. The Grants faced each other from either side of the table. Dinners were not allowed to drag. Two hours and the guests were moving on to the Blue Room or the Red Room for fifteen minutes of chat before the President gave the signal to retire.

William H. Crook, who had been bodyguard to Lincoln and served as an usher for the Grants, rated Mrs. Grant as the most popular of all the wives he had seen in the White House. He found her warm-hearted and kindly. She knew the Executive Mansion from cellar to garret and "any morning her stout, comfortable figure might have been seen making the rounds of kitchens and pantries, and stopping to hold colloquies with maids or men." She took a keen interest in all the servants and their family affairs, helping them when in trouble and encouraging them to be thrifty. She urged them to buy little homes so that they might settle down eventually in independence.

Crook was impressed with Mrs. Grant's influence over the President. It showed in ways both large and small. When he refused to see a caller and the man reached Julia with his plea she promptly sent Crook to the President with a card: "Dear Ulyss — Do please make this appointment. Julia." The man got what he wanted and Crook kept the card as a souvenir.

He believed that Grant thought Julia "absolutely perfect" and that he could not get along without her. He liked to humor her in all her small fancies as well as on larger issues, and sometimes she had whims.

He was always up at seven and read the Republican or Post until breakfast was announced. Then he would knock at Julia's door.

"Is that you, Ulyss?"

"Breakfast is ready."

"I will be there in a few minutes, General."

But Julia was dilatory and Grant waited patiently in the library until she appeared. They invariably went down to breakfast arm in arm. The fare quite often was broiled Spanish mackerel, steak, bacon and fried apples, buckwheat cakes and coffee. The days of cucumbers and coffee for breakfast were over. Grant usually finished quickly and pushed back his chair but Mrs. Grant lingered for another cup of coffee. However, he always waited for her and escorted her back to her sitting room, where they usually had another chat before he set out for his morning walk.

He settled down to his desk at ten and worked with concentration until three o'clock, when he knocked off for the day, unless special business was pending. Except for private parleys business was not transacted in the evenings and Jay Cooke, the banker, warned Grant that "God win not bless us unless our rulers are righteous," when he showed signs of using the Sabbath for worldly purposes. But Julia saw to it that the family went regularly to the Metropolitan Methodist Church. She was one of its most active workers and the President was a trustee. The Rev. John Philip Newman was a close family friend and, in time, one of his most ardent defenders. Grant always looked gravely content in his church pew when Julia's clear voice rose in worship and Nellie shared his hymn book.

"He didn't like musical gymnastics, as he called them, but he often asked me to sing," Mrs. Grant recalled in a newspaper interview in 1901. The old Civil War airs brought up memories. Once, in the White House, she was singing Lorena without music. Her hands slipped from the keys for she had forgotten the accompaniment, and then she noticed that the newspaper had fallen from Ulysses' hands and he was watching her closely.

"That was very pretty," he said.

"Were you listening?" Julia asked. "I didn't know it."

Grant maintained his military habits in the White House and surrounded himself with disciplined officers and a clockwork regime. At no time in the history of the White House did so many soldiers call on the President. Julia always gave a specially warm welcome to the numerous delegations of Union veterans who called to pay their respects to their old chief, and a "loyal Union soldier" was a phrase often noted in the President's letter book.

When dining alone the family usually assembled at seven o'clock. There was sure to be merry play with the children. Grant rolled bread into little balls and threw them at Nellie and Jesse. When he made a strike he went over and kissed the victim on the cheek. "He was a most loving father," Crook observed. But rolling bread balls became an unconscious habit and eyebrows went up when he was observed doing it also at Lady Thornton's table.

The children went to bed at nine and Julia usually followed them before eleven, when she was not entertaining or being entertained. Grant, who liked to stay up late, often strolled across to the Fish home on Scott Square after dinner. He could discuss foreign affairs with his host, and Mrs. Fish was one of the few women with whom he grew eloquent.

Thomas F. Pendel, the White House doorkeeper, found Julia kind and charming but singularly absent-minded. He always stood close to her at receptions since she invariably arrived without her fan, or her handkerchief, or her white kid gloves, or sometimes even her earrings. He made countless trips upstairs to pick up forgotten items. And he caught many glimpses of the Grants off-guard. One day as he arrived with a card announcing visitors he found the President thumping the piano keys in the library.

"Ulysses, shall we see these people?" Julia asked.

"Mrs. Grant, that's your funeral, not mine," he replied.

Both laughed and Julia went downstairs to spread balm.

Neither she nor Ulysses lost their old love of country living when they moved into the White House. They were always alert to the world of nature around them. It was a mutual joy going back to their courting days. Grant rode little after he became President and Julia not at all but they went driving at every opportunity — not often together, however. At the end of his working day the President usually indulged in a fast drive in a racing buggy with his magnificent trotter. As soon as he left his office at three he visited the stables. His favorite, Cincinnatus, was the dark bay charger that Lincoln had ridden at City Point. Julia's two carriage horses were St. Louis and Egypt Jesse had his Shetland ponies Billy Button and Reb. Nellie had her own saddle horse, Jennie. The other family standbys were Jeff Davis,

Mary and Julia. There were five vehicles in the carriage house — a landau, a barouche, a light road-wagon, a buggy and a phaeton for the children.

Julia became nervous when she drove with Grant on one of his mad afternoon sprints. Pendel reported that she made him turn back and leave her at the White House on more than one occasion. But she found real pleasure in leisurely jaunts in her landau, with Jerry and Albert on the box. Taking Nellie or some of her many friends with her she drove often to the Soldiers Home and through Rock Creek Park, particularly when the dogwood, laurel and Judas trees were in flower. Waves of perfumed air flowed over her as she drove along the Piney Branch Road, reviving memories of her White Haven days.

Sometimes she felt the need of getting away from surrounding pressures. The large tribe of Grants and Dents were natural targets for office seekers of all kinds. Friends, relatives, acquaintances, had axes to grind. When Jesse was in Washington he was pursued by petitioners and Grant had to dampen down this ancient urgency on his father's part. Julia was pliant where her friends and relatives were concerned, and Grant felt he had no peace from this kind of pressure. He was pursued even when deep-sea fishing at Long Branch. "The fact is, I am followed wherever I go, at Long Branch as well as here," Grant wrote to his sister Mary on October 26, 1871, explaining why he had not seen a Mr. W. she had sent to him. For the first time in his life he had arranged to go deep-sea fishing. He had engaged the fisherman and boat and was not told that the suppliant had arrived. "I sometimes shake off callers, not knowing their business, whom I would be delighted to see," he added.

By this time many tales of nepotism surrounded the family and Olivia took note of the number of Dents who came and went but added: "Are they to blame because a President happened to drop into their nest?" Nellie Dent, now Mrs. Sharp, was constantly in view, charming, and helpful to Julia. In time, Emma also appeared and sometimes took her place beside the President. Nellie's husband, Alexander Sharp, was marshal of the District of Columbia. Emma's husband, James F. Casey, by this time was collector of the Port of New Orleans. George Dent was appraiser of Customs at San Francisco and John was an Indian trader for New Mexico. Louis Dent ran for the Governorship of Mississippi on the Democratic ticket and was badly beaten. Grant gave no aid to Louis, a driving figure often engaged in controversy.

Sumner, Carl Schurz, Horace Greeley, and Frank Blair all played on the nepotism theme. "A dozen members of the family billeted upon the country!" Sumner exclaimed in the summer of 1872 in a savage attack on Grant for gift-taking and nepotism. In June of that year the National Quarterly Review said that the ring nearest to Grant was the Dent family ring. Colonel Dent was a fixture at the White House and Julia insisted on the utmost deference being shown him. When she received, he occupied a chair behind the line in the Blue Room, and "every lady who passed down the line was reminded that Father Dent was there, while all were delighted to pay their respects to the courtly but venerable gentleman," said Mrs. Logan.

He laid down the law from the day he arrived and said he would be damned if he would drink tea out of such coarse china. "Papa was an old Jackson Democrat," said Julia, apologizing for his strong language. Another set of china was ordered at once for the private dining room. All his whims were indulged by his daughter. The Colonel held court daily in the White House office reception room, and politicians and soldiers alike stopped to chat with him. In his estimation Grant was "really a staunch Democrat but did not know it." He thought him wrong on many issues and did not hesitate to tell him so.

The fur flew in the family quarters when Jesse came visiting. Dent chose to treat him patronizingly as an older, feebler man who should be humored. This outraged the spirited Jesse. Hannah chose never to visit the White House in spite of repeated invitations from Julia and Ulysses. But the children went to visit her in Covington and enjoyed her quiet ways and her tasty ginger snaps.

Julia was diligent in charitable and church work. At Christmas the asylums, hospitals and orphanages received generous donations from the Grants, often in the form of barrels of fruit and confections. Toy merchants and jewelers counted on Mrs. Grant's bounty, for she bought freely for the young and frequently led a parade of unidentified children through the shops, making them happy with her gifts.

She also made up packages for her absent sons and prided herself on smuggling good fare into West Point for Fred. "They were great boys to have friends," she said of them. Jesse had a small menagerie in the White House and he organized a boys' club in the gardener's tool house. It had mystic symbols and the President called it the "Kick, Fight and Run Society." There were children's parties at the White House nearly every

Saturday. In some respects Jesse was as spoiled as Tad Lincoln. The Grants were notoriously indulgent with their children. It soon became a matter of comment in Washington that they were allowed to do what they liked and that their schooling was neglected.

Nellie was appearing regularly at the levees in 1870 with her long hair hanging down her back and her "beautiful eyes as gentle as those of a gazelle," an observer noted. She attended a girls' school in Washington and for a time Julia sent Jesse to the same school. He resented this indignity, objecting to it almost as much as he did to the kilt his mother made him wear. Jesse was the family wit, and a constant source of delight to Grant, even when he jumped on the rostrum and mimicked Father trying to make a speech.

When Nellie was sent to Miss Porter's School in Farmington, Connecticut, her father took her there personally, saying that if Julia went she would "only cry and bring Nellie back." But she left with her mother's fond promise that if her teachers made her study too hard she need not stay.

Nellie was homesick from scratch. "I shall die if I must stay here," she telegraphed her father.

Governor Marshall Jewell of Connecticut, a family friend, went back and forth between Hartford and Farmington, talking to Miss Porter, telegraphing to the White House, listening to Nellie. It was all to no avail. Nellie was brought home and that was the end of her schooling. Mary Clemmer Ames, one of the capital's best known correspondents, smacked hard at Julia for her handling of Nellie, saying it was a sad thing to see a President's daughter "launched into the wild tide of frivolous pleasure" while the daughters of Senators and Cabinet Ministers were studying and learning how to live in a disciplined fashion. At seventeen she was spoken of almost exclusively as the driver of a phaeton and as the leader of the all-night German, said the disapproving Mrs. Ames. Various conservative mothers frowned on Nellie's early plunge into the social whirl. They thought her much too young to be leading the cotillions that were then known as Germans. Ben Perley Poore noted that the General's pet unquestionably was Nellie, "who was bright and beautiful, and whose girlish prattle was far more attractive to him than the compliments of Congressmen or the praises of politicians."

A year later Jesse was sent to school at Cheltenham, near Philadelphia. But he, too, was homesick and wrote to his mother: "I do not believe I am making satisfactory progress here."

"It is too soon to determine this," Mrs. Grant replied. "When you have been there longer you will like it better."

He then appealed to his father, saying that he wished to come home. Grant promptly wired back: "We want you, too. Come home at once." That night he was back in the White House.

Early in 1871 Grant was writing encouragingly to Fred about his final examinations at West Point and was urging him to be of "good cheer." He would pay his bills up to five hundred dollars. A month later, perhaps remembering his own early struggles with farming, he offered to put up from six to eight thousand dollars, and twenty-five hundred a year thereafter for three or four years, in order to get Fred started on the land. Grant suggested that his son grow olives, figs, almonds and fruit. But Fred never became a farmer.

The whole family went to West Point to see him graduate that year. Afterward he went West to do some surveying. By the end of the year he sailed for Europe as an aide to General Sherman, who was making a grand tour of the Mediterranean. This stirred up fresh blasts of censure for the Grants. Fred was on leave from the army and again the charge of nepotism was raised. It was known that Julia had strongly urged his appointment as an aide. Sherman characterized Grant's love for his children as an "amiable weakness, not only pardonable, but attracting the love of all who did not suffer the consequences." Both he and Sheridan thought that Julia was unwise to push her son's interests on the military front but both were fond of her and could deny her nothing.

Fred was received like a Crown Prince in Europe and Sherman wrote to Grant from Rome on February 21, 1872, that he thought the youth would profit greatly from the trip. "You may assure Mrs. Grant that I will watch his health with a parent's eye," wrote General Sherman. "He sees many pretty girls here who are enough to tempt any boy — but I will try to prevent his making any serious attachments. He promises me on this score that he will confide absolutely in his mother."

Nellie, too, had gone abroad by this time. Suitors were already swarming around her in spite of her youth and Julia thought that travel might remove this hazard and also broaden her outlook on life. She gave her into the keeping of Mr. and Mrs. Adolph E. Borie, experienced travelers — so experienced that Grant feared they would stay in a few favorite places and not do the grand tour of Europe that he wished Nellie to have. Borie was a merchant and financier who served briefly as Secretary of the Navy.

But much to her chaperone's amazement Nellie was treated in England like visiting royalty. Queen Victoria received her at Buckingham Palace. Adam Badeau, now serving in London as American Consul General, feted her at a garden party, where she "smiled with democratic grace on duchesses and marchionesses as they made her the same curtsy they made to royalty." Some learning must have sunk in, too, for her father wrote proudly to Jesse that Nellie's letters were much better than those of the boys. "Her composition is easy and fluent, and she writes very correctly," he noted. "She seems to have made a very good impression where she has been."

The third member of the family to go abroad was Buck, by then an extraordinarily handsome youth. He planned to study in a small German village for a year and then return to Harvard to take his examinations. For the time being only Jesse remained within reach of his mother. But she was content in the thought that all were improving themselves and were seeing the world. This left her free to try an experiment that she had long had in mind. Since entering the White House she had worried considerably about her squint. She was much on display in public places. Her photographs were in circulation. During the war she had consulted St. Louis physicians about remedying the condition but she had been advised that it was too late. Now she intended to risk a simple operation in Washington, on the chance that it might be successful. But at the last minute the "General overturned everything," according to Crook and Emma.

Grant told General George Pickett the whole story when the Confederate General and his wife visited the White House after the war, and they fought out Gettysburg at the dinner table — with a spoon, a blue pencil and the tablecloth. Then Sallie Pickett laughingly recalled the day that she and her husband, on horseback at the Bermuda Hundred line, had seen Julia through field glasses, as she stood between Grant and Ingalls. The Federals were shooting in their direction but Sallie had jested that Mrs. Grant was too cross-eyed to know which way the shots were going. She now told this story apologetically and Grant immediately launched into the tale of the operation that did not come off.

As the time drew near for the corrective surgery he began to worry about it? he said. When he watched Julia putting on her bonnet and packing her bag with odds and ends he had the feeling that they were making a great mistake. She was walking out when he held the doorknob and checked her, saying:

My dear, I know that I am very selfish and ought not to say what I am going to; but I don't want to have your eyes fooled with. They are all right as they are. They look just as they did the very first time I ever saw them — the same eyes I looked into when I fell in love with you — the same eyes that looked up into mine and told me that my love was returned. I have felt and seen that expression in them through all the years since then, and I don't want it changed now. This operation might make you look better to other people; but to me you are prettier as you are — as you were when I first saw you. ...

Julia responded with enthusiasm. "Why, it was only for your sake that I was even thinking of having anything done," she said.

Grant untied her bonnet strings and they both felt light-hearted and relieved. The subject never came up again.

Julia had been in the White House less than a year when she showed her strength of purpose by snubbing Mrs. John D. Cox, wife of the Secretary of the Interior. When Cox resigned suddenly the New York Herald of November 5, 1870, noted that "little disagreements and unpleasantnesses in the female department have served to heighten the new formed dislike between the Grantites and Coxites." Cox advocated Civil Service reform. When Mrs. Cox cut out a newspaper article critical of the President's policies in this field and sent it to Mrs. Grant anonymously, she carelessly put it in an envelope bearing the family monogram. Moreover, Julia recognized her handwriting. She promptly put the scurrilous piece in a White House envelope and sent it back with the comment: "Returned to Mrs. Cox, with the compliments of Mrs. Grant." After that, neither one spoke to the other, and Mrs. Cox was missing from the receiving line.

The social pace quickened with each year that the Grants were in the White House. Fierce battles raged in Congress and these were reflected in the drawingrooms as old friends drifted apart and new alignments showed up. The good will which had attended the first Grant inauguration lost some of its glow as the President coped with the Alabama claims, the gold conspiracy, inflation, graft charges, tariff problems, Civil Service reform and race troubles in the South. His first and fiercest battle involved the proposed annexation of San Domingo. He lost it to Sumner, who later was toppled from his throne as chairman of the Foreign Relations committee, a fallen giant who still cast rocks at the White House and made a blazing attack on Grant in the Senate in May 1872. The constructive moves the President made were lost in the clamor over scandals among the men with whom he had surrounded himself. His home life, however, was some solace for the conflicting elements that raged around him.

The social picture, dimmed during the days of the war, was vitalized again in the 1870s with, a reckless surge to make up for the lost years. A boisterous note was apparent as entertainments mounted in number and throngs turned out to enjoy them. The belles set forth by gaslight, their gowns rustling, their eyes glittering like their jewels, to spend endless hours in receiving lines or swinging around ballroom floors.

Diamonds were back in fashion after the wartime blackout Great equipages drove along the Georgetown Road again. New faces appeared at state dinners. Northern and Western hostesses had taken the place of the plantation dowagers who had held the field for so long. The lobbying was bold; the pace was often hectic. Ten pairs of lavender kid gloves for a season, hemstitched shirts for young blades, basques and bustles in place of hoops, tiny, tilted Watteau hats instead of bonnets — the scene was changing fast. The plain chignon that Julia favored was going out of fashion and puffs of false hair were in style. The Civil War festoons of flowers were no more. They had gone out with the wartime song Lorena.

Sumner, ignoring Grant and Fish, had frequent gatherings at his stately home. Henry D. Cooke, the banker, gave ostentatious parties on Georgetown Heights, often attended by Julia. Zachariah Chandler's great mansion blazed with lights night after night. Music floated out to the street as the guests danced and clustered around tables heaped with ices fashioned into temples, towers, minarets and pagodas. The faraway days of Grant in Detroit were forgotten and Chandler now sought his favor. Mrs. Sprague's parlies were the ultimate word in elegance. Mrs. John A. Creswell, cushioned with riches and good taste, her features delicate and cameo clear, was a favorite hostess of Julia's. Mrs. William W. Belknap, a Kentucky beauty who had bloomed for a season, caused havoc, and died at the end of 1870, soon was followed by her sister "Puss," who took her place as wife and hostess in Seward's old house on Lafayette Square.

Schuyler Colfax, the Vice President was a formidable host with a fragile wife who usually stood beside Julia in the receiving line. The Colfaxes entertained once a week and among their guests was Mark Twain, wearing lavender kid gloves in the fashion of the hour. Mrs. Sherman, now occupying the Grants' old house on I Street, stayed locked up in her study, reading, writing and praying, but occasionally she and Julia had intimate talks of days remembered from the past. She went down to the ship when

Fred sailed off with General Sherman and brought back some flowers from Fred for his mother.

Admiral Porter brought out the Navy brass and Grant was observed doing a passable dance at a midshipmen's ball at Annapolis in 1871. "He has at last succumbed to his dogged resolution to perfect himself," the New York Commercial Advertiser reported, although his "peculiar ballroom 'shuffle' does not thrill the bosom of the goddess with anything like the enthusiasm she feels for Sheridan's 'Gallop' or Sherman's 'Lancers.'"

Julia no longer floated around the ballroom with the easy grace of her youth. She did not put Ulysses through the torture of dancing with her when she knew how much he disliked it, but at a pinch she could still whirl around with Sheridan and hold her own on her feet with some of the younger matrons. Her New Year's Day reception in 1872 was considered a brilliant function. Washington was full of ranking officers and every member of the diplomatic corps was out in full court dress, with jewels and decorations. The Marine Band, conducted by Professor Scala, played in the corridor. The Blue Room was softly illumined and decorated with flowers.

Julia was gowned in Venetian red velvet and looked her best. Madame Catacazy, wife of the Russian Minister, moved smoothly past her, tall and statuesque, her hair a bright gold ornamented with a dull-gold arrow. She had a story and a past, but her home was filled with treasures, her heart with memories. She knew, and Julia knew that day, that Catacazy was on his way out and that Grant was his executioner. The Minister had been meddling in political affairs and the President had asked for his recall. Madame Catacazy had always been a conspicuous figure in Washington as a beauty who had run away from her first husband to join Catacazy and eventually to marry him.

Lady Thornton, tall, spare and dignified, was ever punctilious with Mrs. Grant as their two husbands ironed out their international differences. Madame de Noailles made witty remarks in passing but it never troubled Julia that she could not converse with her in French. She was natural and friendly with Madame Garcia, wife of the Peruvian Minister, to whom Mrs. Fish showed an unwonted chill. The Latin beauty had coquetted boldly with the President at the grand ball given for Prince Arthur. It was noted that Grant "watched her, amused in his quiet, grave, scarce-smiling way." She was voluble, plump, and had written a daring novel. She rode around Washington swathed in white ostrich tips in a carriage lined with white satin. But Julia, in her unassuming way, was a match for Madame

Garcia, as she was for most of the types, diplomatic and otherwise, that passed her in the receiving line.

Adam Badeau thought that Mrs. Grant understood both the petty craft and the important ambitions underlying much of the social interchange in the capital, and that she gave her husband the benefit of the advice of a "woman who understood other women." When Grant was "overmodest, or willing to let himself be passed by, there was always the mentor to caution and urge and stimulate and advise; and sometimes the mentor was needed," Badeau noted.

A new social hierarchy had risen around the Grants, and James G. Blaine, Speaker of the House, moved strongly into the picture at this time. Both Mrs. Blaine and Gail Hamilton, her cousin who lived with them and was a correspondent, made frank notes on the Grants. "He is quite simple and unpretending; so is Mrs. Grant," Gail observed after a White House reception. She found the President "highly intelligent and intelligible" on foreign affairs but deficient in the "touch-and-go talk of society."

At a dinner given in February at the Chandler home Julia talked freely of her early days in Missouri. General Sheridan, with broad shoulders and an eagle glance, held them all spell-bound as he talked of the Franco-Prussian War and its leaders. The guests discussed the Chicago fire, the freshet at Rome, Anna Dickinson, and Mrs. Isabelle Beecher Hooker, who was pounding away for suffrage. Susan B. Anthony and Elizabeth Cady Stanton were on the rampage at the moment, and Julia was interested in the fact that one of their number, Victoria Woodhull, was setting herself up against Ulysses for the Presidency. But Miss Anthony as a matter of expediency backed Grant against Greeley for the second term, and Julia thereafter sponsored the suffrage movement,

Mrs. Blaine, a plain and candid woman who contrasted oddly with her handsome and magnetic husband, "the plumed knight," felt some concern about her costumes as she observed the Worth creations worn by Mrs. Sprague and Mrs. Belknap. But her worries ceased when she noted at an elegant luncheon given by Mrs. Creswell that Mrs. George S. Boutwell's skirt "had evidently felt the deadly pressure of an iron." Mrs. Grant was never sufficiently chic to put her entourage to shame, but the newspaperwomen challenged her to name a fashion dictator, to swing American fashions away from the Empress Eugenie influence. She immediately proposed her most honored friend. "In matters pertaining to good sense and fine tact, I rely upon Mrs. Fish," said Julia.

The Secretary's wife picked up the challenge adroitly but with her tongue in her cheek. She hoped that every woman would seek her own convenience and comfort "whilst thinking of other things than dress" She felt perfectly comfortable herself, she added, in the new short street dresses with neat fitting basques, and she approved of American fashions for American women instead of those dictated by people "who differ with us in the spirit of our institutions."

There was reassurance in this for Harriet Blaine and also for Julia, who gave her clothes much thought, bought the best of everything but did not top the field in style. Mrs. Blaine confessed to being quite unprepared for the "womanliness, cordiality and thoroughly unaffected kindliness," as well as the social skill displayed by Mrs. Grant in welcoming the Japanese delegation in March 1872. She stood at her left and Mrs. Coif ax at her right as the ten Japanese marched toward them in the Red Room. They were elaborately attired in purple and black and carried heavy swords. Gail Hamilton made a note of the President's pride in his wife's performance. He admitted to her afterward that Julia had done much better than he, for his knees were trembling throughout.

"What! A brave man like you," Gail exclaimed to the conqueror of Vicksburg.

"Yes," he said, although she noticed that he had a prepared speech in his hand.

Julia was looking forward confidently to a second term in the White House, which she had come to appreciate and to love. She thought, too, that she was watching the growth of a man. All the public abuse had not dimmed her pride in Ulysses. She was convinced that her great soldier was proving himself also to be an able President. But the public was divided in its opinion.

CHAPTER XII: LONG BRANCH

THE WAVES ROLLED IN at Long Branch through a shimmering heat haze. Carriages whipped up dust along Ocean Avenue. Brass bands played on the lawns of rambling hotels. Faint breezes stirred the thin brush on the sand dunes and rustled through the stunted cedars. The Grants rested on the porch of the summer White House after their midday meal. Julia sat in her favorite rocking chair, wearing a sunbonnet, flattened at the sides, open at the back, and wreathed with violet flowers.

Jesse had come in with some sandpipers he had shot and was entertaining the President. Buck sat on the porch railing with his usual grave and dreamy look. Suddenly he came to life, vaulted lightly over the railing and was gone. Jesse recalled in after years that his father turned to Julia with a "slow, whimsical smile" and said:

"Did you see that, Julia? Now if you were sitting here alone, and the railing extended across the steps, and the cottage caught fire, you must be rescued or burned,"

"You think so!" Julia exclaimed.

She was now forty-six and no longer the sylph he had known at White Haven. But she jumped up from her rocker, vaulted the rail with a great flourish of striped petticoats, and stood laughing up at them.

Observers thought that Grant never seemed quite at ease in the sunny, alfresco life of the summer resort. While at the Stetson before they had their own cottage he wore broadcloth and a tall hat which he gravely tipped to the ladies who paraded past the piazza. But Julia was her happiest at the summer home which George W. Quids, editor of the Philadelphia Ledger, had persuaded them to take. It stood next door to his own. She spent hours on the porch chatting with friends or watching children at play She enjoyed her drives and the cool nights when the breeze blew in on them and a string of lights flashed through the velvety darkness. She attended the camp meetings, sometimes with her friend, Mrs. Newman, and tried to ignore the ceaseless newspaper attacks on her family.

The President was accused of spending too much time away from the White House; of using a naval vessel to get to Long Branch; of accepting valuable gifts; of putting relatives into office; of concentrating on horses;

of sending his children to Europe like royal emissaries; of turning the Executive Mansion into a "military camp"; of getting entangled with a faction that the New York World described as the "clique of money-changers." Julia's own name was introduced not infrequently in connection with gifts and nepotism. But at Long Branch the clamor from the opposition press that grew as election time approached was somewhat dimmed.

The summer White House was roomy and unpretentious. It was two and a half stories high, and had an octagonal porch. A New York Tribune reporter thought it a "mixture of English villa and Swiss chalet" A flight of stairs ran up the exterior and all damp and sand-caked children were induced to use this approach by a crock of cookies placed by Julia along the way.

Long Branch, founded in 1788 as a holiday resort for Philadelphians and originally a focus for blue laws and religious meetings, had become a worldly paradise, aping Saratoga and Newport unsuccessfully but maintaining a dizzy pitch of its own behind its cast-iron trimmings and gingerbread fretwork. Julia's camp meetings were the only echo left of its earlier intention. Racing and gambling, shooting galleries and billiard rooms, high living and segregated bathing for the two sexes, were an essential part of the picture. The beach parade was a sight in itself, with the bolder females wearing low-necked, spangled evening dresses chopped off at the knees. Pop and gingerbread were sold in striped tents.

The Grants had a private beach, with swings in the nearby pines for visiting children. The President still rose at seven, then drove alone for twenty miles along the ocean front in his buggy. On his return he read the papers, looked over his mail and chatted with Julia, or any member of the family who chanced to be around. Jesse fished and hunted. He went on long jaunts after yellowlegs and plover, or came home laden with ducks, squirrels and rabbits. At first the passing ships ran in close to shore and saluted the President. The Grants responded by running up a flag and, in time, Jesse added a cannon salute.

There was no escape from the flow of important visitors, the constant surveillance that plagued them, and the certain knowledge that James Gordon Bennett, Horace Greeley or Charles A. Dana, no longer Grant's friend, would observe who came and went. The President's wealthy friends at this time, in addition to Childs and Bone, included Levi P. Morton, A. J. Drexel and Cyrus W. Field. Roscoe Conkling was another favorite and

Julia frequently invited his wife to stay with them at Long Branch. "Bring the Senator, too, just for company while traveling, and to look after the baggage," she jested lightly on one occasion, but Mrs. Conkling had no wish to be seen in the company of her flamboyant husband at this particular time. She was living in retirement in Utica while the capital buzzed with gossip about Roscoe and Mrs. Sprague. Although not censorious, Mrs. Grant had her own conception of the beautiful Kate, who worked zealously to get Grant out of the White House and her father in. Julia's sympathies were all with her friend, Bessie Cockling, but as Roscoe gained ground with her husband and became one of his chief advisers, she found him irresistible, too.

"My judgment is that it will be better that I should not attend any convention or political meeting during the campaign," Grant wrote to Colliding from Long Branch on July 9, 1872. "I am no speaker and don't want to be beaten." He preferred to mark time until he saw what the Baltimore convention hatched. "I have no doubt but it will look like a full moon, with spectacles on the man in it," he wrote, alluding to Greeley.

Grant won, although seven candidates opposed him in a free-for-all nomination. Greeley lost and suffered most. He had a breakdown and was dead within a matter of weeks. The President went to New York for the funeral. Julia remembered Greeley at her dinner table when he still thought Ulysses a great man. She had never understood the moods and whims of the powerful editor, but they had been hurtful to her husband and had given him much concern.

Grant feared that he would lose Hamilton Fish as Secretary of State for the second term and he dreaded the prospect. "As much as I liked the Governor before he came into my Cabinet I now like him better," he wrote to A. E. Borie. "The State Department was never better conducted than under his supervision. I wish he could stay with me."

Fish did, but Grant still sweated over the preparation of annual messages or speeches of any kind. He confessed to Borie that he always felt miserable until the task was completed. "I believe I am lazy and don't get credit for it," he wrote. "The fact is circumstances have thrown me into an occupation uncongenial to me."

However, the Grants were all in good spirits on the second inaugural day. The wind blew at gale force from the southwest and the temperature was four above zero. Flags and decorations were ripped from their moorings. Tree boughs crystallized. Icicles dangled from the eaves of houses. A few of the Army and Navy cadets dropped out of line. The bands struck odd notes or none at all as the musicians' breath froze in the biting wind. Bayonets flashed like blue fire as the President's guard marched past in dark blue, with yellow trimmings and black-plumed hats. The crowds were out, although Grant was less popular in 1873 than when he stormed into office in 1869 on his soldier's laurels. Sherman was in full rig, with bright yellow kid gloves.

Julia drove with Henry Wilson, the new Vice President and one of her husband's most zealous supporters during the war. This time Grant kissed the eleventh chapter of Isaiah as Chase, all hope of the Presidency gone at last and himself about to die, swore him into office. The Chief Justice looked strange to the crowd, with a full beard grown out around his shattered face. A stroke had ended his career and stilled his ambition at last.

The wind almost wrenched the manuscript from the President's hand as he read his second inaugural speech. Few heard his words. But Julia listened, no longer apprehensive about Ulysses as a speaker. On her return to her now familiar home she put a young West Pointer to bed and gave him restoratives. He had been overcome by the cold. Then she prepared for the inaugural ball that night, a function that would be remembered as the chilliest, most uncomfortable social event in presidential history.

The city was lit up early. Colored lanterns were festooned among the frosted trees. Candles burned in windows. Fireworks were set off in the park south of the White House and the sparks fizzled in all directions. The dome of the Capitol shone with light. When she arrived at the barnlike building flimsily put together and known as the Muslin Palace Julia shivered visibly in her white and silver brocade gown, made from material given her by the Emperor of China. A short sweeping train fell from a bustle and touches of Chantilly lace trimmed the close-fitting bodice. Mrs. Fish was huddled in ermine and Mrs. Henry Cooke wore emerald green. Mrs. Colfax and Mrs. Creswell were in the official party and Nellie, back from her European trip, stood by her mother's side, white flowers in her dark hair, her gown white silk swathed in tulle.

Twelve pilasters supported the carpeted platform on which the Grants stood, surrounded by flowers and potted palms. Kate Chase Sprague had sent Julia a floral arrangement of sunrays that had cost a thousand dollars. She had backed Greeley when all hope for her father was gone, but was now making the beau geste. The pink cambric that lined the building bathed the interior in a rosy glow but hundreds of canaries felt the chill and would not sing. An American eagle hung suspended from the roof. Festoons of flags radiated from a huge illuminated sun behind the presidential platform. But tar rags, used to seam the roof, blew like mad imps among the dancers.

The guests, both men and women, danced in their wraps. The diplomatic corps soon went home. Smiles froze on the lips of shivering guests. One woman with bronchial trouble died on the dance floor. The champagne and punch were neglected for coffee and chocolate, although Mrs. Logan reported that even the coffee was frappeed. Julia worked hard to spread cheer but when the ball broke up unceremoniously the Grants were glad to get home.

By May Chase was gone from the scene. He had led the parade of Supreme Court Justices past the President and Mrs. Grant on New Year's Day, 1873. Julia, standing a pace behind Ulysses in pearl gray silk with point-lace flounces, had seen how ill he looked. Mrs. Conkling, in black velvet and lace, had made one of her rare public appearances. Across the room from her was Kate Sprague, with turquoise ornaments in her red-gold hair and a yellow satin gown, a Worth creation, outlining her famous shape.

Grant offered the Chief Justiceship to Conkling, who refused it. Many felt that he took this stand because of Kate. The Civil War giants were falling, one by one. General Meade had just died. Henry Wilson would be next. Jesse Grant, who had alternately plagued and interested his son all his life, died at Covington at the end of June. He had never fully recovered from his fall at Grant's first inauguration, and had told Ulyss in December 1872 that unless tie saw his son that winter he would never see him again.

Colonel Dent, too, was on his way out that year. The Grants had planned to join the Blaines in Maine but the President wrote to the Speaker that he did not think the Colonel would "survive Mrs. Grant's absence for a week." He had forgotten every bitter thing ever said to him by his father-in-law and treated him with the utmost courtesy to the end.

On the December day before he died Dent sent for Crook and said: "Do you know, Crook, I'm just like a candle. Ill snuff out." He was eighty-nine and Grant wrote to Corbin that "it was a clear case of life worn out purely by time, no disease, care or anxiety hastening dissolution." The Grants had been out dining that night and returned to find him already in a coma. Julia had always adored her father and Grant found it hard to comfort her on this occasion. Funeral services were held in the Blue Room with the Rev. Dr. O. H. Tiffany, of the Metropolitan Methodist Church, presiding. The Colonel's body was sent to St. Louis for burial and Ellen, Julia's mother, was reinterred at Bellefontaine with him. The President, Fred Grant, Alexander Sharp and James Casey went west for the funeral, but Julia, Nellie and Emma stayed at the White House.

While these personal sorrows were affecting the Grants the President was in the midst of another political crisis. The Credit Mobilier scandal, which had been in the making for a long time, burst wide open as the banking house of Cooke crashed unexpectedly in 1873. Oakes Ames, deeply involved in Union Pacific Railroad operations, had sold shares of Credit Mobilier stock to members of Congress when an investigation threatened. Some of Grant's friends, as well as Cabinet members, were involved. Ames was censured by the vote of the House. An attempt to impeach Vice President Schuyler Colfax failed, but the administration suffered under the revelations. It was an old issue that had arisen to plague Grant.

With the fall of Ames the house of Cooke fell, too. The banking brothers had been heavy investors in railroad stock. In September Grant was with Jay Cooke at Ogontz, the banker's country home in Cumberland County, Pennsylvania, when the news came that his bank must close, but Cooke kept quiet about the disaster until the President had left. Grant had gone to place Jesse in another school nearby and had stopped over briefly at Ogontz, a favorite holiday spot with both of the Grants. Cooke had just given Jesse a fishing rod and creel to make him happy over the prospect of entering school.

Julia visited Ogontz each summer. She liked the white-bearded banker who looked like a patriarch in his great cape cloak and wide-brimmed, soft gray hat. He was genial and devout, worldly and simple, all at the same time. After family prayers each morning he got up and clapped his hands, exclaiming: "Now, let's get jolly." His turreted house on Put-in-Bay had roaring fires, picture windows looking over the water, and a fine library. Women as diverse as Julia Grant, Kate Sprague and the solemn Mrs. Carl Schurz enjoyed his hospitality.

Like countless others, Mrs. Grant was stunned to learn that the Cookes had failed. All through the Civil War their bank had seemed like the Rock of Gibraltar. There was instant panic on the Stock Exchange. Firms were suspended. Banks were mobbed. The panic of 1873 went down in history as a major financial disaster and great numbers of unemployed walked the streets that winter. Among others, Governor William Sprague of Rhode Island, Kate Chase's millionaire husband, was ruined.

With two deaths in her immediate family and all the political distress of the year Julia hesitated about holding her New Year's Day reception in 1874. She finally decided to stay long enough to receive the diplomatic corps, the Supreme Court members and the Cabinet members, but not the general public. She was bitterly criticized for her act and took no further part in social affairs for several months. Don Piatt, who published The Capital, took this occasion to enlarge on the ill-will that now surrounded the Grant family. Julia was both hurt and angry when she read: "Two weeks precisely after the loved form of an aged father had been carried in tears to his last resting place, the daughter and granddaughter took part in a public reception, in which the crepe they wore made a ghastly feature. To say that this was positively shocking is to use very mild language."

Piatt compared Mrs. Grant's public appearance with Mrs. Lincoln's reception while her son Willie was dying upstairs. He wrote of the Grant children "being carted over Europe by our flunky diplomats as specimens of the so-called American court and blood royal ... the fact is, this family does precisely what it pleases, and it pleases to do some very rough things . . ." Piatt, like some of his colleagues, resented the Grant reserve. He noted that the "military rule of the White House treats us to large slices of cold shoulder expressed with the sauce of contempt."

But by May 21, 1874, all Washington was en fete for Nellie's wedding to Algernon Charles Frederic Sartoris. On the way home from Europe, while the Bories were seasick, Nellie was bewitched by Sartoris, a nephew of Fanny Kemble. He was handsome, twenty-three years old and had attended Oxford, but he was considered an unsuitable match for the President's daughter. Even his own parents, Edward and Adelaide Kemble Sartoris, of Warsash House in Hampshire, wrote to President Grant that they had had much trouble with Algy and were not optimistic about the marriage.

Nellie was not quite nineteen when young Sartoris walked into Grant's study in the White House and said:

"Mr. President, I want to marry your daughter."

"It took a bold man to say that to General Grant," Badeau observed. The President argued that she was too young. But Nellie's own pleadings served to weaken the resistance offered at first by Julia and Ulysses. It was much like their own romance all over again, with Colonel Dent opposing Grant. Sir Edward Thornton, who was Algy's host, thought that Nellie, "who had been petted and indulged more than any child he had ever known," would be bored by English country life. He hoped that she might find some comfort in her mother-in-law, a charming and clever woman. No one seemed to think that she would find much comfort in Algy.

Gail Hamilton dined with the Grants immediately after the engagement was announced. Julia, wearing black with a "low neck, short sleeves, and her own black, glossy hair beautifully smooth and shining, done in puffs with a high comb," sighed at the mere mention of the marriage, The President seemed "to feel badly about it." Miss Hamilton, herself an established spinster, was astounded to hear him say that he would prefer Nellie to be an old maid, but if she must marry, he thought she should choose an American husband.

Many of the Grants' more intimate friends protested the match, but Nellie, as always, had her way. She was married in the East Room on a shining May day. Outdoors, magnolia and catalpa trees spread shade and perfume in gardens and parks. The city was a riot of blossom as seventy carriages brought two hundred guests to the White House. Their names were famous as warriors, statesmen and millionaires. Washington was filled at the time with officers who had won their spurs in the Civil War. The diplomatic corps was in full rig and Sir Edward Thornton sponsored the bridegroom.

Did Ulysses remember the narrow stairs in the little house in St. Louis down which Julia had come to join him in her watered silk and gauze veil, as he followed Nellie's bridal party sweeping down the wide western staircase of the White House? Her gown was of heavy white satin trimmed with point lace and priced at two thousand dollars. Her veil had been ordered from Brussels by her father. Nellie was of medium height and gracefully fashioned, with creamy skin, a mass of dark hair and her father's thoughtful eyes. She was pale and so was the bridegroom, who broke all precedent by carrying a bouquet of his own — orange blossoms and tuberoses with a center of pink buds from which a tiny flagstaff protruded. Its silver banner bore the word Love, a theatrical touch worthy of his famous aunt.

Nellie's eight bridesmaids walked in pairs — Edith Fish, Bessie Conkling, Sallie Frelinghuysen, Lillie Porter, Jennie Sherman, Anna Barnes, Fannie Drexel and Maggie Dent. They wore white corded silk draped with tulle. Their sashes were arranged in graceful loops from the waist downward. Four carried bouquets of pink flowers and four of blue.

All of the official family were present, from the Vice President to the bride's brother Fred, now a White House aide, who was best man for Algy. The East Room was a bower of bloom. Flowers had been brought in from Florida — masses of tuberose, spiraea, lilies of the valley. The dais where Nellie was married stood in front of the east window and was covered with a rug given the Grants by the Sultan of Turkey. It was canopied with ferns and vines, and was surmounted by a wedding bell of snowballs and white roses that hung suspended by heavy ropes of smilax. Rings with the couple's initials swung at either side of the bell. More flowers were massed at the windows, wreathed the columns, and formed arches in the doorways.

Dr. Tiffany performed the wedding ceremony at eleven o'clock in the morning. The President walked beside the bride with his usual air of gravity but Mrs. Logan noticed the tears in Julia's eyes. Since she was in mourning she wore a gown of violet faille in shaded tints, with bell cuffs of lace and a high lace yoke and ruff. It had small clusters of pansies, a favorite flower of Julia's, and pendant crystals gave it glitter. Instead of her usual plain chignon her hair was dressed a la grecque, with a ringlet dangling down the back.

The crystal and silver chandeliers shed soft light on the wedding party. The air was heavy with the scent of tuberose. The Marine Band played softly for Nellie, one of their favorite girls. All were sentimental about Grant's daughter, and to Crook she was "springtime and freshness." The banquet was served in the state dining room and the cake was a sensation. The menus were of white satin with a bridal knot of ribbons, and the fare ranged from soft-shelled crabs on toast to a chefs mysterious Epigraphs la fleur, de Nelly Grant. President Monroe's gold spoons were in use.

The wedding gifts were on view in the library. Drexel gave a dinner service valued at forty-five hundred dollars. Childs had selected a dessert set of eighty-four pieces. Hamilton Fish gave Nellie a silver tankard; Creswell an ice cream service; Babcock a lace fan; and A. T. Stewart a five-hundred dollar handkerchief. Her parents gave her a necklace and earrings of diamonds, a point-lace fan, a bouquet, a lace handkerchief and a check for ten thousand dollars.

But Grant was an unhappy man that day. Jesse recalled him "silent, tense, with tears upon his cheeks that he made no movement to brush away." And Crook reported that after Nellie had left no one could find the President until they looked in her room. There he was, sobbing without restraint. The young pair traveled to New York in a specially decorated

Pullman car, the bride wearing a blue redingote costume and jauntily tilted blue felt hat with a wing. Her trousseau included three Indian shawls, a sacque of black Brussels lace, and a variety of costumes in delicate shades — blue, yellow and rose, the colors that best became Nellie.

The Grants went to New York on the same train to see them off on the Baltic, taking Anna Barnes, Nellie's closest friend, with them. Anna lived across from the White House and the two girls had been inseparable. It was freely predicted that Nellie would soon be on her way home, or would be suing for divorce. But when Marshall Jewell visited them in England some time afterward, he found her still infatuated with Algy. She was already well liked by his parents and was contentedly sampling county life.

Five months later Fred brought a bride into the Grant family. If Julia was unhappy about her son-in-law she was enchanted with Ida Marie Honore, the sister of Mrs. Potter Palmer, of Chicago. Grant thought her as "charming for her manners, amiability, good sense & education as she is for her beauty." They were married at the Honore country home on October 28, 1874. The President and Mrs. Grant were guests, but Potter Palmer, in a gray topper and gray gloves, with a single large pearl in his cravat, and his wife in a gray gown fringed with cardinal red, drew most of the attention. Bertha M. Honore had married Potter Palmer, twice her age, four years earlier and he had given her the Palmer House as a wedding gift. Their baby, Honore, was at

Ida's wedding.

The bridal couple knelt under a canopy of camellias and orange blossoms, cape jessamine and carnations. Ida wore a Paris gown of lace and satin d'orange, and her satin corset was stiffened with a hundred bones. Her trousseau was much discussed in the press. Fred, then a lieutenant colonel on General Sheridan's staff in Chicago, drove up to the house in an open wagon drawn by four well-curried army mules with jingling harness and burnished hooves. Potter Palmer gave Ida ten thousand dollars' worth of diamonds and Julia gave her pearls. General Sheridan and his staff were there, but General Sherman was in the mood to snub the wedding when Mrs. Honore invited him to the reception and not to the ceremony itself. "Unless I am notified by noon tomorrow that this is a mistake ... I will simply send my regrets to Mr. and Mrs. Honore . . ." he wrote to Fred.

Buck, whom Miss Hamilton considered the most outspoken of the Grants "a pleasing young man, a little nervous, but rather winning and gentle" at this time was working in a law office in New York while he attended the Columbia Law School. Jesse had just entered Cornell, "without a condition," his father wrote proudly to Badeau, "although he has never attended school but three years, then in an infant class." He noted that his boys were growing up. Fred weighed 193 pounds and had no surplus flesh. Buck was 160 pounds — "twenty pounds more than I weighed at forty years of age." He added affectionately: "They are all of good habits and are very popular with their acquaintances and associates."

After his trip to Europe with General Sherman Fred had done some surveying in Montana and Arizona, and then was appointed a lieutenant colonel on General Sheridan's staff. By the winter of 1874 both Nellie and her husband were back at the White House and Julia had her daughter and her daughter-in-law to assist her in her social duties, for Fred by this time was stationed in Washington. Her Saturday afternoons became doubly popular when these two young matrons with their good looks, stunning clothes and fine manners, took their stand beside her.

But by Christmas time Julia was involved in an open battle on the social front. She was giving an elaborate reception and state dinner for King Kalakaua, of the Hawaiian Islands, when Mrs. George H. Williams, wife of the Attorney General, approached her. Julia cut her dead. A few days later she told Mrs. Fish that although she wished her to be present at the New Year's Day reception, this invitation did not hold for all the Cabinet ladies. Mrs. Williams was the one whom Julia wished to ostracize. Mrs. Fish protested this discrimination. Her husband mentioned the matter to Babcock, who consulted the President. In this case Julia was overruled, and a tactful letter was then sent to Mrs. Fish by Babcock, saying that all would be welcome.

Williams was in heavy trouble at this time and Julia was convinced that blackmailing letters reaching the Grant family were inspired by his wife, who was bitterly disappointed when her husband was not confirmed by the Senate to succeed Chief Justice Chase. At that time she made all manner of threats. When he was about to be ousted as Attorney General her acid gossip and the letters brought on the crisis with Mrs. Grant. They were thought to be the joint work of Mrs. Williams and H. C. Whitley, a former Treasury Department detective. Casey, husband of Julia's sister Emma, was named in them in connection with some Custom House operations in New Orleans.

Mrs. Williams lived fashionably on Rhode Island Avenue, and entertained on an elaborate scale. She was the daughter of a steamboat man and had eloped at fifteen. In the course of a second marriage she helped to run a tavern in California. Williams was her third husband. She was a lively and shrewd member of the Cabinet set and her feud with Mrs. Grant attracted much attention. Like her husband, Julia could be stubborn when she wished, and she was as unforgiving to Mrs. Williams as to Mrs. Cox. She had a strain of iron in her and was uncompromising where her husband's enemies were concerned. Among them she numbered Andrew Johnson and Sumner. She was equally loyal to his friends, and Mrs. Logan, who thought her "incapable of hypocrisy or deceit," considered her astute in business "and quick to see the best side of a proposition."

The Grants at this time were suffering the profound embarrassment of the Whiskey Ring exposures. The ring had been operating for some time, and defrauding the government of huge sums through a coalition of distillers and revenue collectors. Grant was caught in the web through having accepted the bounty of the collaborators without knowing anything of what was going on. When he, Julia and Babcock visited St. Louis in 1874 they were feted by one of the conspirators and were put up at the Lindell House. To their horror Babcock, who seemed like a member of their own family, was named in the ultimate disclosures of the ring. He had delivered Grant's last letter to Lee. He had done innumerable services for Julia and the children. He had been in their counsels for years, and Grant had given him one appointment after another.

The conspirators were convicted but Babcock went free. He was solidly backed by Grant. Jesse said that they all loved him and could believe no ill of him. They had him back as secretary at the White House after the trial but his position was untenable. Eventually he drowned off Key West after Grant had appointed him superintendent of the Lighthouse Board at the end of his administration. Horace Porter, the second military aide who had been close to the Grants for years, on the battlefield as well as in the White House, had left some time earlier and allied himself with the Vanderbilt railroad interests. He was now vice president of the Pullman Company, and still a good friend of the Grants.

The Whiskey Ring was one of Julia's most painful experiences in the White House and it ended the family connection with St. Louis, since its focus was there. In the following year, 1875, she and Ulysses stopped off there on their way to Des Moines to arrange for the sale of their personal property and the lease of the White Haven estate. All their dreams for retirement to Julia's early home were abandoned. During the war Grant had pictured himself settling down on his St. Louis farm and raising horses. He had jestingly suggested that he would sit in a big arm chair in the center of a ring "holding a colt's leading line in my hand, and watching him run around the ring."

Before the Whiskey Ring investigation had died down the Belknap scandal developed and again the President faced a crisis. His Secretary of War was accused of graft in connection with Indian-post traderships on the frontier. The charges against Belknap involved both his wives, the Kentucky sisters who had radiated charm and beauty in the capital. Both the dead and the living were accused of lining their luxurious nests with ill-gotten gains from Indian traderships. The arrangement had begun with the first Mrs. Belknap and had continued with the more sensational "Puss," who had the smallest and most beautiful feet in Washington; whose Worth gowns, emeralds, coral-headed parasols and entertainments were famous.

The Belknaps had been close to the Grants. "Puss" had been conspicuous in Julia's receiving line. When impeachment threatened, the Secretary, who was a large man of military bearing with a long beard, hurried to the White House. In a painful interview, the red-eyed, desperate man, contemplating suicide at the time, had a brief exchange with Grant. His resignation was promptly announced. Jesse always maintained that his father demanded it. But the President was criticized for countenancing such a move. Impeachment proceedings dragged along and finally were dropped. Belknap practiced law, and "Puss" and her daughter spent most of their time in Paris thereafter. Grant stood by Belknap, as he had by Babcock.

In the midst of all this uproar Julia became a grandmother when little Julia Dent Grant was born in the White House on a June day in 1876. She was the child of Fred and Ida and she was baptized in the East Room by Dr. Newman, with members of the Cabinet looking on. Small Julia, who later became Princess Cantacuzene, was carried in for Julia's New Year's Day reception in 1877, wearing a long dress of mull and old Valenciennes lace that her grandmother had worn at White Haven. Years later President McKinley escorted the Princess up the White House stairs to show her her old room.

The Centennial was ushered in at Washington in 1876 with damp, fog, and the bells of Julia's church playing Pleyel's Hymn. Grant had been asked to permit a portrait or bust of himself to be placed on exhibition. He would not listen to this proposal made by his old chaplain friend, Eaton. Julia tapped his shoulder with "characteristic heartiness and good nature, saying, 'You know, Ulysses, you and Lincoln and Washington stand together, you ought to let them have something.'" But Grant refused.

On another occasion, when Julia wished a picture of Grant for a cameo, she told him at breakfast that he should present a clean, clear profile. He misunderstood her and came home that night with his chin shaven.

"I fairly gasped as I said: 'My dear! What have you been doing to yourself?'" Julia later recalled.

"Why, didn't you ask me to have a clean-shaven profile picture taken for your miniature?"

However, he had his picture taken before his beard grew out again.

There were ninety-two Stock Exchange failures in 1876, inflation was in full play and echoes of graft and corruption would not die down. The Ouster massacre had stirred up indignation. There was desperate unrest in the South. A bitter struggle was on for the presidency. The Grant administration had lost all prestige except in the field of foreign affairs, but Julia had become a little drunk with power and she hoped and believed that Ulysses might be re-elected for a third term. He had no desire to seek the office again and, aware of her powers of persuasion, he acted swiftly without her knowledge.

The question came up for discussion at a cabinet meeting early in the summer of 1875. Julia was in the room as the group assembled. Grant, always courteous to his wife, hesitated to ask her to leave but she soon saw that he was uneasy and she went out of her own accord. After she had left, the President told of his intention to write to the chairman of the Republican State Convention at Philadelphia, making it clear that he had no intention of running again. When the Cabinet dispersed he wrote the letter in his own hand and went out to post it personally. But first he showed it to Badeau and told him that he was sending a copy to the press without his wife's knowledge, for he was sure that the news would be disagreeable to her, and he wished his decision to be irrevocable before she learned of it. But Julia, suspicious by this time, asked him what had occurred at the cabinet meeting. After some hesitation he said:

"Well, my name is being mentioned for a third term, and I've been unable to answer until the nomination was offered; but today the question came up in such form that I have written a letter against the third term."

"You must not send it," said Julia imperiously.

"But I have sent it," he answered quietly.

"Well, go get it back instantly."

Ulysses told her that it was already in the post box. Years later, when she discovered that Badeau had seen the letter, she reproached him "more than half in earnest for not striving harder to prevent its issue." She was angry and disturbed when the news broke, but she had always known that Ulysses was an obstinate man. The die was cast. He meant it.

Badeau found it hard to think of Grant apart from his family, and in writing about them he gave weight to Julia's influence over her husband. No one denied that it was great, and many believed that the President's favor might be obtained through her intercession. But she made little headway in the political field although to Badeau her instincts sometimes seemed better than the President's judgment. "He would not overthrow a man whom he trusted," the writer observed, "though there were occasions when it would have been better for him had she succeeded."

"He had as much confidence in his wife as any man that ever lived," Badeau wrote, but he thought that Julia's love sometimes outweighed her judgment and that if she wished a man upheld or deposed it was because she believed him true or false to Ulysses. She shared many of his secrets but not all. His reticence occasionally extended to Julia, too. Even in personal matters he could be immovable at times. In general Badeau thought that Mrs. Grant advised her husband "simply and strongly to do what he thought right, and perhaps induced him to do it; although he, as little as any man, I believe, required such inducement."

Although Julia and Badeau quarreled at the end, his tribute to her as a wife stood untouched, and he wrote of the Grants:

No more beautiful life can ever be known. General Grant's regard for his wife was constant, tender, true ... In the first years of my intercourse with Grant I was greatly impressed with the influence of his wife, and the impression deepened until the last. Nobody can understand his character or career who fails to appreciate this; no one who did not know him intimately can ever say how much Mrs. Grant helped him; how she comforted him, and enabled him to perform his task, which, without that help and solace, I sometimes thought might never have been performed . . . She soothed him when cares oppressed him, she supported him when even he was downcast (though he told so few); she served him and nerved him at times when he needed all she did for him.

One of the worst storms in Washington history blanketed the White House for the Grants' last New Year's Day reception. As the day wore on the streets became impassable but the public flocked out for this final view of their soldier President. Julia received in the Blue Parlor. She wore black velvet, embroidered with jet Her basque bodice had a heart-shaped neckline and she wore a diamond cross, Ulysses' gift to her on their twenty-fifth wedding anniversary. Ida's dark beauty was shown off with a claret velvet gown, the basque clasped in front with diamonds. Nellie looked sumptuous in a gown of rare white lace over pale blue silk, with a long blue train and a glitter of diamonds on her basque.

In a sense this was a farewell party. Pendel noticed how reluctant Mrs. Grant was to leave the White House. But Grant had a different point of view. "I never wanted to get out of a place as much as I did to get out of the Presidency," he remarked later. Julia and Buck went over the mansion together, taking an inventory of their personal things, saying good-by and making final preparations for the incoming Hayes family. Julia moved through the rooms, some stately, some shabby, where birth, marriage and death had filled out the cycle of life, great functions had been held, and gray nights of worry had plagued them at times. She stocked the larder for Mrs. Hayes and the President ordered various wines, not knowing that Lucy Webb Hayes would make the White House bone dry and become known as "Lemonade Lucy."

The Grants gave a state dinner for thirty in honor of the incoming President and his wife, who were staying with the Shermans on I Street. After the inaugural ceremonies Julia was hostess for the last time in the White House at a friendly luncheon given for their successors. She observed Mrs. Hayes' brunette good looks, her sturdy competence and crisp ways. As the Grants were leaving Mrs. Hayes stood bareheaded at the entrance while the President remarked: "General, if I had a slipper I'd throw it after you."

Both of the Grants had changed in these eight years. They had become used to softer living, to flattery and applause, as well as to censure. They had learned to cope with massive gatherings and public tumult Both looked more prosperous, better dressed, more self-assured. The General's weight had increased from 150 to 185 pounds. His reddish-brown hair and beard showed touches of silver. He now used eyeglasses for reading. He wore a cutaway and his watch chain was a single heavy strand of gold.

Julia was stouter and some threads of gray showed in her glossy dark hair. She moved with more assurance and rather slowly. Still naive in spirit, she was now sophisticated in experience. She had been deferentially listened to for so long that she had assumed an air of authority. Mrs. Alphonso Taft, a new social figure coming into view as the wife of the Attorney General, observed that she had the appearance of a person who had never been criticized or "taken down." But she found her "simplicity itself almost flat sometimes ... & although impulsive and governed by her prejudices one cannot help liking her because she is so genuine." Mrs. Taft, whose son, William Howard Taft, would one day be President, thought Ida a "thorough society girl but winning," and Fred and Buck "pleasant unaffected fellows, like our boys, only I don't believe they are so smart!" She considered them on the whole an affectionate and happy family, "disposed to have a good time and not worry over the hard things said of them." But she found Mrs. Blaine "bright and smart, one of our sort of women."

Grant went out to applause as well as to condemnation. Julia never let people forget that the ratification of the Treaty of Washington, settling the difficulties with Britain in 1871, was one of his triumphs; that he vetoed the inflation bill; reduced the national debt and taxes; established Yellowstone Park; promoted Civil Service reform; worked for better educational facilities through the country; interested himself in the well-being of the Negro; and inaugurated the principle of arbitration in international disputes. The physical world around them was changing, too. The telephone was coming into use. Typewriters were on the market but were regarded still as curiosities. George M. Pullman, a friend of the President's, was revolutionizing railroad travel.

The Grants were not well-off when they left the White House but they had come to a decision about what they wished to do. Grant had always hoped to see the world. They had money invested in mining stock and railroad bonds. Mrs. Grant owned real estate in Washington. They still received rental for White Haven. Adding it all up, they decided to tour Europe and perhaps go farther afield.

With the warm good will of their intimate and official friends, and the applause of the crowds who remembered soldier Grant as well as the President, they sailed on May 17, 1877, on the Indiana. Steam whistles, salutes and flags, the inevitable Grant accompaniment, sped them on their way from New Castle after a farewell party at the Childs home in

Philadelphia. Jesse went with them. They would not be back until September 1879, and by then they would have seen the world through a brilliant spectrum and recovered the old Grant prestige that had been dimmed in the last days of the administration.

"Having learned a lesson from my predecessor, Penelope, I accompanied my Ulysses in his wanderings round the world," said Julia, looking back on the hour of their departure.

CHAPTER XIII: PENELOPE FOLLOWS ULYSSES

QUEEN VICTORIA and Mrs. Grant faced each other at Windsor Castle on a June night in 1877 in a state gallery hung with the portraits of royal ancestors. The two acknowledged matriarchs chatted about their children. They were of the same height and resembled each other to some degree in build. The court was in mourning for the Queen of the Netherlands and Julia wore black satin with Chantilly lace and diamonds.

The Queen spoke amiably of Nellie, who had been presented to her on her first visit to England. Julia responded with warmth, pointing out that her daughter had been so pleased with her welcome that she had become one of the Queen's subjects by marriage. When the Queen made a reference to her official duties Julia quietly responded: "Yes, I can imagine them. I, too, have been the wife of a great ruler."

The three Grants were none too happy at the moment, since nineteen-year-old Jesse had just succeeded in imposing his will on Queen Victoria behind the scenes. He had been assigned to sit with the Royal Household but he felt that he should dine at the Queen's table with his parents. Jesse had not wished to come to Windsor in the first place. He had been invited to a young people's ball in London. But his mother had urged him to share in an experience that he would remember all his life.

The Queen was out driving when they arrived. The Grants were shown to a spacious suite looking out toward the Great Park, and Jesse and Badeau were quartered together. Shortly before dinner Sir John Cowell, Master of the Queen's Household, strolled in and explained that Jesse and Badeau would dine with the Royal Household, not with the Queen. Jesse, impulsive like his mother, immediately started packing up to leave. He announced that he was going back to London if he had to walk to the station.

Edwards Pierrepont, the United States Minister, was called in for consultation. He was furious that "Jesse's folly" should imperil the harmony of an evening carefully arranged by the Earl of Beaconsfield to offset some of the chill shown by certain nobles who had backed the Southern cause. He said he would tell the boy's father. That suited Jesse. They all marched off to his parents' quarters where the Duchess of

Roxburgh was tactfully explaining to Julia that when the Queen did not feel her best, a large number at table made her dizzy.

Jesse, dark-haired, lean and good-looking, with a stubborn, indented chin and hair parted in the middle, angrily stood his ground when Pierrepont told his story, winding up with the exclamation: "And Jesse here says that he will go back to London!"

"I think that is what I would do, if I were in Jesse's place," said the General, according to his son's version of this encounter.

Julia was disturbed and suggested compromise but Grant listened attentively to what Jesse had to say. They all remembered that they had entertained Prince Arthur at the White House. Word soon reached the Queen that trouble was brewing. In no time at all Sir John returned, bland and smiling, with the announcement that Her Majesty would be pleased to have Jesse at her table. It had all been Sir John's fault and he could not forgive himself for his blunder! Later that evening, according to Jesse, Sir John confessed to him that the Queen had said "Well, let him go," until he pointed out that this would whip up a rumpus. It was then proposed that the American Minister should smooth out the matter.

The Grants were received by the Queen in the gallery leading from her private apartments. She talked first to the General and seemed all too anxious to put him at his ease, he told Badeau afterward. General Grant had not felt overawed. Then she turned to Julia and they had their brief chat. They dined in the Oak Room with the Grenadier Band playing outside in the quadrangle of Windsor. Lord Derby escorted Julia, who took interested note of the small imperious figure, representing such worldwide power. Jesse conducted a merry conversation with the Countess of Derby at dinner and had every opportunity to study Queen Victoria at close range, although the exacting Badeau thought him much too far below the salt. The Queen rose at ten, chatted briefly with her guests and made a stately departure after two ladies-in-waiting had thrown a lace shawl over her shoulders.

The party now scattered. The band played softly in one of the drawing rooms. The General was beaten at whist by the Duchesses of Wellington and Roxburgh. Julia chatted with Lord Derby and other peers. At eleven all the women retired and Grant and Jesse went down to the billiard room with the Queen's youngest son, Prince Leopold, who was garbed in a smoking suit of purple and yellow satin. It was the only spot where smoking was allowed. They played billiards until two in the morning and Jesse won twenty royal shillings.

In after years Julia was inclined to think that Badeau had precipitated the fuss. He was greatly concerned that the Grants should be treated like visiting royalty. This was the last thing they wished for themselves and they were much embarrassed when the newspapers pounced on this incident and pictured Jesse as flouting the Queen. The story took wings on both sides of the Atlantic. An American youth, the son of the great General Grant, defying Queen Victoria! It was unthinkable. Julia, an independent in spirit but a conformist in practice, was concerned. She said it was all a misunderstanding. After that the reporters took note of Jesse's doings and he became a natural headline target.

But the visit to Windsor was only an incident in a triumphal tour of Great Britain. They were feted from the moment they arrived at Liverpool and Julia stepped ashore wearing a smart flounced costume, with her bonnet set well back on her head and an umbrella in her hand. Cheering crowds, flags, parades, banquets and speeches, triumphal arches, public holidays and the freedom of cities, became their constant fare. Grant was a public hero all over again, and Julia, always at his side but unobtrusive, delighted in the ovations.

At this time John Russell Young moved into the intimate Grant circle. An Irish-born journalist of considerable reputation, he had served as a Civil War correspondent for the Philadelphia Press and was an occasional contributor to the New York Tribune. James Gordon Bennett assigned him to cover the Grant world tour for the New York Herald. He became a close friend of both of the Grants, as well as being the official chronicler of their travels. Julia was particularly fond of him and he accompanied her on many of her sightseeing and shopping tours. Young sent dignified accounts of their doings to the Herald, and the American public wakened up to a fresh view of the traveling General and his wife.

At the first opportunity Julia and Ulysses broke away to go down to Nellie's home near Southampton. Grant, now reconciled to the marriage, had given Algy a trotting horse and light American buggy, and Sartoris and Jesse rode all over the countryside. Although rumors of marital unhappiness persisted, the General's letters to the end of his life showed nothing but friendliness toward Algy, with constant invitations to visit the Grants in America, and to bring his parents with him. Julia was delighted to find her daughter so well established in her new sphere.

Wherever the Grants went they encountered celebrities they had entertained in Washington or officers who had fought in the Union army. When the Prince of Wales gave them a dinner at Marlborough House the Empress of Brazil reminded Julia of her visit to the White House. Here Julia met the great Disraeli, then Prime Minister and newly created Earl of Beaconsfield. One function followed another. Lily Langtry sat at one side of Grant at Lord Houghton's and Julia Ward Howe at the other. Grant had little to say to either of them, but both his dinner companions were eloquent conversationalists. Lord Strathnairn, of Alma and Inkerman fame, was present on this occasion, sharing his military interest in Grant with Sir Garnet Wolseley, who rated Lee the genius among American generals and Jefferson Davis his bedeviler. The Indian Mutiny, the Crimean War, the Civil War, were fought all over again.

Kate Field and Olive Logan, two American correspondents, took notes on Julia at the reception given the Grants by the Pierreponts at the Embassy. They observed her having an earnest conversation with Mrs. Gladstone, who wore pale blue with a cluster of diamonds holding a long blue plume in her hair. Mrs. Pierrepont was in scarlet and black and Julia looked well in burgundy velvet with a pale yellow satin overdress. She was greeted by John Bright, a good friend of the North. Kate Field observed how pasty-faced both Bright and Gladstone looked beside the sturdy Grant All the grandes dames of England were present, but the "American belles carried away the palm for style and beauty, as they usually do on such occasions," she commented. Years earlier Julia and her luckless young husband had often sat in the theater run by Kate's father in St. Louis.

The world had changed radically for Julia since then. Now it was resonant with violins and applause in a wholly new setting, but she never forgot that she had presided at the White House. Great names in the arts now figured in her receiving line — Anthony Trollope, just finishing The Duke's Children; the hearty Robert Browning who held her tiny hand quite gently in his; Arthur Sullivan, busy on Pinafore with William S. Gilbert. She persuaded the General to wear his uniform when they went to Covent Garden to hear Madame Albani sing Martha. The diva added the "Star Spangled Banner" in Grant's honor and Julia suddenly stood in a blaze of light and blinked at all the glitter.

She sat in the famous Waterloo Chamber of Apsley House at a dinner given by the son of the Iron Duke, and talked to him about music under a life-sized portrait of Napoleon. He was quiet, unassuming and more interested in the arts than in soldiering. His Duchess, who had Grant at her right, was a favorite with Queen Victoria.

When Roscoe Conkling dined with the Grants in London he wrote home to his daughter Bessie in Utica that Mrs. Grant had found none of the great ladies she had met "so easy or knew so well the right thing to do as Mrs. Fish or Mrs. Conkling." Roscoe's handsome figure was much observed in London at this time. His red hair and Titian beard, his foppish attire and noble carriage, his lordly manner and eloquent speeches, made him conspicuous wherever he went. Ever the political strategist, as well as the family friend, he saw much of the Grants and kept a third term in mind, but Ulysses felt far removed from the political scene at this time. He was relieved to be away from it and he viewed his reception strictly as a compliment to the United States. "I love to see our country honored and respected abroad, and I am proud that it is respected by most all nations, and by some even loved," the General wrote to Childs before his tour was finished.

They went to Epsom Downs, where he compared notes on the horses with the Prince of Wales. He received the freedom of London and Julia took part in the reception given him at the Guild Hall. A delegation representing a million British workmen called on him at Badeau's house. "There is no reception I am prouder of than this one today," the General commented. They toured the manufacturing districts of England, visited Tynemouth and watched a great demonstration of workingmen at Newcastle. The General rode out to the moors in the trades procession which had banners bearing his own phrase: "Let us have peace." Julia read with astonishment next day that Ulysses "looked like an ordinary Tyneside skipper, open-browed, firm-faced, bluff, honest and unassuming." In Birmingham they stayed with Joseph Chamberlain, monocled and eloquent statesman, then busy reorganizing the Liberal Party with John Bright. Grant received addresses of welcome from the workingmen in Birmingham and Newcastle, as well as in London.

By autumn they were in Scotland, where they first visited Edinburgh and Abbotsford. Grant had read Walter Scott to Julia in their courting days and she viewed his home with the keenest interest. They toured the Speyside and were welcomed at Granton to the home of their clan. They went over the Craigellachie region, always identified with the Grants and their motto: "Stand Fast." Julia had a passion for legends and lore, which she could indulge in this setting. She walked the quiet streets of Inverness, where the provost welcomed them to the capital of the Highlands. Here Jesse came into strong collision with the kilt and tartans his mother loved.

But as they traveled farther north the Grants were absorbed in the countryside the bronze and purple shades of autumn settling on the moors, the grouse in full flight, the Dornoch Firth sweeping out from the small, beautiful town where Andrew Carnegie, one day to be a friend of Julia's, would make his summer home at Skibo Castle. They attended a horticultural show in Dornoch, one of their favorite forms of entertainment in Britain, since their love of flowers was a shared taste that never left them.

The Duke of Sutherland entertained them at Dunrobin Castle and his Duchess showed Julia through the great baronial halls, with stag heads mounted on oak shields inscribed with the names of the sportsmen who had bagged them. Jesse and his mother thought they had never seen such an array of famous names, but when the Duke urged Ulysses to add the name Grant to his collection with a deer head, he refused. "Twice in my life I killed wild animals," he said, "and I have regretted both acts ever since."

They went on to the little fishing town of Wick, the Castle of Thurso and John O'Groats, the most northerly point of Britain, where they looked out on the Pentland Firth as a wild gale blew. Back in Glasgow Grant received the freedom of the city and the Lord Provost called him the Wellington of America. They visited Ayr, toured Loch Lomond and were guests of the Duke of Argyle at Inverary. The Grants always looked back on this particular visit with special pleasure. The Duke had been a stout ally of the North during the war and was one of the more liberal peers of Britain.

All that summer and autumn they moved from place to place. In Brussels King Leopold gave them a state banquet after calling informally at their hotel to welcome them. In Switzerland Mont Blanc was illuminated in their honor and Grant laid the cornerstone of a new Episcopal Church in Geneva. He showed great interest in the town where his own international negotiations had had their focus, and the Alabama claims had been settled by arbitration.

Julia was captivated by the mountain scenery and in "ascending and descending the beautiful mountain passes . . . always regretted she could not have some of her old friends like Mrs. Fish to help her enjoy herself," Grant wrote to Hamilton Fish. Badeau thought that Grant, too, was uncommonly moved by the Swiss scenery "all the stupendous grandeur of the scene was as apparent to him as if he had been a poet," he commented.

The General was genial and carefree, after years of strenuous effort. Julia was her most flirtatious self, and even a little coy at times. During their travels she kept a watchful guard on Ulysses, since women both subtle and determined laid siege to the unresponsive General. "Mrs. Grant always awed even Princesses if they paid too much attention to her great husband," Badeau noted. She was particularly chilly to a Russian princess, American by birth, who deceived them about her operatic background when she entertained them at her villa on one of the Italian lakes, "Nevertheless the villa was beautiful, the lake was Italian, and the Princess was real, like her lace and her red rose," Badeau commented.

Before leaving Italy they had a glimpse of Fanny Kemble, who walked through their garden gate holding a black ruffled silk parasol over her aging head. She curtsied low to General Grant, who at first had some difficulty placing her until she told him that she was Algy's aunt. She asked him to use his influence in getting a pension for a Swiss peasant who had served in the American army, a favor that he was unable to grant.

Julia and Ulysses had many small adventures as they toured Central Europe. Once at a chalet in the Brunig Pass Julia disappeared and Ulysses feared that she might have fallen over a precipice, but she was only playing a game of hide and seek. Again, Badeau observed how reluctant Grant was to have his wife leave his side as they traveled from Interlaken to Grindelwald. They seemed like young lovers, although Julia was fifty and Grant was fifty-four.

The General was a strenuous and relentless traveler. He walked day and night in the streets of strange cities. He cared more for the ways of the people and the practical problems of agriculture and industry than he did for museums. Julia trudged dutifully through the art galleries, followed the trail of the poets, made reverential visits to the churches, and enjoyed the classical music that Grant abhorred. She was also an inveterate shopper, a keen observer of the children wherever she went, and she liked to take stock of the work of the Christian missions.

Their visit to Paris was delayed while General MacMahon, Marshal of France, engaged in a political struggle of his own. They finally arrived there in October 1877, at a moment when France was burning with excitement over its republican victory. They stayed at the Bristol Hotel and again were feted and entertained. They saw the obelisk lying in the mud after the Commune, and moonlight falling on the gilded dome of the Invalides. They viewed the ruins of the Tuileries and paid a formal visit to the Elysee. MacMahon wished to stage a military show for the General, but he would not permit it. Peace was his mission.

Julia drove along the Champs Elysees in an elaborate equipage as the autumn leaves whisked through the Bois. She shopped happily under the Palais Royal arcades and spotted historical landmarks. Ulysses bought her a jeweled pin in Tiffany's Paris branch, and together they selected a cloak for Nellie on the same day that they dined with the Marquis de Talleyrand. Both parents constantly sent gifts and money to their only daughter. Julia stocked up on gowns for her further travels and sent trunks containing her old ones back to America. Her shopping expeditions at times kept the patient Ulysses waiting for hours, but he always listened attentively to her tales of fittings and linguistic mix-ups when she returned, and had good-natured comments to make on her selections as she paraded before pier mirrors. Julia had the knack of always making things seem funny to her adoring husband, one of her most potent weapons in keeping alive his interest.

But he was not enamored of Paris. He stole off at every opportunity to sit in the New York Herald offices and study the American papers. "I have seen nothing here that would make me want to live in Paris, or elsewhere outside of the United States," he wrote to General Beale on November 4, 1877. The only thing he found to commend was that people minded their own business and did not interfere with their neighbors.

"It is a beautiful city but I am quite ready to leave," he wrote to Borie two weeks later, adding a note about Julia, whose shopping operations were always of great interest to the merchant prince from Philadelphia. "Mrs. Grant is quite well acquainted with the places we most hear of: Worth, Bon Marche, the Louvre, fashionable dress and bonnet makers, etc. . . ." the General noted.

Mrs. John W. Mackay, with the profits of the Comstock lode newly behind her, gave a great dinner and ball for the Grants at her magnificent home looking out on the Place de l'Etoile. The garden was illumined with flags and emblems silhouetted by gas jets. Footmen in crimson and gold lined the entrance and stairway. The menus were printed on silver tablets. The guests included the Marquis de Lafayette and M. de Rochambeau. Mrs. Mackay, a hearty dowager who knew the mining West and the pioneering frontier days, had his favorite brand of cigar for Ulysses and some lively American chitchat for Julia.

Early that December they boarded the American cruiser Vandalia at Villefranche, planning to spend the winter in Egypt. They found Naples dirty and disappointing. The sun did not shine on the glorious bay, Vesuvius was in a lazy mood, and Julia sat on a chair at Pompeii and watched a loaf of bread being dug in their honor from the ruins of an ancient bakery.

Palermo loomed up through a violet haze as they sailed south, and here the officers of the Vandalia gave a Christmas festival for Mrs. Grant. The hatchway was turned into an arbor. The ceiling bloomed with vines. The mast was leafed. Christmas bells rang out in the town. Songs and cheers greeted the Grants from other ships in the harbor and fireworks lit the sky. They ate turkey and plum pudding and toasted the "loved ones at home," Julia's constant thought while at sea. "It was a merry, genial, homelike feast," Young noted. Julia wore a dress with a ruche around her neck, a nipped-in waist and long earrings. She was in "capital health and spirits" and Grant, deeply tanned and much stouter, seemed "much younger and brighter than I have seen him for many years."

The General had gained forty-eight pounds since leaving Washington, and Julia was straining the seams of her new dresses. Her jolly spirit made her popular with the crew and her traveling companions. Young wrote affectionately of her "considerate, ever-womanly and ever-cheerful nature." They read the Odyssey together before sailing through the Straits of Messina and she promoted much fun and nonsense about Ulysses, Scylla and Charybdis. They passed Stromboli in the rain and Scylla at eight in the morning, while they were still asleep and deaf to siren voices.

Their man-of-war rolled heavily. Jesse swung in a cot. Grant had a cabin in the bow of the ship. Julia, with her maid, rose to the beat of drums and found everything on the ship "strict, steady and precise." She interceded for prisoners in the brig. She laughed when Ulysses read snatches of Innocents Abroad to her as they sat on deck. The General was an excellent sailor under all conditions, but Julia became seasick when the weather was rough. They rolled so violently as they approached Egypt that she begged the Captain to anchor his ship.

She had not recovered sufficiently to meet Henry Stanley, fresh from the African wilderness, at a dinner given for them in Alexandria, but Ulysses had a long talk with the explorer. They made a dreamlike trip up the Nile to the First Cataract in a flat-bottomed vessel given them by the Khedive. There were ten in the party and they tied up at night and watched the Bedouins make bonfires on the shores. The desert was flushed with purple as night fell. Julia thought she had never seen such sunsets, as she watched the palms fade like ghosts into the shadows.

Torch bearers accompanied them back to their boat after official receptions along the way. They visited Luxor, Karnak, Thebes, and Memphis, and were awed by the mighty ruins. At Karnak a broken column was carpeted for Julia to sit on as they lunched in the shade of the ruins. She wore a helmet swathed with a heavy silk veil, and colored spectacles. At Aswan she and Young went shopping for ostrich plumes. Her companion found her an easy prey to Arab bargaining as she listened to woeful tales of family sorrows and starving children. She protested the beating of the water girls, and the donkey boys who pursued their party for baksheesh.

When a message arrived that Gordon of Khartoum, then the Governor General, wished to receive them, Grant rode off on a splendid Arabian horse, after getting Julia safely fastened to a donkey. Bella, her Scottish maid, had little use for donkeys and her stern Presbyterian nature was unresponsive to Egyptian ruins. But Grant considered it great fun getting Julia hitched to a donkey. He wrote to Fred:

Your Ma balances on a donkey very well when she has an Arab on each side to hold her and me to lead the donkey. Yesterday, however, she got a little out of balance twice, but claims that the saddle turned. Of course it did. How could it have done otherwise with 185 Ibs. in a stirrup on one side and the donkey only weighing 125 pounds. But she rides a donkey very well on the whole. I wish Ida was along to keep her company.

The Khedive offered the Grants a palace to live in while they were in Cairo and Julia felt as if she were part of an Arabian night's dream as she lounged among purple and gold cushions on deep divans and clapped her hands for giant Nubians who arrived with coffee, braziers of willow charcoal, and long pipes for Ulysses.

The General called on the Khedive wearing plain evening dress but his wife distinctly felt that women were of small account in Egypt. They remained in Cairo for several days, visiting the Pyramids and other sights. Julia haunted the bazaars and urged all members of the party to prepaid for their visit to the Holy Land by reading the Bible. They traveled toward Jerusalem by wagon through a plain where lilies and scarlet anemones bloomed. The orange trees were bowed with ripening fruit. The almond trees were just coming into bloom. They saw the mountains of Judaea through intermittent rain and Grant observed that the plain of Sharon "under good government should raise wheat enough to feed all that portion of the Mediterranean."

Young picked anemones, buttercups and daisies for Julia as an offering from the Holy Land. She was alert to every Biblical landmark along the way. Her devout Methodist upbringing and Grandfather Wrenshall's precepts had left their mark, and she primed her companions on what they ought to observe. To their dismay they finally rode into Jerusalem like a conquering army instead of a small band of devout pilgrims.

"I didn't want to parade into Jerusalem, Julia," said Ulysses apologetically. But the Turkish Governor was determined to honor the visiting General. They were met with banners and armed men, bands playing, colors falling, and crowds out to greet them. Desert chiefs had ridden great distances to see Grant of Vicksburg. Having left the warmer plains they found snow lying on the ground in Jerusalem as the Governor welcomed them to the Holy City with a military band.

They walked along the Via Dolorosa and climbed to the Garden of Gethsemane. Here a monk gathered flowers for Mrs. Grant from the Tree of Agony and gave the others twigs and leaves. Bella felt better away from the heathen gods. They climbed the Mount of Olives and viewed the land of Moab, the Valley of the Jordan and the Dead Sea. They saw Pisgah and Damascus Gate. Grant wore gloves for his ride to Bethlehem and Julia "by various friendly processes" was again securely fastened on a donkey. Greek priests welcomed them at the Church of the Holy Sepulchre but the Grants found the scene confusing.

Smyrna was crowded with ships of all nations as the Vandalia took them to Constantinople. World famous war correspondents were there and they took a lively interest in Grant. The Treaty of San Stefano had just been signed and they had prime stories to tell of the Russo-Turkish War. Julia visited the bazaars but found the prices exorbitant.

In Greece they were received by the King and Queen, and the Parthenon was illuminated in their honor. The ruins "blazed with a thousand Bengal fires." Julia studied the sculpture with appreciation but Grant found more to interest him in the ancient battlegrounds and the plains of Marathon. From Greece they worked their way backward to Italy and by April 20, 1878, Julia was methodically touring the Uffizi Gallery in Florence and buying trinkets for friends and relatives. She continued this in Venice and spent blissful hours riding through the canals in gondolas. In Milan they attended an opera at La Scala and everyone seemed to know who the visiting American General was. All through northern Italy there was interest in Grant the soldier. His feats were familiar to the Italian officers who had fought with Garibaldi.

In Rome the General was received by the Pope and talked to him for an hour. There were complications in the arrangements — a question of whether to visit the King or the Vatican first, but the General solved it by arriving very simply on his own with Jesse. The youth was giving trouble by this time. He was desperately homesick and wished to get back to America. He suspected that his mother shared his feeling but would not voice it as long as his father wished to keep on going. Neither one had ever seen the General happier, in spite of his boredom with art.

While in Rome he wrote to Buck asking him to join them on his vacation. His second son was prospering. He had been assigned to look after his father's investments, with good results. Grant, who feared at first that he might not have enough money to keep him going for long in Europe, was now slightly better off. Buck was too occupied to make the trip, but when they returned to Paris for the opening of the Exposition it was arranged that Fred, who liked to be in the thick of things, should join them for the rest of their travels, while Jesse returned home.

By this time the Grant tour was becoming legendary in the American press. The General's old aura had returned to some extent. The scandals of his administration were fading into the background. Talk of a third term persisted and Julia listened attentively. Letters and newspaper clippings arrived, all pointing in one direction, but his backers wished Grant to keep on traveling until the convention of 1880. They felt he would have added status by that time and would arrive home on a rip tide of enthusiasm.

One of the more memorable stops along the way was their visit to Berlin and their meetings with Bismarck. Grant rated Beaconsfield, Bismarck, Gambetta and Li Hung-chang, Chinese viceroy and warrior, as the four greatest men he met on his tour around the world. They stayed at the Kaiserhof in Berlin and the General explored the city on foot with extraordinary energy. Kaiser Wilhelm was recuperating from an attempted assassination so that he could not receive them, but Bismarck appropriately played host. Grant had a severe cold as he reviewed the Prussian Guard and could scarcely mount his horse. A downpour doused the scene as cavalry, artillery and infantry engaged in a sham battle on the Tempelhof grounds. The event as a whole was depressing and Grant felt so miserable that Young thought it a good thing they had the unquenchable Mrs. Grant with them. Everyone else was cheerless and damp but the General's wife had a nature that "would see as much sunshine in Alaska as in Italy, on whom tempest, rain or snow never makes an impression," he reported.

On their return to the hotel Prince Bismarck made a special call on Julia. He wore full military uniform and a gilded helmet pulled down to his heavy brows. He welcomed her to Germany and hoped she would take home only the best impressions of the country. She assured him she would. Julia had already had a long talk with the Crown Princess, discussing children and household affairs, wedding anniversaries and domestic manners in Germany.

The Grants were entertained at his palace by Bismarck. Like Ulysses, the German enjoyed a cigar but his doctors had banned them and he now sat nursing a pipe two feet long between his knees, hunched forward as he did so. A Danish hound lay at his feet, creating a picture that Julia always remembered. The two warriors talked of the assassination of Lincoln in connection with the attempt on the Kaiser's life; of German officers who had served with Grant; of Sheridan, whom Bismarck admired. Grant sturdily told him: "No better general ever lived than Sheridan."

Julia was observed in the liveliest conversation with the Princess. She was always particularly interested in the wives of the world's warriors and felt a special kinship with them. She observed that Ulysses was showing his usual reserve with Bismarck but her own merry flow of talk went on unabated. When their host showed them the war chamber where an international commission was sitting to settle the terms of the Russo-Turkish War he indicated to Julia the chair that Beaconsfield occupied. She asked at once why Germany was involved, and Bismarck replied: "To tell you the truth, Madam, Russia has taken too much Turkey and we are helping to digest it."

The General wrote to the Rev. M. J. Cramer in Copenhagen a few days later: "He is no doubt the greatest statesman of the present time." He and Julia soon were guests of the Cramers. After touring Germany from end to end and meeting Richard Wagner at Heidelberg, they moved on to Copenhagen and the Scandinavian countries. Cramer, who had married Ulysses' sister, Mary Frances, was now the American Minister to Denmark. The Grants were received by the King and Queen at Bernstorff

Castle. Julia took a copy of Hamlet with her to Elsinore but Grant teased her for her faith in superstitions and legends.

A great gale blew their ship about as they sailed across the Baltic from Sweden to Russia. They sailed into Kronstadt and were received by the Emperor in St. Petersburg. The Civil War was discussed and the Grand Duke Alexis, whom Julia had entertained at the White House, bemoaned the death of General Custer. But the Catacazy ouster lay like a shadow around them all. The Imperial yacht was put at their disposal and Julia saw St. Petersburg in its day of jeweled pomp. They found Moscow and Warsaw gloomy and soon moved on to Vienna, arriving there in August 1878.

Both decided that this was their favorite capital in Europe. The Emperor Francis Joseph entertained them at Schonbrunn. A diplomatic dinner was given at the American Embassy, followed by a ball, which drew out the flower of Viennese society. As Julia watched the swinging couples, gorgeously attired, dancing to Strauss waltzes, she thought she had never seen such joie de vivre. "Vienna is one of the most beautiful cities in Europe, if not the most beautiful," Grant wrote to Fred on August 22, 1878, not knowing that his son would soon be the American Minister there, and that Ida and her daughter Julia would become prime favorites in Vienna.

He was waiting for Julia as he wrote this letter and he finished on the indulgent note he always used with her: "Your Ma is now out shopping and it is less than an hour to the time when we are to be at a dinner party and she has to dress after her return. Ladies never do take notice of time."

Unpunctuality was one of Julia's weaknesses, a great trial to her army-trained husband, but he never complained. He merely jested with her about it. Grant thought the shops of Vienna superb, better than those in Paris. His only complaint was that "everybody retires so horribly early." The streets were almost clear by ten o'clock at night. In Paris he had tramped about until two o'clock in the morning.

They were welcomed by the rulers of Spain and Portugal and Julia was a great conversational help to Grant, who became doubly reserved in face of linguistic difficulties. In Madrid James Russell Lowell, the American Minister, thought her self-possession inimitable at a royal function when she kept up a running fire of conversation, smiling and bowing, as she sat between two guests with whom she could not exchange a single intelligible word. Lowell thought this curious show the ultimate in courtesy.

But Julia moved around with skill in conversational encounters and did not let language barriers defeat her. She now talked fluently, if not always soundly, on public affairs and turned readily from discussing domestic matters and fashions with queens and princesses to sturdy war talk with Bismarck, shipping with King Leopold, music with the Duke of Wellington, or Shakespeare with the King of Portugal, who was engaged at the time in doing a translation of the dramatist's works. Between interpreters and her own animated intervention Julia impressed her entourage with her usefulness in this field. The General could be deathly still unless he had a strong opinion he wished to voice, or the subject under discussion was one on which he was well informed. He had no small talk.

Back in France, the Grants visited Pau, and the General, pondering on what he had seen, wrote to General Beale from there: "The fact is we are the most progressive, freest and richest people on earth, but don't know it or appreciate it." Mrs. Lincoln was in Pau while they were there, a wretched exile, forgotten except for her eccentricities. Julia later maintained that she was unaware of her proximity or she would have visited her.

By this time the Grants had decided to prolong their travels and see the Orient. Julia in particular urged that they take this route home. Fred and Mr. Borie had now joined them. They revisited Egypt but this time without pomp or circumstance, and on January 1, 1879, they sailed from Suez for India on the Venetia, a Pacific and Orient passenger steamer.

All her life Julia would remember the singing birds of Agra at dawn and the Taj Mahal with the gardener there adorning her with roses. At Benares they moved uneasily among the holy men and pilgrims. At the Palace of Amber the Maharaja of Jaipur entertained them in a hall lighted with tall torches. He showed them his stables and his dancing girls. He decorated Julia with a gold and silken cord and sprinkled some attar of roses on her handkerchief, the symbol of friendship. Grant did not wish to go on a tiger hunt in Jaipur but Fred went out with a pig-sticking expedition.

They were all exhausted from the heat and the discomforts of their railroad traveling by the time they reached Delhi and were shown the ruins of Lucknow. Young thought that Julia had stood the journey well and "justifies the reputation for endurance and energy which she won on the Nile." But she became seriously ill in Lucknow. When she was out of danger Borie wrote facetiously to his wife about their travels in India. He and the worldly John Russell Young surrounded Mrs. Grant with a light spray of raillery, focused sometimes on her piety and her determination that they should read religious books to her. Julia could always laugh at herself as well as at others, and Fred and General Grant shared in these jokes at her expense, although none was irreligious in spirit. As they journeyed across India by train Borie took note of General Grant, Fred, Dr. John M. Keating and the Maharaja of Jaipur playing Boston, a simplified version of solo whist, in one corner of the car, while Young and Borie sat with Julia in another, reading Richard Baxter's Saints' Everlasting Rest to her.

While recovering from her illness Mrs. Grant cheerfully entertained them all by mapping out a fantastic will. "The scene was most affecting," Borie wrote blithely to his wife, adding:

She gives three millions of dollars to a fund for supplying the Hindoo gentlemen with warm clothing, four millions to be spent on necklaces, earrings, ice-cream knives, samite-chuddahs and umbrella-handles for her friends at home. She leaves eleven millions to the General in the event of his marrying again within three months after her departure. If he does not, then the money is to go to Mr. Childs to purchase larger type for the Ledger. The remainder of her fortune she leaves to Mr. Young. Bella she leaves to the Colonel — allowing him $117 a year for her support. But happily Mrs. Grant has recovered.

In this same letter Borie wrote that Fred could make his mother believe virtually anything, even that cloves, chewed after a drink of brandy, were good for the complexion. They all found her trusting, credulous and affectionate in her ways. Borie was traveling chiefly for his health and he and Julia were allies in many small matters involving their daily plans. Both preferred the sedan chair to the elephant's howdah after giving the more lordly method a brief trial. Julia was pleased to have an expert shopping ally in the wealthy Mr. Borie. Wherever they went he might be found sitting with a swarm of peddlers around him, calmly inspecting jewels, silks, ivory, brass, and chaffering relentlessly. Grant wrote reassuringly to Mrs. Borie that her husband was enjoying the trip greatly, "though I think he would be rather glad to avoid the swallow-tail and white cravat at dinner occasionally."

At Calcutta they were entertained in royal fashion by the Viceroy, Lord Lytton, whom Julia knew also as the writer Owen Meredith. The state banquet was memorable for the magnificent costumes and jewels of the maharajas. But by this time even Grant was wilting from the heat and they all welcomed the cool sea trip across the Bay of Bengal. They slept on deck and watched the sun rise. The General had long talks at sea with Young, while Julia sat nearby, fanning herself and occasionally throwing in an interpolation. When these interviews appeared in the New York Herald they caused a sensation, since Grant talked with uncommon candor of the war, of the generals on both sides, of his terms in the White House, of the political scene in Europe. His afterviews of the war were fresh and challenging. His comments on European politics brought repercussions.

"I am both homesick and dread going home," he wrote to the Cramers from Singapore on April 4, 1879. "I have no home, but must establish one after I get back. I do not know where."

A great storm blew up as they sailed from Singapore on the fourteenth anniversary of the surrender of Lee, and they all talked of this event. Grant bivouacked by the wheel that night. Julia stayed on deck as long as she could, then deserted her blankets, shawls and cushions and went below. Their visit to Siam was dizzying in its novelty. Julia and Borie came close to drowning when their boat almost capsized as they were trying to board the royal yacht in a great storm. "We complimented Mrs. Grant upon her calmness and fortitude at a time when it seemed inevitable that she would be plunged into the sea under the moving paddle of a steamer," Young reported.

Fred now supplied the uniformed dash that his father avoided and Julia wore yellow satin at the state dinner given them by the King of Siam. The Celestial Prince escorted her into the dining room with a flourish of trumpets and two bands played Siamese and European music alternately. Julia conversed with the Queen in an inner room, since his consort could not sit with the King. She left Siam with memories of an elephant review held under black clouds, the royal wats flashing brilliant colors and strange angles, and the people bustling over unidentifiable tasks. Grant and the King of Siam engaged in correspondence after this meeting. Wherever the General went in the Orient he was consulted about political affairs.

Hong Kong was a shopping paradise for Julia, but sailing up to Shanghai their vessel rolled so badly that "Mrs. Grant arose and prayed and so saved the vessel," Young wrote to Borie, who had left the party by this time and had returned to the United States. "We did not know until the next morning that the ship had been in danger, or that Mrs. Grant had saved it. I am afraid that while the prayers were going on in the cabin, there was an exciting game of Boston going on in the ward-room." In this same letter

Young observed: "It looks like the General again for President. I am sorry."

Canton left an unforgettable picture of densely packed crowds, silent and staring. At Tientsin they met Viceroy Li Hung-chang, the Bismarck of the East. He and Grant had long political discussions. They were the same age. Their victories synchronized, and they had much in common as warriors. During this visit the Viceroy's wife gave Julia the most extraordinary party in her vast experience. She broke all precedent by inviting the women of the American colony to the dinner given in Mrs. Grant's honor. Most of them had never even seen her. They were uncertain how to dress and Julia consulted the General. He jestingly urged her to go easy, lest the question have some bearing on the future domestic peace of the Viceroy. In the end Julia advised all the guests to wear their best attire — French models and jewels if they had them. They had considered simple effects but gladly chose sophistication.

The dinner was served in European style with French china and English silver. Chopsticks were in evidence, too. The American women politely tried to use them but soon gave up. The Viceroy's wife wore brown velvet brocade trousers and tunic encrusted with pearls and jade. The back of her head was entirely covered with small jade butterflies. Through an interpreter she asked them all how old they were, how many children they had, what their husbands did, how long they had been married, how many servants they kept. Then, to show her interest in them, she chose to examine their jewelry at close range. They stripped off their earrings and bracelets and passed them around. The young girls of the household, wearing gorgeous tunics, had long gold fingernails and tinkled as they moved.

After dinner a pantomime was staged, followed by decorous dancing. Some of the Chinese women sang Christian hymns. One did a Tyrolean yodel. A crowd watched these strange proceedings from outdoors and the Viceroy could be seen peering over their heads to see how the ladies were enjoying themselves. When observed he withdrew. The party was an experiment that opened the way for freer social interchange in China.

Julia found Japan fascinating in a different way. Jushie Yoshida, the Japanese Minister in Washington, had been brought home to manage the entertainment of the Grants. Madame Yoshida was a particular friend to Julia, who had always considered the Japanese lady the most decorative figure at her receptions, and charming to boot. General Grant planted memorial trees in Nagasaki. They were entertained in the style of the feudal lords of Japan in an old temple in the heart of the city. A plum tree in full blossom was placed before Julia. Their days were a perpetual pageant of fireworks, plays, crowds and colored lanterns. They failed to see Fujiyama because of the clouds. They sailed through the Inland Sea but made no landing because of a cholera epidemic. They passed some days at Nikko in the quarters of the priests, enjoying the mountain scenery, visiting the waterfalls, strolling around the temple.

Ito, Saito, Inouye and Iwakura, the latter an old friend of Grant's, all were on the scene, and Prince Dati made them welcome to Tokyo. They were quartered at the summer palace of Enriokwan, an island home with romantic grounds. Julia wrote to Nellie that she did nothing, when alone, but wander around and admire the lovely things in view. The grounds had all the traditional elements of the Japanese garden — grottoes, arched bridges, small lakes and flowering shrubs. The house itself was filled with treasures. Merchants came from the bazaars to display their wares for her benefit. Fred had chosen several gowns for Ida and Mrs. Sheridan, Julia wrote, and she was getting some for Nellie. She had sables for her daughter, too.

On July 4 the Emperor gave a state dinner for the Grants. While Julia sat on a sofa beside him she rubbed her hand over the smooth lacquer arm and remarked on the beauty of the finish. On her return to America the entire set, sofa and chairs, was sent to her as a gift. She used them always in her sitting room a superb assemblage with gilded chrysanthemums set in black lacquer. They supplied her with a conversational theme on many occasions and always brought back a picture of the Mikado.

Four days after this dinner the Emperor and Grant together reviewed the army, an event that had no precedent in Japanese history. The Mikado arrived with a flourish of trumpets. Drivers in scarlet livery sat on the box of the royal coach. Its panels were decorated with the imperial flower, the chrysanthemum. Before they left the country a great festival was held in Ueno Park for the Grants. The Japanese could do no more than they had done to honor the visiting American General. He had held a number of discussions with political figures but had not established the same warm relations as with Li Hung-chang.

Julia, as usual, observed the missions and she and Ulysses toured the military and naval schools in Tokyo, as well as colleges and normal schools. By this time she was insistent on getting home. The General wished to visit Australia and not return to America until spring. "But when mother longed for home the tour was over," Jesse commented. When they put in at Hong Kong they received a telegram from Buck saying: "Rumor Nellie's death untrue." The elder Mrs. Sartoris had died in England. Since they had not heard the rumor they were spared this anxiety.

After that they steamed across the Pacific through a smooth sea. Julia lay in her deck chair and thought eagerly of home. She had seen so much in these two years that the images were confused at the moment. The world would never look the same to her again. Others had toured the globe but none had done it so exhaustively or been so royally received at every point as the Grants. As Badeau summed it up: "No other man was ever received by both peoples and sovereigns, by savants and merchants, by Presidents and Governors-General, by Tycoons and Sultans and Khedives, and school children and work-people and statesmen, like Grant."

And Julia had shared in it all, except for the few occasions when the presence of a woman would have violated etiquette. Beyond doubt it had been a happy interlude in Grant's life. He now had a more expansive view of the world, a sense of international fellowship that he saw might be an asset in the White House. The man who had left California in 1854, penniless and under a cloud, to return to his wife in St. Louis, arrived in San Francisco on a September day in 1879 to such tumult and shouts as the youthful city had never known. This time Julia stood by his side, their two-year Odyssey ended, their prospects bright at the moment.

Buck was the first to greet them on their arrival. "Princely. . . . Old World Splendor Eclipsed," said the San Francisco Daily Evening Post of their welcome. "I cannot venture in the streets except in a carriage for the mob of good-natured and enthusiastic friends, old and young," Grant wrote to Borie on September 28, 1879. Senator William Sharon, D. O. Mills, J. C. Flood and other newmade millionaires were their hosts. The Sharon party at Belmont was discussed across the country. The Grants journeyed to Yosemite and took long drives through the Sierras. They toured Oregon and Nevada. The mines and mills were decorated for their coming, and cheering crowds awaited them in Virginia City and elsewhere. At Leadville, where Buck had mining interests, Julia donned a miner's outfit and went down in the tunnel.

Hannah read of these events with her customary detachment. While the uproar was still going on, she wrote to Childs in her careful script: "I hope my son will ever so act during the remainder of his life as to command the respect of the people and win the love of all of his acquaintances."

Fred and Ida, with their small daughter, Julia, joined the elder Grants at Omaha. From there they journeyed to Chicago, with demonstrations all along the way. Their welcome home reached its climax when the veterans of the Army of the Tennessee, led by General Sherman, gave Grant a thunderous reception at the Palmer House. A great parade, with floats and banners bearing the names of his battles, brought Chicago traffic to a standstill. Once again Julia saw General Sheridan ride past in full command, this time as Chief Marshal.

Galena again claimed its soldier son with jubilation, and Julia and Ulysses were glad at last to close the door on crowds and settle briefly in their house on the hill. Everywhere the impression spread that this was a monster build-up for Grant as a presidential nominee. His backers had done much to stir up the excitement but his popularity with the public was real. If the world at large thought so much of Grant, why not his compatriots? It was promotion on a massive scale and Julia's hopes were high again for another term in the White House.

By January 1880 they were touring the South and she was watching anxiously for favorable reactions while Grant was insisting that it was a matter of "supreme indifference" to him whether or not he was nominated. But while saying that he did not seek another term he left the door ajar, and Julia was openly advocating his cause. That winter they visited Cuba and Mexico, where the General showed her some of the battlefields linked to their courtship days. They were back in Galena when the Republican National Convention was held in Chicago in June 1880, and James A. Garfield was nominated. Conkling, Cameron, Logan and Washburne had pushed to the last ditch for Grant, and he therefore found himself in the situation he had most wished to avoid. He had made it clear to Washburne that his name should go in only if the party seemed overwhelmingly for him, and it was to be quickly withdrawn if serious opposition arose. Their close friendship ended after this, although he showed no feeling when the news reached him in Galena.

Grant learned of his fate in William R. Rowley's office. He lighted a cigar, slipped out a side door, leaned against the old-fashioned hitching post and after a few moments of thought tossed away his cigar, returned to his waiting friends and quietly said: "I can't say that I regret my own defeat. By it I shall escape four years of hard work and four years of abuse, and gentlemen, we can all support the candidate."

Julia was stricken until her customary optimism reasserted itself. She had not believed it possible that his party would reject Ulysses. He gave Garfield campaign support and they went to New Mexico and Colorado later that summer but she spent most of the time resting — a most unusual procedure for her. She was exhausted, disappointed, and uncertain about the future. They had little money, no home but the house in Galena, and once again Ulysses was looking for a job.

It was all a great blow to his pride and no one doubted that Julia had counted on his nomination. But Grant wrote philosophically to Nellie on June 27, 1880: "I felt no disappointment at the result of the Chicago Convention. In fact I felt much relieved. . . . Had I been nominated there would have been the most violent campaign ever known in our country made against me. This I have avoided."

The Grants were back in Washington in December 1880 for the first time since they had left the capital. As their train came in the chimes of the Metropolitan Church rang out "Home Again." A salute of seventeen guns was fired. Congress adjourned when the General visited the Capitol. President Hayes gave a dinner in their honor and Julia watched Lucy Hayes with her bright good looks and cheerful manner presiding with great assurance, although her husband's sun was setting.

It was only a matter of months until Garfield was dead and Chester Arthur had moved smoothly into office. His first state dinner was given in honor of General and Mrs. Grant. Julia wore a white satin dress with a long train closely flounced with lace, and her most impressive diamonds. Again she found it a strange experience to sit at the familiar table and study the plateau mirror centerpiece, and the gilt epergnes overflowing with Marechal Niel roses. Fourteen courses were served and eight wines, a change from the Hayes' regime. The Van Buren silver had been given a new plating of gold. There were many sophisticated touches, for President Arthur was fastidious, a scholar, an epicure, an expert in significant detail. All deferred to the General, but Julia knew that the curtain had fallen for him in Washington. They were finished with Galena, too. The moment had come for them to start another cycle — and this time it would be in New York.

CHAPTER XIV: A MANSION OFF FIFTH AVENUE

THE GRANTS had a brief period of affluence in the early 1880s when the General became a nominal partner in the firm of Grant & Ward on Wall Street. Buck had gone into partnership with Ferdinand Ward and James D. Fish in 1880 and was doing so well that two years later he invited his father to join them. Accompanied by his old friend, Matias Romero, the General had made two unsuccessful trips to Mexico, hoping to promote railroad, commercial and mining interests between the United States and the country south of it that he had come to love.

But his future was uncertain, his course vague, when he settled down to work among the millionaires who had long been his friends. He paid daily calls at the office during the winter months, but rarely made the trip in to town once his family had moved to Long Branch for the summer. His working links with the house were little more than nominal but his name gave it prestige. For the first time in his life he felt that he was providing financial security for his family. After crossing the continent in the summer of 1883 to watch the golden spike being driven that symbolized the completion of the Northern Pacific Railroad he wrote to Nellie: "As a family we are much better off than ever we were before. The necessity for a strict economy does not exist, or is not so pressing as it has hitherto been." A month later he sounded even more confident when he wrote: "The family are enjoying as much prosperity as we ought to expect."

Practically penniless when they returned from their trip around the world, and with nothing in prospect after the presidential nomination fiasco, a group of twenty friends — including Childs, Drexel, Hamilton Fish and J. P. Morgan — had raised a fund of $100,000 to be invested for the General's benefit. In the meantime George W. Jones, editor of the New York Times, had raised a separate large sum. The $100,000 was then used for the purchase of a house for the Grants. Julia soon was established in a four-story mansion with bay windows at 3 East Sixty-sixth Street, and was enjoying the metropolitan life of the 1880s. On top of this her husband and Buck were prospering in a most unexpected way.

The city was growing fast. The tide of fashion had swept uptown from lower Fifth Avenue. Four4n-hands, tandems and dogcarts had replaced the trotters and pacers so popular in the 1870s. Bustles and flounces, flowered and feathered hats were in fashion. Julia enjoyed being close to Central Park. She responded readily to the carnival touch of early spring tulips and hyacinths on display, children rolling hoops, lights beaming softly through leafing trees and the soft roll of carriages. The Metropolitan Museum and the American Museum of Natural History were new and diverting. Delmonico's had moved north to Twenty-sixth Street and drew a sophisticated following. Men's clubs flourished and Grant was feted at the Union League Club in 1880 at one of the most notable functions in its history. A great tide of immigrants was flowing into the country and the population had reached a total of two million by the time Brooklyn Bridge opened in 1883.

Old friends now surrounded Julia, and her children were established and doing well. Ida and Fred, with small Julia and Ulysses, lived in Morristown, New Jersey, and were "as happy as clams at high tide, have a great deal of company and ... are very popular," Grant wrote to Nellie. Buck had married Fannie Chaffee, daughter of Jerome B. Chaffee, a Colorado Senator and millionaire, who had invested heavily in Grant & Ward. They lived on West End Avenue and owned Merryweather Farm, a country estate near Salem Center in Westchester County. Both Julia and Grant, inveterate farmers at heart, took great interest in this choice spot. Jesse, who had mining interests, had married Elizabeth Chapman of Minneapolis and their daughter, Nellie, was born at Long Branch in 1881, in the same year as Fred's son, Ulysses. Elizabeth had auburn hair and large beautiful eyes and Grant wrote to Nellie that some thought her "quite pretty," as well as being amiable.

Ida by this time was a universal favorite, a charming young matron who was like a second daughter to Julia. Her sister, Mrs. Potter Palmer, had become one of the best known women in the country and often visited the Grants. By 1883 Nellie had three children — Algernon Edward, aged six; Vivian May, aged four, and Rosemary Alice, aged three. Nellie and Algy brought their children to America nearly every year, to stay with their grandparents either in New York or Long Branch.

Julia was extravagantly happy to have a fresh batch of small children around her. She spoiled them all and told them to appeal to her if their parents or nurses denied them what they wished. They frequently took her at her word, and Grandmama was always surrounded by small fry, who helped her to dress, buttoned her boots, borrowed her ribbons and snapped open the small gold locket she wore at her wrist to look at the daguerreotype it contained of Grandpapa as a young lieutenant. They all liked to drive downtown with her to shop.

"The fact is that Ma and I are very proud of our grandchildren," the General wrote to Nellie from Long Branch in July 1883.

Other relatives came and went. Julia's sisters, Nellie and Emma, still visited her, bringing with them memories of the early days at White Haven. Grant's widowed sisters and nieces were always welcome. But in 1883 Hannah, who would never visit Julia, died in Jersey City. After Jesse's death she lived with the Corbins in Elizabeth, New Jersey, until Abel's death in 1879. Then she settled in Jersey City with her widowed daughter. Grant visited her at times and went to church with her but his wife and mother saw little of each other in their later years. However, Julia was still the family focus, the hospitable matriarch to whom they all turned for Christmas and other celebrations.

She became an acknowledged dowager whose carriage often was recognized although she was instinctively unobtrusive. She rode down Fifth Avenue in a landau behind Major and General, two staid horses for a Grant to own, and often she had little Julia Grant at her side. She was using the magnificent silks she had brought from the Orient to dress herself and her family. She was now in her late fifties and her hair was noticeably touched with gray. She had a matronly look and paid more attention to rich materials than to fashionable cut in choosing her wardrobe, although Ida and Nellie were chic to the last degree. She often called on Mrs. Fish at 251 East Seventeenth Street, her New York home, or visited her up the Hudson at Glenclyffe. They played bezique together and Grant jested with Fish about his agricultural operations. Julia admired his wonderful roses. "I do not think that we weary either of the other," Fish wrote of his wife in 1879. And thus it was with the Grants.

"I have never seen a case of greater domestic happiness than existed in the Grant family," said Childs of them. "Perfect love had indeed cast out all fear ... for his family, he had the most supreme love and tenderness."

Everyone knew the General from the moment he stepped out of his front door in the morning. He was now in his early sixties, and his shoulders seemed more rounded than ever. His eyes sometimes had the look of steel, sometimes the flash of blue fire that went with it. He wore frock coats of excellent cloth and a tall hat. He always looked grave and meditative, even when he was returning salutes in the street. To the public he was doubly interesting, as a former President and a great General. He was unmistakably General Grant.

Their town house was a storehouse of treasures. It held the gifts they had received on their travels. One of Julia's prized possessions was a gold lacquer cabinet eleven hundred years old given them by the Mikado. The black lacquer furniture in her sitting room had been his own set. Teakwood cabinets, jade and porcelain from Li Hung-chang, cloisonne from Japan, malachite and enamels from Russia, golden and jeweled caskets with scrolls symbolizing the freedom of various cities, and the medals, swords and souvenirs of Grant's military life gave character to their home. The General sometimes lifted his small grandson to his shoulders and carried him around the rooms, showing him his trophies and explaining what each one meant. The library, in which he spent much time, was finished in Venetian red. Its books were the gift of the city of Boston, a valuable collection of carefully selected volumes. Persian and Turkish rugs and a Bengal tiger skin covered Julia's floors.

She had a long visiting list of well-known people and was deferred to wherever she went. During this period of apparent prosperity the old White House links brought her visitors from various parts of the country. She held receptions, and tea in her sitting room was always a festive affair. Ulysses often went out in the evening without her. He was sought out by men of prominence and he had cronies with whom he liked to play cards and talk horses. He was a familiar figure at the men's clubs and Julia was always glad to see him surrounded by congenial companions.

Both of the Grants enjoyed the theater and they were often invited to opening nights. William Florence was a personal friend of the General's and they sometimes went to see him play. When the General walked in on an Edward Harrigan show with a party of ten, the audience rose and cheered and the orchestra played the national anthem. Grant had learned to take these ovations in an impassive, subdued way, but Julia could never conceal her pleasure when the General was recognized. She bowed and smiled and enjoyed any side allusions made to him in a play.

But opera was another story. Ulysses flatly refused to accept the numerous invitations they had to attend the Metropolitan. On one occasion when Roscoe Conkling was dining with them Julia announced that they were going to the opera that night. A poker game had been arranged by the General. Conkling caught the appeal in his eyes and volunteered to take

Mrs. Grant. This worked out happily, since he was one of her favorite companions, never failing in his devotion to Grant.

When they went to Washington, as they frequently did at this time, they always stayed with General Beale in the Decatur House built by Latrobe in 1819. Here Henry Clay, Martin Van Buren, John Quincy Adams, Edward Livingston, Judah Benjamin and Howell Cobb had lived at one time or another. Mrs. Beale and Julia were most harmonious and General Beale was a horse fancier who liked to take Grant out to his farm. Their daughter, Emily, a favorite of Julia's, had recently married John R. McLean of Cincinnati. Their oldest daughter was the wife of George Bakhmeteff, who was at the Russian Legation in Vienna. When she came to Washington she was regarded as a striking sight, walking about with a massive Hungarian boarhound.

But the Grants were unable to accept the Beales' invitation to visit them at the end of 1883, for the General had fallen on the sidewalk on Christmas Eve just as he stepped from his carriage at his own front door. One leg was severely injured and he was laid up for weeks. After that he had to walk on crutches and he suffered from neuralgic pains. He never wholly recovered from this injury and limped for the few remaining months of his life.

He was still not at his best when Ward called to see him early in May 1884, and told him that the Marine Bank of Brooklyn, with which Fish was associated, was in difficulties. Special demands had been made on it and they needed $150,000 for twenty-four hours to tide them over. Otherwise the bank, which handled the Grant & Ward accounts, would fail. Ward asked Grant if he could raise this sum, while he tried to find a matching amount.

The General went straight to the newly finished mansion of his friend, William H. Vanderbilt, at 640 Fifth Avenue and asked him if he would lend him $150,000 for one day. He explained the circumstances. It was a Sunday morning but Ward had impressed the General with his urgency.

"I gave him my check without question, not because the transaction was businesslike, but simply because the request came from General Grant," Vanderbilt later wrote to Julia.

The check was turned over to Ward, who promptly absconded, leaving the Grants to face fresh disaster. The General drove down to Wall Street behind his black horses on Tuesday, to find Buck waiting white-faced for him and Fred. He told them blankly that the firm had failed. There was no record of the Vanderbilt check. It had not been deposited in the Marine Bank. Only a few securities remained in the safe.

Ward, a handsome and persuasive swindler, had used the General's name for his own ends and Grant, characteristically, had trusted him until it was too late. Julia had never been wholly persuaded that Ward was the great financier her husband thought him to be, but her faith in Ulysses' judgment was unshakable. Some of Grant's more conservative business friends had shown concern over the rapidly mounting fortunes of the firm, and Sheridan was dismayed to see the great soldier "sitting around Wall Street discussing investments and debentures." The General had become used to the company of millionaires.

Once again he was faced with a major crisis and his name was back in the headlines. The whole country learned within forty-eight hours that Grant had crashed on Wall Street. They were literally penniless and Julia did not even have means to buy bread and butter until their old friend Romero, the Mexican Ambassador, called when news of the crisis reached him. He offered Grant funds. The General said he would consult his wife. When he left the room Romero slipped away and on his return the General found a check for a thousand dollars on the table. A stranger, Charles Wood, of Lansingburg, New York, sent him another check for the same amount with a note calling it a "loan on account of my share for services ending in April 1865."

Grant's sons, his widowed sisters, his wife, his nieces, Senator Chaffee, and a number of friends were involved as well as the general public. He had hoped it would mean a bonanza for them all. As always, when an emergency arose, Julia's spine stiffened. She held much of the real estate in the family and with Ulysses she decided that all their assets must be offered at once to Vanderbilt. This was a personal obligation that had to be met.

Vanderbilt received the General sympathetically on his second visit, saying that the whole country felt for him in his fresh misfortune. He would gladly have canceled the debt but Grant insisted on turning over everything he owned to meet an obligation "which I so justly owe you." Within the next few days he and Julia sent him the deeds to their joint properties and offered him their household treasures from far and near, and the swords, medals and souvenirs of the General's war years. They had property in Washington, Philadelphia, Galena and St. Louis. The house they occupied was in Julia's name and Grant had given her he Long Branch cottage while he was President.

Vanderbilt returned the deeds, then left for Europe. But the General and Julia gave his lawyers the mortgages on their real estate, and securities to their treasures which they thought equated the $150,000 due. When Vanderbilt came back he sought to wipe out the obligation in one sweep, providing only that the war relics, which he would deed back to Mrs. Grant, should eventually be turned over to the Government as a national trust. Grant replied for Julia, to whom the Vanderbilt letter was addressed. She felt she could not accept his generosity in toto, the General wrote, although she concurred with pleasure in the gift to the Government. "In this matter you have anticipated the disposition which I had contemplated making of the articles."

Vanderbilt would not accept this rejection. He proposed that as money came in from the sale of the real estate a trust should be set up for Mrs. Grant. The General promptly replied that his "generous determination compels us to no longer resist," but Julia evidently thought differently, for a few hours later, she sent a contradictory note to Vanderbilt: "Upon reading your letter of this afternoon General Grant and myself felt that it would be ungracious to refuse your princely and generous offer. Hence his note to you. But upon reflection I find that I cannot, I will not, accept your munificence in any form. I beg that you will pardon this apparent vacillation and consider this answer definite and final."

Julia proudly decided to turn over the war relics to the Smithsonian Institution immediately. Early in February 1885, President Arthur sent a message to Congress, drawing attention to her gift. He wrote of the "high sense of public regard which animates Mrs. Grant." Fred and Buck carried the relics into the first floor parlor for her inspection as the dray waited outside to take them away. A visitor found her profoundly saddened as these mementos passed in review before her. Fifteen buttons she had cut from Ulysses' coat after various battles. His shoulder straps from the coats worn as he besieged Richmond and St. Petersburg. A gold model of the table in the McLean house on which the surrender terms were signed. Canes, swords, uniforms, medals. A priceless collection of Japanese coins. Elephant tusks from the King of Siam. A Coptic Bible taken by Lord Napier from King Theodore of Abyssinia. The gold pen the General used in writing many of his orders. A gold medal from Congress for the opening of the Mississippi, and many other items. Julia watched with blurred eyes as Fred and Buck handed them over to be carted away.

Eventually Ward and Fish were brought to account and sent to jail. The General gave testimony from his bedroom. The Grants were completely exonerated. Ward's villainy was exposed in court and the public saw that the General once again had been a trusting dupe. Mark Twain said of him at this time: "He was the most simple-hearted of all men." But the humiliation was extreme. Fred, who had invested nearly all his money in the firm, rented his Morristown home and moved in with his parents. Grant wrote sadly of the family ruin to his sister Virginia, and to his niece Clara V. Cramer, calling it the "most stupendous fraud ever perpetrated" but he promised that he and Fred would try to keep them from harm.

There were no more luxuries, no more fast horses. Food was plain and the Grants no longer went to town from Long Branch. Julia expressed herself bluntly on the subject of Ward and Fish. The General gazed out to sea and wondered what to do next, a question answered when Robert Underwood Johnson arrived on a June day to ask if he would write some articles on the war for the Century. Before he would discuss the matter he spoke with extreme bitterness of Ward and Fish and the swindle they had perpetrated. He said they had traded on his reputation in enlisting the funds of others. He seemed like a "wounded lion" to Johnson as he sought to exculpate himself. He was particularly incensed over the fact that Ward had even taken a hoard of twenty-dollar gold pieces, his tokens for directors' meetings, which Julia had kept in a vase on the mantlepiece.

The Century editors had made overtures to Grant before the crash but he now had a compelling motive to write. It was agreed that he should do four articles on his most famous battles at five hundred dollars apiece. "They were undertaken simply to keep the wolf from the door," Johnson observed. The original sum was voluntarily doubled later on.

Julia and Ida were much relieved to see the moping General go to work. A white deal kitchen table was set up in a room looking out on the vine-clad porch and this became his office. It held his books, papers and maps. Fred, Badeau and General Porter helped him to check facts and dates, Julia often came in and sat in a wicker armchair, watching Ulysses pore over army maps in the old preoccupied way. He worked swiftly and determinedly but his first article on Shiloh read like an official battle report. Johnson visited him again and drew him out with questions. He showed him what was needed. Then the General pounded on with a style of his own — clear, effective, dramatic. The articles were a success and the Century circulation leaped by fifty thousand. When his family found that he was writing of Vicksburg without giving any indication that he had been there they protested and had him revise his text.

Meanwhile, the family life went on around him. Julia did her best to keep the children from disturbing Grandpapa but he always stopped to pet and kiss small Julia when she came in view. At times he played cat's cradle with her, or pinched her ear or cheek and said softly "Juliana Johnson, don't you cry." Many years later she recalled that he had a "charming, gentle way of acting always."

Her small granddaughter observed how popular Grandmama was with the important looking men who visited them at Long Branch. She was too young to remember the visit of Oscar Wilde and Sam Ward in the summer of 1882 but in 1884, while the General was writing about Shiloh, George M. Pullman, Cyrus W. Field, Childs, Drexel and Russell Sage, another horse lover, gathered around her on the piazza and she conversed brightly with them all while Grandpapa remained comparatively silent.

When he spoke it was to the point but he always watched Grandmama affectionately to see what she was up to, and small Julia noticed that she was "cute with him," and always got her way. They were inseparable and had periods of contented silence. She never fussed about small things or became cross with the family, and she said the sort of funny thing that seemed to amuse the General. She ran the house and was not dependent on anyone for help or advice.

The children had their own garden patches at Long Branch where they grew flowers and vegetables. Young Ulysses had planted a melon vine in his patch. Every time he told Grandmama that a flower had bloomed on the vine, he found a watermelon or canteloupe in its place by morning. His miraculous vine became a family tradition. Grandmama kept a little box or jar with cookies, prunes, apples, peppermints, and other treats on hand for the children. Small Julia recalled her as an "enchanting companion," who recited poetry, told excellent stories, and was a "human, sunny friend and a sympathizer to little people."

The articles proceeded so well that by autumn the Century editors proposed that Grant expand them into a book. He had many scruples. He did not wish to compete with Badeau or Young, whose books about him had recently been published. Nor did he consider himself a writer. Others had badgered him for his memoirs. While still with Grant & Ward he had refused Mark Twain's overtures over a luncheon of bacon and beans near his Wall Street office. And Charles L. Webster, who published Mark Twain's books by subscription, had asked him in 1881 if he would write his memoirs. But things had changed. He was now in desperate need of money to provide for his family. Sherman had told him of the twenty-five thousand dollars that he had received for his Memoirs. Moreover, he was finding diversion in going over the old battlegrounds. "Why, I am positively enjoying the work," he wrote. "I am keeping at it every day and night, and Sundays."

Mark Twain got wind of the proposed book when he heard Richard Watson Gilder discussing it as they came out of Chickering Hall in November 1884. He had known Grant since 1866 and had high regard for him. He called to see him next day and learned that the General had at last come around to writing his memoirs. He asked to see his contract, which called for the author's usual ten per cent royalty. It had not yet been signed. Twain called it absurd and came up with a proposal of his own. He drew out his checkbook and offered to give Grant a twenty-five-thousand-dollar advance on the first volume and the same amount for any subsequent volume. He proposed a twenty per cent royalty on the subscription list price or seventy per cent on the actual net returns.

Grant hesitated. He felt loyal to the Century editors. Fred leaned to the new proposal. They consulted Childs, who studied the set-up of the American Company at Hartford — Webster's firm — and pronounced it sound. But Grant had qualms over Mark Twain's lavish proposal, thinking the publishers might lose money, which they did in the long run. He had no great expectations for his book and feared that they might suffer a heavy loss.

But the contract was signed, insuring Grant seventy per cent on the net returns. The two-volume set in cloth binding sold for nine dollars. Two thousand sets in calf were issued at twenty-five dollars a set. When he signed the contract, Grant received a nominal sum to cover immediate expenses instead of the twenty-five thousand dollars offered by Mark Twain. He divided the money at once among Julia and his children, but in February 1886, nearly a year after his death, she received a first royalty check for two hundred thousand dollars, which is on display today at The Players in New York. Her second royalty check was for one hundred and fifty thousand dollars.

Interest in Grant's book was intensified by the macabre circumstance that the world soon knew he was a dying man. He had always liked to nibble at fruit, and he had just bitten into a peach one day early in June, soon after the collapse of his firm, when he got up from the table and walked about in acute pain. His discomfort persisted, particularly when he ate anything acid. A few days later while he and Julia were sitting on Childs' porch Grant commented again on his sore throat. He coughed considerably and was persuaded to let Dr. Da Costa of Philadelphia, who was visiting their host at the moment, have a look at his throat. He was promptly referred to Dr. Fordyce Barker, his own physician in New York. Dr. Barker was leaving for Europe and turned him over to Dr. John Hancock Douglas, the leading throat specialist in the city, and an old army man who had been with the Sanitary Commission and had attended Rawlins. But Grant slid along for nearly four months, not paying much attention to his condition. It was late October and they were back in their town house before pain finally drove him to Dr. Douglas with Dr. Barker's card. The specialist immediately suspected "serious epithelial trouble" and Grant asked him bluntly if it were cancer. Remembering that he was a soldier, who would demand the truth, Dr. Douglas gave him a qualified reply.

Treatment began next day. Grant tried to conceal his fears from Julia but she and Fred soon called on Dr. Douglas, who talked to them as optimistically as possible of a "complaint with a cancerous tendency" and told them what must be done. Julia refused to take the fatalistic point of view. She kept her composure and went on believing for several months that Ulysses would recover. "Her behavior was a mystery and a wonder to those who knew the depth of the tenderness and the abundance of the affection that she lavished on her great husband," Badeau observed. "Her calmness and self-control almost seemed coldness, only we knew that this was impossible."

The General seemed to improve with local treatments and he and Julia zealously carried out all the medical orders. Dr. George F. Shrady was associate physician with Dr. Barker and the consultants were Dr. T. M. Markoe and Dr. H. B. Sands. Grant went regularly to the physician's house for his treatments at this time. It was two miles away and he insisted on taking the street car to save cab fare. By December his pains were so excruciating that he finally compromised and drove instead. Except for the children the carefree spirit had gone from the menage. The Fred Grants occupied the top floor of the house and little Julia and Ulysses came running downstairs to play in the park, to dine with their grandparents, to sit in Grandmama's parlor at the end of the day. As always, the General liked to see them, but by degrees they were warned to keep quiet and not to disturb him without permission. Small Julia noticed that her grandmother sometimes smoothed out his frown in passing with her "tiny, beautiful hand." Not only was he ill but the family were harassed by debts.

On November 18 he wrote to Nellie that he had had a sore throat for more than four months and had just had three teeth pulled. He thought the doctor was making "fair progress" with his throat. A month later he refused an offer by Cyrus W. Field to raise funds for him. Some of his more intimate friends felt that he was exerting himself beyond his strength on his book. There were two schools of thought about this. Small Julia would hear one person say: "The book is killing him." Another would think differently and remark: "No, the book is keeping him alive; without it he would already be dead." Just before Christmas he wrote to General Beale that it was nearly impossible for him to swallow enough to sustain life and it pained him even to talk.

Julia ran the household, helped by Ida, but increasingly she stayed within constant reach of Ulysses. She moved softly in and out as he worked. She still made jokes but his responses now came slowly. It hurt to laugh. It hurt to talk. Soon he no longer went downtown and only occasionally ventured out for a drive. Instead of donning his street clothes he wore a dressing gown constantly and a loose scarf around his neck.

His library was upstairs, with the bay window fronting on the street. Behind it was his bedroom and beyond that Julia's, with folding doors open between. She used a small sitting room at the back for social gatherings, and at the end of the day Ulysses joined her there and listened with obvious pleasure to the family chatter. Ida often read to him in the afternoon from books he needed for reference. In the evening he sat and thought and made notes for next day's work. Most of his dictation was given in the morning to N. E. Dawson, a stenographer supplied by his publisher, with Fred and Badeau helping to check official reports and look up documents. As he worked he usually wore a knitted cap with a long peak for his neuralgia and large spectacles with hard rubber rims.

He composed with ease and made few changes. But Mark Twain, who thought his memory superb, discovered that he was sensitive to criticism, although outwardly impassive about it. Fred astonished him by asking Clemens to say a kindly word to his father about his work. "I was as much surprised as Columbus' cook would have been to learn that Columbus wanted his opinion as to how Columbus was doing his navigating," he commented. Clemens told him he thought his writings ranked with Caesar's Commentaries in their clarity, directness, simplicity and justice to friend and foe alike.

Fred resigned from the Army in December, to Sheridan's regret. He declined the offer of an army appointment by Sherman because he wished to devote all his time to his father. There were no parties at the Grant home that winter, but well-known men came and went. They usually gathered in Julia's sitting room and some stayed for the family dinner. Sherman was a frequent guest. Tall and vital, small Julia thought he had a "charming, confiding manner" and he seemed to be a "great resource to grandmama with whom he chummed admirably whether in her serious or lighter moods."

"Tenacity, tenacity, tenacity," his brother John Sherman said of Grant. "He never was discouraged." But General Sherman found Julia much distressed on a December day because Ulysses seemed at last to be profoundly discouraged. It worried her that he settled "into a silent moody state looking the picture of woe," Sherman wrote to his wife. "But he warms up when I or any of his old comrades come to him." He tried to reassure Julia by pointing out that Ulysses had always been a silent fellow. He reminded her of days at headquarters when Grant would sit perfectly still and quiet while he walked up and down and cursed.

But Julia was now convinced that his silence always meant pain. However, he seemed to take heart when the old staff officers arrived. General "Black Jack" Logan often called, his dark eyes burning, his small figure on springs. He frequently broke into "hot eloquence" over some army memory, small Julia observed. General Sheridan, stouter and ruddier than in his service days and with his hair now white, could bring old memories to the surface. General Simon B. Buckner came, too, to talk of the surrender of Fort Donelson. There was neither North nor South in the General's dwindling view of life. All were eager to help him with his book.

The handsomest visitor of all was Roscoe Conkling, "tall, imposing with fine gray curls, grizzled beard, and his head thrown well back," as small Julia observed him. Mark Twain alarmed her with his shaggy mane of white hair. He had a vague way of strolling into a room and moving aimlessly about. When seated he leaned far back, with crossed legs, and his chin thrust upward, his eyelids half-lowered. He drawled in a "curious, rather bored, monotone," and somehow Julia got the idea that he was a crazy man. But Grandmama and Mark Twain could make each other laugh and in one of his more serious moments he commented: "General Grant was a sick man but he wrought upon his memoirs like a well one and made steady and sure progress." Another regular visitor was Romero, small and thin, with a large bald head, and a look of great sadness in his black eyes as he watched the silent General. Senator Leland Stanford came in bearing flowers, to talk of life in California. Childs sent masses of flowers every day and both Julia and Ulysses enjoyed them.

Grant was at a low ebb on the day word reached him that he had been restored to his old rank as General, with full pay. Childs and Mark Twain were with him when the telegram arrived. His face lit up with one of his rare smiles. Julia came into the room and exclaimed: "Hurrah, they have brought us back our old commander." Childs found the scene most affecting. The General bore no ill-will to those who had opposed the measure. But a tempest of applause had greeted the news in Congress. The rebel yell was heard quite clearly through the din.

"It will be a long time yet before I can possibly recover," Grant wrote to Nellie on the eve of his death sentence in February. His sore throat had come to be a very serious matter, he explained. He had lost thirty pounds and he was seeing his doctor twice a day. Algy, who was in New York at the moment, had been up to dine with him. "We have all been as happy as could be expected considering our great losses and my personal suffering," he wrote. Then he mentioned his book with a modest note: "If you ever take the time to read it you will find out what sort of a boy and man I was before you remember me."

A medical consultation at their house in the middle of February confirmed the fact that Grant had lingual epithelioma, or cancer of the tongue. The disease had progressed. His case was inoperable. His days were numbered. The news was flashed around the world and his working tempo was speeded up. It was a race with time. It was also an hourly struggle with pain.

"My tears blind me," Julia wrote on the last day of February to her old friend, Mrs. William S. Hillyer, who had often shared her lot in camp during the war. "Genl. Grant is very very ill. I cannot write how ill."

"Grant is dying," the New York World proclaimed on March 1. But with Joblike patience the General went on with his work. Letters and telegrams poured in on the family. Army clubs and loyal leagues sent messages to the ailing warrior. The sons of Robert E. Lee and Albert Sidney Johnston were among the first to offer good wishes to the man who had conquered their fathers. Jefferson Davis sent a friendly message from Beauvoir. Beauregard, refusing to write about him for a Chicago paper, regretted his sufferings and added: "Let him die in peace, & may God have mercy on his soul." Rutherford Hayes and Robert Lincoln were among his callers. Mrs. Hamilton Fish, whose own husband was ailing, sent round some turtle soup to Julia a few days after the fatal news got out. It had helped Hamilton, she said, and he thought that possibly "our dear General might take some."

No invalid ever saw his march to the grave more clearly defined than Grant, day by day, step by step. He insisted on reading the newspapers and no one could stop him. He analyzed them and separated the true accounts from the false. None knew better than he what was actually going on in his workroom. None knew so well the involutions of pain.

Julia was ill herself after the medical consultation in February. Another in March showed that the disease had made further progress. But both she and Ulysses put on a cheerful front when Nellie arrived from England on March 14. Now a handsome matron with three children and an assured position in England, she leaned tenderly over her father and talked to him in the old sweet way. He drove out in the park with her and Dr. Douglas and seemed greatly cheered. But Nellie was shocked to see the change in her father and she marveled that by mid-winter he could have finished the first volume of his Memoirs, a total of a hundred and eighty thousand words. The answer lay in Mark Twain's comment that he "never flinched or faltered, never at any time suggested that the work be finished by another hand."

A few days after Nellie's arrival Mark Twain came in with a young protege of his, a sculptor named Karl Gerhardt, who had done a bust of Twain that was reproduced in Huckleberry Finn. Now he was at work on one of General Grant and he wished to show it to the family. In the end it was used as a death mask and was widely reproduced in terra cotta. Mark Twain thought it revealed the concealed pain Grant was enduring at the time and suggested his patience and courage.

Julia was, not altogether pleased with it at first. She found fault with the nose and forehead and suggested that Gerhardt be allowed in the General's room to work from life. He was lying in his leather chair with his feet up on another chair. He was muffled up in dressing gown and afghan, with his woolen cap on his head. Julia pulled it off and she and Ida deftly turned him this way and that with affectionate touches. But Julia was not satisfied with any pose he took. Finally she said: "Ulyss! Ulyss! Can't you put your feet to the floor?" He did so at once and straightened up, Mark Twain observed. While this was going on he wore a "pleasant, contented, and I should say benignant, aspect, but he never opened his lips once . . ."

CHAPTER XV: DEATH ON A MOUNTAINTOP

THE GENERAL had his closest brush with death early on a Sunday morning at the end of March 1885. He had driven in Central Park with Julia and Nellie the afternoon before and returned fatigued. He wakened choking in the night. Dr. Douglas and Dr. Shrady were at his side at once and Dr. Shrady gave him quick injections of brandy. It took an hour to revive him. In the meantime all the members of his family were called in and Julia sent for Dr. Newman, after a later collapse.

"Doctor, I am going," Grant murmured as the minister's familiar face swam into view. "I hope the prospect of the future is clear and bright."

Julia kneeled by his side.

"Do you know me, darling?" she asked.

"Certainly I do, and I bless you all with my heart," Grant murmured.

Julia and her children kissed him before Dr. Newman sprinkled water on his face from a silver bowl and baptized him. The General opened his eyes and whispered weakly: "I thank you. I had intended to have attended to this myself."

The watching reporters were quickly aware of trouble as lights went on in the house, messengers sped in all directions and Dr. Newman arrived. "General Grant sinking" said the Herald on March 31. For the next few days a stream of visitors arrived. Hamilton Fish, ailing himself, drove up and Cyrus W. Field arrived with a basket of flowers. Mark Twain appeared but when he learned the General was too ill for visitors he talked to Badeau instead, Leland Stanford came with a basket of lilies.

"Anxious to die," said the Herald on April 5. "General Grant worn by his sufferings and despondent." But another hemorrhage on April 7 helped to clear his throat and for a time he felt better and could talk again. He was in good spirits on April 9, the anniversary of the surrender of Lee. That day a cablegram arrived from the Marchioness of Ely on behalf of Queen Victoria, who was at Aix-les-Bains: "The Queen, who feels deeply for you in your anxieties, commands me to inquire after General Grant." Julia promptly replied through Fred: "Mrs. Grant thanks the Queen for her sympathy, and directs me to say General Grant is no better."

As his interest in things around him revived the General gave out a public message in response to the floods of inquiries that had reached his home: "I am very much touched and grateful for the prayerful sympathy and interest manifested in me by my friends and by those who have not hitherto been regarded as my friends. I desire the goodwill of all, whether hitherto friends or not." The General's first draft of this message was recalled by Julia who insisted that the word "prayerful" be inserted before it was released to the press.

After this crisis Julia no longer deceived herself but acknowledged that Ulysses' end was at hand. She had baffled those around her with her steadfast refusal to face the fact, even when Nellie came hurriedly from England, even though the newspapers proclaimed it day after day. Ulysses bolstered this feeling where Julia was concerned. Understanding her nature as no one else did, and watching her troubled face, he scribbled one of his notes to her: "I don't think I am so bad as you think, I heard some of you say you thought I would have died. I did not think so. I felt certain I could come out of that attack all right, and I did."

Next day the reporters noted that in delirium he was fighting the battle of Shiloh all over again and there was newspaper speculation as to the amount of morphine he was getting. But on April 18 he appeared at the bay window, wearing his smoking cap, and saluted the U. S. Grant Post of the GAR as they walked past to do him honor. He no longer looked the warrior of Vicksburg but a tired man with sunken cheeks who still could straighten up in response to a salute. Again he stood at attention on his birthday, April 27, when the 7th Regiment of the New York National Guard marched past in full dress with plumed shakos.

Julia arranged a party for his birthday. It was his sixty-third and last. She drove with him through the blossoming park and he joined the family in a festive dinner. Sherman and Mark Twain were present, and small Julia noted her grandmother's "delight over some unexpected remark" by Mark Twain that amused the General James G. Wilson called with a birthday gift and had half an hour's talk with his old commander. They discussed points in his book and Wilson came to the conclusion that he surpassed Sir Walter Scott in his heroic efforts to meet his obligations and finish his work. "Publishers, physicians, family, friends, watched this terrible struggle," he commented.

None watched it with more sympathy and grief than Julia, who sometimes moved in a daze and was scarcely conscious of anything that went on outside the house. Crowds stood across the street on Grant's birthday and country carts were noticed among the smart equipages that drove past with interested onlookers. Small Ulysses, aged three, disturbed them all by howling in the night. He wanted an apple and Grandma had secretly instructed him "to shout and make a noise" when he wished for something. Even the General came to his door to see what was going on. Julia found an apple for him although Ida was indignant with her son. But the General liked the vigor and spirit of the "sturdy little grandson who bore his name."

Dr. Shrady, who had attended Garfield and was devoted to Grant, found the General "strangely calm, submissively heroic and philosophically determined" once he knew the worst, and he believed that he knew it from the start. "It is merely postponing the event," he wrote to Shrady after he was snatched back from death at the end of March. "I am ready now to go at any time. I know there is nothing but suffering for me while I do live." He expressed regret that he had not been allowed to die. "I was passing away peacefully," he said. "It was like falling asleep."

The General astonished the physician by the cool and matter-of-fact manner in which he discussed the progress of his own case, and observed his symptoms. He took his own pulse. He followed his daily temperature. He insisted on seeing the official bulletins. The love of his family and his interest in the book alone made his life bearable during these weeks, in Dr. Shrady's opinion.

The General was loyal to his medical attendants and backed their methods when the newspapers ran stories that they were experimenting on him, that they were giving him too much morphine, that he was not getting the best treatment. Letters arrived from all parts of the country, written by cranks who had ideas for saving the General's life. The yard was piled with boxes of quack medicines, herbs, meat extracts, strange waters and nostrums of various kinds.

One of the first taboos for the General was tobacco. He did not complain but one day said to Dr. Shrady: "Doctor, do you think it would really harm me if I took a puff or two from a mild cigar?"

"There was something so pitiful in the request and so little harm in the chance venture that consent was easily obtained," Dr. Shrady reported.

But the doctor neglected to pull down the shades and reporters spotted Grant having his puff. "Grant Smokes Again" ran the headlines and Julia was indignant, but Ulysses and Dr. Shrady kept mum about their defection.

The period from late April to mid-May was a comparatively good stretch for the suffering General. He made rapid headway with his book, talked clearly, felt less pain, and Julia was more at ease during this brief respite. All through their married life she had cheered the General in his darker moments, but the time had passed when she could touch this magic spring between them and scatter his gloom.

The press now kept a death watch on the house. Through parted silken curtains she could see reporters pacing up and down, or leaning against the stone wall across Fifth Avenue. They had jointly rented a house on Madison Avenue and worked in shifts, watching for a gas jet to go up in the middle of the night at 3 East Sixty-sixth Street, for messengers to speed on mysterious errands, for important guests to arrive. They soon ceased to ring the doorbell and make inquiries, but they waylaid visitors coming out. Dr. Newman was a ready talker but soon the physicians clamped down on news, gave out meager bulletins and warned the General's visitors to be on guard. Dr. Shrady, much liked by small Julia Grant, was keen-faced and had a dark goatee. At this time he was the popular editor of the Medical Record. He wrote the bulletins on Grant, and Dr. Douglas, tall and stoutly built, harangued the reporters and sometimes gave them scraps of information. The faithful Harrison, Grant's Negro attendant, also was susceptible to their persuasion. All the papers held forms in readiness to strike off special editions. Julia, who had seen her husband both praised and assailed in the papers for years, dreaded them now more than in the days of the Civil War or the presidency.

By this time the General was on liquid fare. He slept between two leather chairs and never went to bed. He was afraid of choking if he lay down. But he kept on dictating, sometimes as much as ten thousand words a day. By degrees his voice faded to a whisper, then ceased to serve him except for brief moments. He then turned from dictation to scribbled notes. But General Logan, visiting him early in June, thought that his mind was clear and his memory unfaltering. "His physical suffering seems to have nerved his mind to its best efforts," he observed.

Central Park was inviting in May and early June with its shrubs and newly planted trees, its small lakes and flower beds. Since its completion in 1876 New Yorkers had learned to enjoy it, and carriages rolled through it at all hours of the day. Ida, Nellie and Fannie took daily airings but Julia would not stir from the house except for a rare drive with the General. They were now discussing a shift to the country for summer. Long Branch was considered too damp and the mountains too ratified, but when Joseph W. Drexel suggested his cottage at Mount McGregor, in the foothills of the Adirondacks, Dr. Douglas was satisfied. He wanted pure air for the General, but not too much altitude. The simple two-storied house, a thousand feet above sea level, was reached by a narrow-gauge railway from Saratoga Springs, a distance of ten miles. The porch faced east toward the Green Mountains of Vermont.

The entire Grant family traveled north on June 16 in Vanderbilt's private car. Crowds watched them depart and arrive. The General's Prince Albert coat seemed much too large for his shrunken frame. He wore purple and white bedroom slippers and limped painfully. A white silk bandage swathed his neck. He took off his silk hat in the train and wore his small skull cap. Spectators observed how white his closely cropped beard and hair had become. His two leather chairs were installed in the coach and he lay back languidly until they came to West Point. Then Julia leaned over affectionately to indicate where they were. He smiled back at her and waved to Dr. Douglas to look at the castellated Academy where life had virtually begun for him.

The children had lunch in the forward car. Fred and Ida, Jesse and Elizabeth, Buck and Fannie all chatted with Julia. Jesse still had the power to amuse his father, Buck to comfort him and Fred to stand like a steady rock by his side. Crowds came to stare as the train reached Albany. There were groups at every crossroad, silent now, knowing that this was not a triumphal occasion. Reporters tossed off bulletins to waiting messengers at various stops. The General could no longer tweak an eyebrow without press comment.

Drexel met them at Saratoga and escorted them to their mountain home. Grant slept well that night while Julia settled her family in the various rooms. It was a tight fit but they used the Balmoral Hotel nearby for meals and occasional guests. Julia alone would not leave the cottage for an hour. The General showed ambition on his first day at Mount McGregor. He studied the view from the porch, then leaning on Harrison he walked up the incline to the hotel and rested on a rustic bench. The air was crystal clear, with the faint tang of balsam. The June day was warm and sunny. But the effort was too much for Grant. That night he wrote: "All my physicians, or any number of them can do for me now is to make my burden of pain as light as possible." Three days later, after a full day's work on his book he wrote: "I said I had been adding to my book and to my coffin. I presume every strain of the mind or body is one more nail in the coffin."

He sat for hours on the porch, his woolen cap with its long peak protecting his head, A plaid shawl covered his knees. His pad and tiny white stylus pen were always at hand. He preferred his new lapboard to the bridge table he had used in New York for writing. He thought it the best of all the "gimcracks" that had been tried for his comfort.

Julia felt slightly revived in the clear air, away from the constant vigils of reporters and crowds. But soon people swarmed up the mountain to see the General, and soldiers were posted as sentinels to check the inflow of those who did not have passes. Again the press converged. Delegations arrived with good wishes. Old soldiers came singly and in groups. Children brought offerings of wild flowers. Grant read and wrote and studied the papers with thoroughness. On June 30 he noted: "I see the Times man keeps up the character of his dispatches to the paper. They are quite as untrue as they would be if he described me as getting better from day to day. I think he might spare my family at least from reading such stuff." And on another day he wrote: "I had the newspaper article, with a reply to write, to worry me. Mrs. Grant was very much excited on reading the article." When he had a week in July without much pain the papers "gave that as a sure indication I was declining rapidly."

For the time being Mount McGregor was the most conspicuous spot in the world, for the General had traveled in every country and his story was assuming the proportions of a classical tragedy. Here was a great public figure watching himself die. He knew what he had. He knew what the papers were saying. He was a witness to his own agony as well as being its subject. Enemy voices were stilled at last. The peaks and abysses of his career were all in view, but catalyzed in his final show of courage.

The last days of General Grant on Mount McGregor are most truly mirrored in his own penciled notes to Dr. Douglas, now in the Library of Congress. They were scratched off from hour to hour, a summary of his physical decline, showing preoccupation with his immediate suffering, and here and there quick flashes of the sturdy character of General Grant. Many were written on the porch while Julia and members of his family were with him. Others were scribbled in the agony of the night. They show the variations of mood, the drift from painful consciousness to blurred sedation, from strong awareness of past and present to philosophical speculation.

He observed how people pounced on his notes. "I will have to be careful about my writing," he scribbled. "I see every person I give a piece of paper to puts it in his pocket. Some day they will be coming up against my English."

The days went by for Julia in muted sorrow. She dared not show him how she felt and add to his discomfort. As soon as he wakened in the morning she was at his side. He would not let her nurse him, to save her from further suffering. Harrison, their Negro butler, attended to his physical needs in the daytime, and Henry McQueeney at night. Julia talked to him in her old gay way and told him stories, then moved into another room to hide her tears. She was alert to every variation in his state, and dreaded above all the look of hopelessness that sometimes settled on his face. The New York Times reporter, posted at Mount McGregor, observed that her chair was always drawn close to his on the porch, her figure was in view wherever he appeared. "Whenever he wanted company she was part of it, and many hours in his last days were spent with her alone. Often they could be seen together when not a word was spoken, the mere companionship satisfying them."

When the General was asleep Julia spent much time in prayer. But he could not bear to see the haunted expression that at times she could not conceal from him. Catching her in this mood toward the end he wrote; "Do as I do. Take things quietly. Give yourselves not the least concern. As long as there is no progress there is hope." He teased her for the last time when he wrote Dr. Douglas a note about one of Julia's anecdotes. She had presented it as a piece of wit, but the point seemed to be lacking. To the very last Julia could amuse her devoted husband.

The summer advanced, a mockery of radiant days on the mountaintop, although the temperature slipped from eighty to forty degrees on several occasions and fires were lit in the cottage. The woods were bright with wild flowers and the trees rustled in the night. The children lived a separate life, dancing on the outskirts of death with no knowledge of its presence. Louise, their French nurse, kept them playing in the garden or walking in the woods. They were tactfully steered away from the scenes of tension, and were whisked out of the cottage and over to the Balmoral Hotel when Grandmama seemed upset. But Grandpapa had good days, too, when they were welcomed beside his chair — to stroke his hand, to kiss his tired face. Almost up to the end it made him happy to have his family gather around him on the porch. It pleased him to see small Julia and Josie Douglas playing with the swing, or Ida and Nellie, smartly gowned and holding up parasols, strolling toward the cottage from the hotel. Both could beguile him in any but his most desperate moments. He put on his silk hat and drew them all around him to have group pictures taken on one of his better days. He was proud of the solid clan that he and Julia had founded, and of the devotion his children gave him. They all played their part to the finish.

For a time he seemed better in his new surroundings. He showed more strength, wore his ordinary clothing and shared in the family life to some degree. Ten days after his arrival he was wheeled by Harrison to the brow of the hill overlooking the valley. From there he could see the theater of Burgoyne's campaign — his marches, defeats and surrender — not unlike the Chattanooga terrain. Julia was never able to take in a panorama because of her poor vision but Grant had always enjoyed a place with a view.

By the end of June he considered his book almost finished. It was nearly two hundred pages longer than he had intended but he promised himself that he would cut it. Dawson had watched apprehensively the downward curve in his composition. His notes grew blurred and scratchy as his strength failed. McQueeney held a lamp for him by the hour when he wakened in the night and felt like writing. The creative spring was drying up when he was taken off narcotics at the end of the month by way of experiment. His arms and thighs were sore from injections. But the two days that followed were a nightmare of pain. He wrote: "A verb is anything that signifies to be; to do; or to suffer. I signify all three."

Dr. Douglas quickly restored the dosage. Grant revived and put in a good day's work. On July 2 he wrote the doctor a formal letter that he urged him not to show to anyone before his death, least of all to his family. He frankly threw himself on the mercy of his physicians to make him as comfortable as they could until he died. "I would prefer going now to enduring my present suffering for a single day without hope of recovery," he wrote. But he was thankful to have been spared long enough to complete his work and, above all, to have lived to see "the happy harmony which has so suddenly sprung up between those engaged but a few short years ago in deadly conflict." All manner of men had wished him well and "they have brought joy to my heart if they have not effected a cure."

He felt well on the Fourth of July and the family talked about Vicksburg and the coincidence that Nellie and Ulysses 3rd both were born on this significant day. He received a cablegram from the Emperor of Japan and a message from Cyrus W. Field in London. He, John Bright, the Duke of

Argyle and other friends were dining together that evening and would drink to his health.

A sharp summer storm ripped over the mountaintop and lightning struck the cottage. It ran down a defective lightning rod and branched off through the window of the children's room. The flash grazed small Ulysses and knocked him off his feet. It scorched Louise's apron and burned the wallpaper. A sentinel was killed in the grounds.

Two days later Grant sank back in peace in his chair and wrote: "The pain left me entirely so that it was enjoyment to lie awake; but I got the enjoyment from the mere absence of pain." Julia, as well as Dawson, realized that he no longer wished to make an effort. She hovered over him, tempting him to eat, arranging his pillows, touching him softly with her hands. "Eating is beginning to grow distasteful to me," he reported on July 7, as he starved to death. In another of his notes he wrote: "How much may a man reduce in weight who ought to reach 180 pounds, but who has gone up to 195. I am down now to about 130. I was 140 lbs. seven weeks ago." But his own report of himself early on July 8 followed: "I am as bright and well now, for a time at least, as I ever will be." After a visit from some Mexican editors that afternoon, however, he wrote less cheerfully: "I must avoid such afternoons as this. We had company since five and I was writing all the time."

Two days later Buck arrived with the last part of the first volume in galleys. "In two weeks if they work hard they can have the second vol. copied ready to go to the printer," Grant wrote triumphantly. "I will then feel that my work is done." That same day Buckner traveled up to see him. "He is coming up specially to pay his respects," the General wrote with obvious pleasure. It was their last meeting. As he left, Mark Twain arrived. It was also farewell for him. And for Robert Underwood Johnson, who wrote of this interview: "I could hardly keep back the tears as I made my farewell to the great soldier who had saved the Union for all its people, and to the man of warm and courageous heart who had fought his last long battle for those he so tenderly loved."

Next day, July 11, Grant whipped off an agonized note: "I feel as if I cannot endure it any longer." Julia was deeply upset that day, too, from the premonitory signals in the newspapers. Dr. Shrady had been sent for and Dawson reported that "at last he had reached the end of all he could do." No one was a better judge than the stenographer who had followed his heroic effort from the beginning — first fluent dictation, then his voice tapering off to a whisper, then silence and the work switching from dictation to notes. At the end he was able only to scratch down his ideas.

Dawson recorded the joy with which Grant let his family know that his task was done. The date was July 16, a week before his death. "He had intended to have had the whole read over to him and to have revised it all," Dawson recalled. "He was in reality only able to revise the first volume, and during his last hours he was afraid that he would not be able to complete it." But after looking in the mirror for the first time in a week to see whether "I look like a bloat or a ghost," the General summed up the situation in a note to Dr. Douglas:

After all that however the disease is still there and must be fatal in the end. My life is precious of course to my family and would be to me if I could recover entirely. There never was one more willing to go than I am. I know most people have first one and then another little something to fix up, and never get quite through. This was partially my case. I first wanted so many days to work on my book so the authorship would be clearly mine. It was graciously granted to me, after being apparently much lower than since, and with a capacity to do more work than I ever did in the same time. My work had been done so hastily that much was left out and I did all of it over from the crossing of the James river in June/64 to Appomattox. Since that I have added as much as fifty pages to the book. I should think. There is nothing more I should do to it now, and therefore I am not likely to be more ready to go than at this moment.

The two volumes in the end totaled 1231 pages and 295,000 words, and brought the family, within the first two years after publication, royalties amounting to $450,000. The work was completed in approximately eleven months, under conditions unique in literary history. Grant died knowing only half the story. In May he had received a letter from his publishers telling him that with their subscription campaign only half over, sixty thousand sets had already been ordered, ensuring royalties of at least three hundred thousand dollars. Both Julia and Ulysses were astounded. The General was immensely relieved to know that his family would have this provision. It had been his only motive in writing the book although, once started, he was swept along on a tide of reminiscent interest. Dr. Douglas dreaded the day the book would be finished, and believed that it actually prolonged his life.

Two days after his announcement Grant wrote that he regretted the prospect of living through the summer and fall. "I do not think I can, but I may," he speculated. At this point Julia and Fred tried to persuade him to take some alcoholic stimulant. They gave him Tokay. Except for three small glasses of port he had had nothing of the sort since leaving New York. "I do not need or want either," he wrote for Dr. Douglas' benefit. "Mrs. Grant and Fred thought they would help me."

On July 20 he asked to be taken in his bath chair to the observation point on the hill. Fred, Harrison, and Dr. Douglas chose a new route and ran into difficulties. They had to cross a platform used for dumping coal. Grant got out of his chair, walked up three steps and picked his way through the coal while his chair was lifted up. He was deathly pale on the way home and collapsed as soon as he reached the cottage. Next day Julia was with him every minute and was holding him when he sank helpless into his chair, letting his cane fall to the floor. The warrior had taken his last walk, seen his last panorama.

There was no improvement on the following day and the children were brought in to say farewell to their grandfather, although they did not understand what was happening. He was already close to death on the 22nd when he noticed that the clock in his room struck twelve although the time was only eleven. "Fred, hadn't you better take that clock down and wind it up and start it as it should go?" he scribbled.

When he indicated that evening that he wished to be put to bed he was lifted from the leather chairs in which he had passed so many wearisome hours — a sure sign to the watchers that he had given up the fight. Hour after hour that night Julia sat near the head of the bed, holding Ulysses' hand, kissing him from time to time, mopping his brow. Once, when asked if he was in pain, he murmured "No." Fred occasionally put his arm under his neck to support him. Fred, Buck and Jesse and their wives all surrounded the bed and the doctors stood by. Only the children slept at peace upstairs.

The night wore on. Just before dawn Dr. Douglas went out for a breath of air. Moonlight silvered the tall pines, but fog was drifting up from the valley. On his return "there was so much peace and quiet" in the General's attitude that he urged Julia and other members of the family to snatch a little rest and prepare themselves for further hours of vigilance. At seven Henry rushed out to Dr. Douglas on the porch to say that he thought the General was going. Harrison knocked at the bedroom doors and the family converged again around the bed, this time in dishabille, muffled in wraps and shawls.

"There was no expiring sigh," Dr. Douglas recalled. "Life passed away so quietly, so peacefully, that, to be sure it had terminated we waited a minute." He made a final note in his diary: "The intellect remained unclouded and he had been enabled to accomplish his great desire, the completion of his Memoirs."

The time was eight minutes after eight, and Fred stopped the clock, which may be seen at Mount McGregor today, as well as the cherrywood bed in which he died. Small Julia later remembered her grandmother's sobs and cries behind a closed door, and the strange hours that followed. When they loosened the General's robe they found the locket containing a strand of Julia's hair, and a letter addressed to her that he had secretly carried around for fourteen days:

Look after our dear children and direct them in the paths of rectitude. It would distress me far more to hear that one of them could depart from an honorable, upright and virtuous life than it would to know that they were prostrated on a bed of sickness from which they were never to arise alive. They have never given us any cause for alarm on this account, and I trust they never will. With these few injunctions and the knowledge I have of your love and affection and the dutiful affection of all our children, I bid you a final farewell, until we meet in another and, I trust, better world. You will find this on my person after my demise.

The General had already made plain to Fred his burial wishes in one of his last notes. He mentioned West Point, St Louis, Galena, or New York. When Fred read it he gently told his father that Washington probably would be selected for his place of burial. The General then took back the note he had written, went into an adjoining room, possibly to consult Julia, and soon came back with another which read: "It is possible that my funeral may become one of public demonstration, in which event I have no particular choice of burial place; but there is one thing which I would wish you and the family to insist upon, and that is, that wherever my tomb may be, a place shall be reserved for your mother at my side." West Point was his favorite choice but he did not think that Julia could be buried there.

President Cleveland issued a proclamation announcing Grant's death and sent Julia a message of sympathy. There was national mourning as messages and carloads of flowers arrived at Mount McGregor, Julia was prostrated. Her little namesake wandered alone in the woods and made an oak leaf wreath for Grandpapa. She took it back to the house and found her way into the room where the General lay in his coffin. Death was a strange spectacle to the child. "It seemed heartbreaking that my grandfather should be so still, and dead," she later recalled.

Fred put a small packet of mementos in the General's pocket and a ring that Julia had given him many years before was replaced on his hand. He had hidden it away in his clothing when his fingers shrank from illness. The packet contained the strand of Julia's hair, entwined with a lock of Buck's, that he had worn since the days of Fort Vancouver.

On July 30 Julia braced herself to enter the room where Ulysses still lay. She remained alone with his silent figure, kneeling in prayer. She collapsed afterward and was comforted by Mrs. Creswell and Mrs. Newman. Before the funeral services held at the mountain cottage she busied herself draping the leather chair in which the General had sat. Fred and Buck looked after all the funeral arrangements, consulting their mother on the more important decisions. For the most part she stayed upstairs, weeping and praying, while crowds stormed the mountaintop. Five trains a day brought passengers from Saratoga.

Her sister Nellie was with her again, as in the days of Julia's courtship. Grant's sister Virginia and his niece, Clara Cramer, sat sadly in the parlor during the services. Mrs. Potter Palmer had come on from Chicago. General Sherman stared straight ahead as Dr. Newman, nearly six feet tall and histrionic in his delivery, talked for more than an hour, covering every phase of Grant's life in his eulogy. Julia, sitting near the door, looked dazed as he spoke of his family life and of her:

"He, the Doric column to sustain; she, the Corinthian column to beautify. He, the oak to support; she, the ivy to entwine. He, unhappy without her presence; she, desolate without his society . . . She shared his trials and his triumphs, his sorrows and his joys, his toils and his rewards. . . . Lovely and pleasant in their lives, and in their death they shall not be divided. Side by side they shall sleep in the same tomb, and she shall share with him whatever homage future ages pay at his national shrine."

The General's funeral services in New York were not held until August 8. By that time Julia was too reduced to leave Mount McGregor. The cortege moved down the mountain on the 4th without her. Death at last had put an end to pain. The funeral was only a dim echo to Julia high on her mountaintop, although nothing like it had been seen in New York except the outpouring for Abraham Lincoln. Twenty-four black horses drew the catafalque. The New York Times of August 9 focused the picture: Broadway moved like a river into which many tributaries were poured . . .

There was one living mass choking the thoroughfare from where the dead lay in state to the grim gates at Riverside open to receive him. . . . From Fourteenth Street to the top of the hill — pavements, windows, curb, steps, balcony, and housetop teeming. ... All walls and doorways were a sweep of black. . . .

It was the last parade for General Grant. He had been the central figure of many. Julia had approved President Cleveland's choice of pallbearers. Two of her husband's favorite Generals, Johnston and Buckner of the Confederate Army faced Sherman and Sheridan across his coffin. Three Presidents — Cleveland, Hayes and Arthur — were among the mourners. Veterans, white and Negro, sorrowed for the soldiers' soldier. Sherman's head drooped and he wept when taps was sounded. The children seemed to be lost in wonder, as small Julia carried the oak wreath she had made for Grandpapa, and little Nell a bunch of heather, both of which were placed on Grant's coffin.

Soldiers kept midnight watch in the greenish shimmer of the stars at the small temporary brick tomb. Their white tents faced to the Hudson, flowing dark and silent. All members of the Grant family were at the Fifth Avenue Hotel that night except Julia, who kept a lonely vigil at Mount McGregor. The sky was brilliant with stars. The August night was soft with the ripeness of summer. The cottage rooms seemed small and stuffy, with the fragrance of many flowers still lingering in the air. But the world looked dark to Julia, indoors and out, as she mourned the death of her hero.

CHAPTER XVI: "AS THE NEEDLE TO THE THREAD"

WHILE TRIBUTES to General Grant reached Mount McGregor from all parts of the world, Sherman's personal message to Julia penetrated with the swiftness of light the fog that surrounded her at this time. On the day after the ceremonies he wrote from the Fifth Avenue Hotel that "such a funeral never before occurred in America and never will again." Then he added his own personal estimate of their relationship:

May you continue for many years to receive tokens of love and affection and then rest at that majestic spot on the Banks of the Hudson made sacred by the presence of the mortal part of the Great and Good General, to whom you were as true as the needle to the thread, in poverty as in health, in adversity as well as in exaltation.

Julia was prostrated as the tide of eulogy flowed around her. She had given way after the long weeks of strain and waiting. Now the public and the press remembered only the good in Grant. His last heroic fight had wiped out the calumny that, in John Russell Young's words, had fallen with Pompeian fury on the General. In the stifling August heat Julia read messages from Queen Victoria and Li Hung-chang; from Gladstone and John Bright; from Longstreet and Sheridan; from statesmen and plain soldiers. Hamilton Fish was too ill at the time to act as a pall-bearer but Mrs. Fish wrote to Julia that "all felt that enough could not be done to honour the greatest man of the century." Americans met in London and Paris to draft resolutions of sympathy for Mrs. Grant. Gladstone, standing throughout, with his ear cupped in his hand, listened to the eulogy by Canon Frederick William Farrar at a memorial service held in Westminster Abbey.

Julia returned to New York to find her house no longer warm with the breath of life. In December the General's book came out and created a sensation. The circumstances under which it was written gave it unique interest. Beyond that, the clear, forceful text was applauded, and the General's fairness was self-apparent. Julia sent copies in all directions, including one to the Pope. She had it read to her over and over again. She agreed with Matthew Arnold that its chief value lay "in the character which, quite simply and unconsciously, it draws of Grant himself."

Her sons and Sherman stood firmly by her in the early days of her grief. The General stopped in frequently to talk to her as she coped with all the business affairs that entangled her after Ulysses' death. Sherman ultimately gave up his home in St. Louis and moved his family to New York. Julia saw much of his wife for a few months but soon was consoling Sherman, for his devout Ellen died almost immediately after they had settled in a house on West Seventy-first Street.

"Wait for me, Ellen, no one ever loved you as I love you," the General cried as he rushed upstairs at the end, but it was too late for her to catch his penitential cry. After that he became a familiar figure at first nights, at the Union League Club, and The Players, which he helped to organize. Disliking carriages, he rode downtown on the elevated and his striking figure was always noted with interest around the city streets.

Webster was as amazed as the Grants over the fortune the General's book brought in, but complications followed for Julia. Ever since her husband's death she had been plagued by Badeau for payments to which she would not assent. She had ordered him out of the house shortly before the General's death when he claimed authorship of the book and demanded more money for his work than the sum originally agreed on.

Grant had been much upset over his claims and had written him that their working relationship must end. Badeau's proposals would have made him a partner with Grant's family as long as the book found sales, and this was preposterous, the General pointed out. He had given Badeau a memorandum promising a certain amount and there the matter must stand. "My name goes with my book and I want it my work in the fullest sense," Grant wrote. "It would be a degradation for me to accept honors and profit from the work of another man, while declaring to the public that it was the product of my own brains and hand."

The public was familiar with his plain style, the General reminded Badeau. Had he not always written his own army orders and his presidential messages? But with a final gesture of kindness to the small, rotund man with graying beard and fussy ways, who had been so close to him since the last days of the war, he added: "Your prosperity in life will gratify me. You can always be the welcome visitor at my house that you have been heretofore . . ."

But not to Julia. She was more angry with Badeau than she had ever been with anyone in her life. Both she and Fred thought him intemperate and unreliable as he helped with the General's papers at the end. They let the case go into litigation after various attempts at settlement. They did not deny the secondary help that Badeau had given but they fought him to the last ditch on the amount he claimed, not because of the money involved, but for the doubts he had raised about the authorship of the book.

The case was settled in 1888 on the eve of trial. Fred at that time decided to release to the press all the family correspondence, including his father's last letter to Badeau and Badeau's note to him, written nearly three months before the General's death, in which he said: "I have no desire, intention or right to claim the authorship of your book. The composition is entirely your own. What assistance I have been able to render has been in suggestion, revision or verification."

Badeau received $11,254 in all for his work and there the matter ended. Roscoe Conkling was fighting the case for Julia in March 1888, when he collapsed in the snow as he walked from his office to his home during the great blizzard of that year. He died soon afterward from the effects of exposure and Julia had lost another of her most valued friends.

Now that she was a woman of known wealth many, claims were made on her. She had trouble with Gerhardt over the ownership of the death mask he had made of the General. And she was reproached in the newspapers when Dr. Douglas, who had had a stroke, wound up in a charity hospital. He was beset by misfortune and went south to try the water cure and to re-establish himself, while his wife opened a boarding house in Bethlehem, Pennsylvania.

Julia insisted that Dr. Douglas had been paid twelve thousand dollars in all seven thousand in recognition of his bills, and an extra five thousand that the General had wished him to have. She denied having criticized in any way the physician's care of her husband. These issues were intensely painful to her and with the Badeau case pending, neither she nor Fred attended the unveiling of the bronze statue of Grant in St. Louis in October 1888. Caroline Ruth O'Fallon, granddaughter of her old friend, drew back the flags and Sherman made the presentation.

That autumn Julia urged a diplomatic post for Fred. China was suggested first but President Benjamin Harrison sent him to Vienna instead, a happy choice for the Grant family as a whole. "I feel certain that he will do honor and credit to your administration, and that you will find him loyal and true" Julia wrote on April 8, 1889, a prediction soon confirmed by President Harrison himself.

Julia decided to spend the summer in Europe with Fred and Ida. She had lost all taste for Long Branch and had tried Lake George but it had too many associations with Ulysses. Her family thought that a total change of scene might do her good. Her namesake, by this time an overgrown schoolgirl of thirteen, with long hair dangling down her back, was a special pet of Julia's. Ida and her daughter attended one of Queen Victoria's drawing rooms on their way to Vienna and the Queen recalled the family visit to Windsor. Mrs. Grant, in mourning, visited Nellie, whose marriage was now admittedly a failure.

When they reached the Austrian capital, the court was in mourning for the Crown Prince who had died mysteriously at Mayerling Lodge. The Emperor Francis Joseph rode through the streets, a green plume rising from his helmet above his snowy side whiskers and rubicund cheeks. He welcomed Julia back to Austria but nothing cheered her now. She could smell the cyclamen blossoms in the Vienna woods. She could listen to the Strauss waltzes, and see Fred off for a hunting trip with the Emperor. But wherever she went she was reminded of Ulysses and their memorable tour of the world. However, the boy soldier of the Civil War was in his element in this riding, hunting, mountain-climbing milieu and Ida, with her Paris gowns and good looks, was a distinctive hostess even among the Viennese beauties. When Fred and Ida left for Baden in August, Julia decided to return home. Sherman was urging her to sell her house on Sixty-sixth Street and to live with Buck on West End Avenue.

She now faced a new problem. An inkling of it had already reached her when the New York World cabled to Fred in Vienna about a proposal to move General Grant's body to Arlington. This was followed by a vote in the Senate for national burial. Fred now wrote all official letters for his mother and he replied that she would consent only if provision were made for her to rest by his side. She was equally reluctant to have him moved to Galena, when overtures were made in connection with the monument being erected there. There was confusion from the start about the burial place of the General. The family's first choice was the Mall in Central Park but when this plan was abandoned they had readily assented to the Riverside Park site, overlooking the river. At the same time Julia had received a guarantee from Mayor William R. Grace that she would be buried there in accordance with her husband's wishes. When in New York she visited his grave regularly, taking white roses with her. At first she went nearly every day. When she was out of town, she still sent flowers and she always superintended the decoration of his grave on anniversaries.

But at this time there was much agitation over the fact that Grant's tomb was a mean-looking red brick vault and that a drive to raise funds for a mausoleum was getting nowhere. Sherman noted with concern when he drove past on an October day in 1888 that it remained exactly as it had been on the day they buried Grant. "Thousands visit it and gaze into the tomb containing the casket visible through the grated door; but as to a monument not a thing has been done," he wrote.

With Congress urging burial at Arlington, Horace Porter took firm hold of the drive for funds in New York. A whirlwind campaign for five hundred thousand dollars brought a fresh response. The papers helped with reproachful editorials. But 1890, on the whole, was a black year for Julia. For a time she was in a deeply depressed state. Thomas P. Ochiltree, writing in the New York World, described her as shutting herself up in her house, with the blinds drawn and few lights on, refusing to see visitors or answer letters, and spending hours brooding over mementos of her husband. He described long vigils at Grant's tomb, where she knelt weeping and praying with her face pressed against the iron bars until her coachman with the crack of his whip would warn her that someone was approaching.

But this was not the picture of her that Sherman sent to Fred and Ida in Vienna. "I saw your Mama a few days ago," he wrote cheerfully on March 30, "and I never saw her look better. She is resolved to hold on to that big house, and on the whole I guess she is right. She wants to be mistress wherever she is, and has the right to be so."

Mrs. Leland Stanford found her in equally good spirits at this time and Sherman wrote again to Fred nine months later that he had never seen his mother "in better health and spirits years surely sit lightly on her brow." Mrs. Sheridan, he added, still occupied her old house in Washington, "every room of which tells of Sheridan."

But in 1891 Sherman followed Sheridan and Grant to the grave, and Julia felt that she had lost a friend second only to Ulysses. His funeral brought another great assemblage to Fifth Avenue. His body was taken to St. Louis for burial with his wife and Willy. Tom, his remaining son, had become a priest. Ellen's teachings had prevailed over Sherman's earnest wish that he should go to West Point with Fred Grant.

Julia was constantly invited to veterans' gatherings and memorial meetings but at first she shunned all public appearances. However, she went to Chicago in October 1891, for the unveiling of the Grant Monument in Lincoln Park. She reviewed the marching soldiers from the porte-cochere of the Potter Palmer home on Lake Shore Drive. Then she and Mrs. Palmer joined in the fourth section of the parade and drove past cheering thousands.

The crowd saw a portly, grave-faced woman with a heavy crepe veil standing in the shadow of the granite pedestal on which the equestrian statue of the General rested. Around Mrs. Grant was a mass of "silk hats and bright bonnets, and long lines of plumes and helmets." Henrietta Strong, eighteen-year-old daughter of General William E. Strong, who had stood by her side at the Planters House in St. Louis after Vicksburg fell, unveiled the statue. Before leaving Chicago she held a reception for the officers of her husband's old regiment, the 21st Illinois, and other veterans of the Western forces he had commanded. Many whom she had known well and seen in the field bowed over her lace-mittened hand. She had asked that none refer to the past, lest she break down before them,

The following April she again made a public appearance, this time for the laying of the foundation stone of Grant's Tomb on his birthday. It was a squally, fitful day and Julia felt scarcely able to drag herself out of the house. Again there was a great demonstration and the General's widow was the focus of attention. President Harrison laid the cornerstone and Chauncey Depew, with his glance fastened on Julia, reminded the assembled crowd that "as son, husband, and father, his care and devotion were constant and beautiful."

Depew thought Grant would have preferred burial in the churchyard where his father and mother were interred. Sherman, before his death, expressed the view that the General would not have liked a marble mausoleum. But the tomb went up in Doric style and became a shrine for visiting thousands every year. Julia protested at once when she learned that the architect proposed to have her buried in the same sarcophagus as the General. "Gen. Grant must have his own sarcophagus and I my casket beside him," she wrote to General Charles H. T. Collis. "Gen. Grant's identity must remain distinct. Hereafter when persons visit this spot, they must be able to say, 'Here rests Gen. Grant.'"

On the day the foundation stone was laid Julia attended the commemorative dinner held annually at Delmonico's on the General's birthday. Augustin Daly and Joseph Jefferson were present at the first dinner. In 1890 Horace Porter presided, and Joseph H. Choate, Chauncey Depew, Elihu Root and Sherman all were present Now, in 1892, Sherman, the vitalizing spirit of the group, was gone. Julia, seated as usual in the music gallery, missed him as the men stood up to toast her, the General's widow. Little Vivian Sartoris, wearing a large black hat with a wreath of flowers, sat downstairs with Chauncey Depew and William M, Evarts, then moved up to join her grandmother. The elder Sartoris had died in 1890, leaving Nellie a house in Cadogan Square and a comfortable income. She had finally separated from Algy, who lived in Italy until his death in 1893.

Julia took pride in her growing family and she frequently visited Buck at his turreted blue limestone home of Norman architecture near Salem Center. The windows looked out on hill, dale and woodland, and maples and elms shaded the house itself. By 1893 Buck had five children — Miriam, Chaffee, Julia, Fannie and Ulysses, 4th. Jesse had two — Nellie and Chapman. Fred had Two — Julia and Ulysses, 3rd.

With Fred's daughter Julia in Vienna little Nell now rode down Fifth Avenue with Grandmamama, as she called her. She was always frightened as they passed the huge dark reservoir at Forty-second Street. Her nurse had told her that giants lived there. Her grandmother invariably held her hand as they passed and diverted her attention by asking: "What shall I buy my pet today?" Then they would drive on downtown and go on shopping sprees. One of Julia's favorite occupations was buying gifts for persons she loved, from dolls for little Nell to umbrellas for Mrs. Beale. When she gave Nell a watch she told her that it was the same as the one she had given to the Empress of Siam. Nell always remembered in after years that the Empress had held it to her ear and crowed over the little wheels and hammers inside. She also had strong memories of her grandmother's visions and dreams. The whole family talked of her premonition on the day of Lincoln's assassination. The second most important of her dreams concerned the big bird with smoke coming out of its wings that hastened the departure of the Grants from Chicago before the city burned. They were due to attend a reception, but when Julia had her visions Ulysses might protest but he did not attempt to cross her. It was an accepted fact in the family that Grandmama was psychic. Badeau believed that Grant took some stock in such matters himself. All were impressed with Lincoln's dreams.

Julia was also zealous in reminding all her grandchildren to study the catechism and say their prayers. In Nell's time she kept an elephant stuffed with marshmallows on the table beside her to share with the children. On the General's birthday each year she gave every grandchild a five-dollar bill with his picture on it. She was a personage of great consequence to the younger members of the family and when Nell visited Constantinople in her early twenties the Grand Vizier recalled that when her grandparents were the guests of Abdu-l-Hamid II, the Turkish Sultan, Mrs. Grant paid little attention to the official doings but concentrated on the children in view. She put her hand on the heir's head and said: "For you I see a great future." Now he seemed immensely tall, and his fez added several inches to his height as he looked down smilingly at Nell and observed: "And now I am the Grand Vizier."

When the Cleveland administration came into office Fred returned with his family from Vienna, although the President had asked him to stay on. Before leaving, Ida presented Julia, aged sixteen, at the Austrian court and when they all joined Grandmama at Cranston's on the Hudson in the summer of 1893, the debutante had thrilling tales to tell of the court pomp, her Drecoll gowns, the splendid fetes and picnic balls she had attended, and the Hungarian gypsy bands that had charmed her.

Julia saw that her namesake had grown into a striking looking girl, exceptionally tall and now quite beautiful. The Fred Grants moved on to Chicago to visit Mrs. Potter Palmer and the World's Fair, and that winter they settled in an attractive small house on West Seventy-third Street in New York. Mrs. T. J. Oakley Rhinelander sponsored young Julia for The Patriarchs. She was soon a popular figure at the more notable parties and a joy to her grandmother, to whom she always turned as someone young in spirit. Ulysses, meanwhile, was doing well at Cutler's and would go on to West Point after a year at Columbia University.

In 1893 Jesse moved to California. Buck soon followed, taking his mother with him to Santa Barbara in 1894. After staying for a time at the Coronado Hotel, where Julia was in her element with seven grandchildren whooping around her, Buck bought a large house on the hill in San Diego and they all moved in. He hoped that the climate would benefit Fannie, whose health was delicate. The Jesse Grants stayed with Buck until their own house was built, and Julia took little Nell shopping again, this time at Marston's, which was only a one-room shop at the time but later became an impressive store.

Julia thrived in the sunshine of California. She wrote to Mrs. Beale that the climate was glorious. But she had no intention of making her permanent home there. Nellie returned from England with her family and Julia, on her return East, went scouting for a house in Washington that they might share. She thought the McLean mansion "quite beyond her reach financially." After staying briefly at 2018 R Street, in a house once owned "by General Halleck, she paid fifty thousand dollars for the mansion at 2111 Massachusetts Avenue that had belonged to Senator George F. Edmunds, of Vermont. She had sold her New York home for a hundred and thirty thousand dollars when her sons moved West. In addition to the profits from the General's book Julia now had a five-thousand-dollar yearly pension from the Government.

She was at Fred's house in New York when Li Hung-chang called to see her in 1896 after he had visited the General's grave and planted trees from China in its vicinity. He and Julia had kept up a lively correspondence after her husband's death. She had written him a sympathetic letter when he was shot at Hiroshima and he had sent her a copy of his peace terms for Japan.

The Bismarck of China arrived gorgeously attired, with a train of secretaries and interpreters. He was past seventy and looked fragile as he sat with Oriental calm across from Julia. They discussed the past and talked of the General. He had brought with him statuettes in ivory and wood, rare porcelain cups, jade, rolls of silk and splendid brocades but, to Julia's consternation, his servants brought in a wheel chair for her. It had all the latest devices and he had found it irresistible. He thought it would be helpful to the General's widow, who now suffered from rheumatism.

"Between gratitude, amusement, and annoyance, her face made a queer study," young Julia recalled, "but she rose to the occasion and thanked him charmingly." He kept reminding her that he and she were both very old, but Julia pointed out after he left that he was her elder by several years.

Fred at this time joined Theodore Roosevelt as a member of the New York City Board of Police Commissioners and at Ida's table Julia dined with such men as Joseph Choate, William Evarts, Elihu Root, Mark Hanna, Roosevelt and Chauncey Depew. All enjoyed the bright conversation of the General's widow when she came up from Washington to visit her son.

She and Nellie were now comfortably settled in the capital. They were close to Mrs. Beale, who still lived in the Decatur House, and to Mrs. McLean, another intimate friend. They all attended the wedding of Harriet Blaine and Truxtun Beale, a union that did not last Walter Damrosch played the wedding march and the guests thought that Nellie Sartoris looked more beautiful in her maturity than in her girlhood. She was well remembered in Washington and all doors were open to her from the start.

Her daughter Vivian had Kemble blood in her veins and hankered to go on the stage. She had an oval face, her grandmother's hazel eyes and a flawless complexion. She danced well and was a bicycle enthusiast. Julia presented her to Washington society at a tea in 1897. Rosemary at this time attended the Georgetown Convent. She was a tall slender girl with dark hair and eyes, and she had the Grant look. Young Algernon was still at Oxford.

Mrs. Potter Palmer gave her niece Julia her American debut in Newport and Mrs. John McLean launched her in Washington with a ball. Her grandmother called her in to look her over when she was all dressed for this occasion. She lifted a rope of pearls from a velvet box on the table beside her and tall Julia bent over her small but imposing grandmother while the pearls were clasped around her neck. "These are Julia Grant's pearls and will bring you luck," she said.

Soon after this young Julia went to Europe with her aunt, Mrs. Palmer, and while on the Riviera fell in love with Prince Cantacuzene, Count Speransky, of the Russian Court. He came from an old Rumanian line and Julia again was faced with the prospect of an international marriage in her family. The papers pictured "Grandmother Grant's despair over the match" but she and Potter Palmer walked around arm in arm beaming happily when the young pair were married in All Saints Chapel at Newport in 1899. Palmer was eighty, and Julia seventy-three. She was captivated by the stunning-looking Prince in Russian uniform who conversed amiably with her in the gardens of Beaulieu.

It proved to be a happy marriage and for the few remaining years of her life Julia followed with the closest attention her granddaughter's experiences at the court of the Czar. The Prince was on the staff of the Grand Duke Nicholas. Julia did not live long enough to know that the Cantacuzenes fled to the United States with their three children, Michael, Bertha and Ida, after the Bolshevist Revolution. Her granddaughter was still one of the dowagers of Washington in 1959, while her grandson, Ulysses S. Grant, 3rd, bore his grandfather's name proudly and continued to serve the Government.

The dedication of Grant's Tomb took place on a memorably cold day in April 1897. Julia shivered as she looked up at the huge marble mausoleum in which Ulysses now rested. Many eyes were turned toward her at this one last gesture on her husband's behalf. For five hours soldiers had marched in a great parade to gather around the tomb. East and West, North and South were represented.

"A great life never dies," said President McKinley, his voice almost lost in the whistling wind. "Great deeds are imperishable, great names immortal ... but brilliant as was his public character, we love him all the more for his home life and homely virtues. His individuality, his bearing and speech, his simple ways, had a flavor of rare and unique distinction. . . ."

In the spring of 1899 President McKinley, with three generations of General Grant's family present, dedicated the equestrian statue in Fairmount Park, Philadelphia. Vivian Sartoris, in a pink silk costume braided with black, unveiled the bronze figure of her grandfather on horseback, his most characteristic pose. Young Algernon, serving in the Spanish-American War, had come from Cuba. Fred had just arrived from Puerto Rico, where he had been functioning as military governor. He dashed to the ceremonies, meeting his mother there for the first time since his return.

As the GAR marched past with their battle flags Julia waved her handkerchief, then mopped her eyes with it and put on dark glasses. The veterans were getting old by this time. But so was Mrs. Grant. She leaned heavily on a cane as she greeted Major General Nelson A. Miles, the ranking officer of the army. She lunched with the President's party and attended a dinner in the evening given by Mrs. Joshua Lippincott in honor of Mrs. McKinley and Mrs. Grant.

Julia's last days were filled with cheerful activity. She headed the Women's National War Relief Association during the Spanish-American War, working with Mrs. Fitzhugh Lee and Mrs. Logan. Their first supplies were sent by hospital ship to Manila. It was an old story to Julia — comforts for wounded men. She wrote an article for Harper's Bazaar in 1900 on the women who waited at home during war, and she urged scholarships for soldiers' children.

"I must keep active to be contented," she said to an interviewer at this time. "I no longer take a very great interest in social pleasures." But she and Nellie were much in view at the turn of the century. The social notes of the period show Mrs. Grant giving a dinner for the daughter of Benjamin Harrison, lunching with Susan B. Anthony at Mrs. McLean's, attending a

McKinley reception and giving a "violet luncheon" for a group of friends. Nellie went regularly to the White House receptions and Julia upon occasion. Everyone did her honor when she appeared. She was not forgotten as a notable First Lady and the widow of General Grant. Julia had never aroused the malice of anyone.

She wore nothing but black now except in summer, when she appeared in white dimity or soft mulls with frills. She had always been fond of finding the "little dressmaker" who would make up her gowns, and she and Mrs. Webster, who discussed early St. Louis with her by the hour, joined forces on this. "Would you mind sending me the address of the dressmaker that made your blue cashmere beaded with gold braid," was a note typical of this exchange.

At home in the evenings she usually wore black velvet gowns with short trains. Her tiny hands were always in lace mittens indoors and in black kid gloves when she went out. She continued to wear a widow's bonnet with long veil up to the time of her death. In spite of her poor eyesight Julia did not wear glasses. She would pick up a book or envelope and hold it a few inches from her eyes. Mary McAuliffe, her maid-secretary, read to her and took her dictation. Among her favorite authors in her last days were Bret Harte and Dr. Weir Mitchell, who had been a surgeon with her husband's forces.

F. G. Carpenter, a newspaper correspondent who called on her at this time, found her in high fettle as she reviewed for him some of the "wonderful events of her career." He thought her one of the "youngest old ladies in Washington." She looked no more than sixty to this experienced observer. Her face was full and free from wrinkles. Her hair was iron gray and luxuriant. She talked to him in a "low, pleasant voice" about the memoirs she was writing, and insisted that Grant, contrary to the popular conception of him, as a well-read man. "During the greater part of our life he read for hours to me every evening," she recalled. They had worked their way through all of Dickens and Thackeray in this fashion.

Julia denied indignantly that anyone had ever done any of his writing for him, and recalled how much she used to torment him with interruptions when he was preparing his final reports in Georgetown at the end of the war, and later in the White House when he sought her quarters for quiet. He liked her gossip and stories at other times, but would beg her to keep quiet when he was composing. At times she had been an irrepressible chatterbox and had had to be quelled. He was always most punctilious about correcting her impulsive misstatements of fact in army matters, and would let nothing stand in error, she told Carpenter. At the same time she made known through this reporter that she had completed her memoirs and hoped to have them published. Some time earlier she had considered having the General's letters to her brought out by Webster but this plan was abandoned. She also had many qualms about the memoir, and in the spring of 1894 she wrote that her work was almost completed, but when he considered "submitting it to the world and [thought] of the criticism, controversy and misunderstanding which it might provoke, I shrink from the final task of publication."

From time to time in the 1890s she dictated to Mary McAuliffe and Marias Romero, Leland Stanford and Elliot Shepard all encouraged her about her work. Shepard considered buying the memoir for publication and offered her twenty-five thousand dollars in advance for it, but when it came to the point, she felt timid about, the plan, fearing that she had been too personal about her family. She went to work on it again, modifying it to some extent. Then she wrote to her friend, Andrew Carnegie, on November 12, 1901, asking him if he would consider its purchase for a hundred and twenty-five thousand dollars. Julia continued:

I wish now to sell it outright. I cannot undergo the anxiety and care of publishers' exactions. I fear you will think I value the manuscript at a high figure . . . My dear Mr. Carnegie I do not feel that I am at all indelicate in making this proposition to you, for I assure you it is a very valuable little book, costing me months of labor, and as well giving me weeks and months of real pleasure, I living over again as it were my historic and happy happy past. I feel too that in coming to you, I am addressing one who can afford to be generous, and who will do me full justice and then too, I think you would be delighted to have it for your many libraries.

But before there was time to pursue the matter Julia died and her memoir was laid away by her descendants. Up to that time Carnegie and C. P. Huntington had been giving her advice about her investments and she wrote jestingly to the steel king: "Do you not think I am something of a financier?" She thanked him for letting her become "in a small way, a partner in your great industry" when she invested money in the Homestead Steel Works.

But the stage was becoming empty. She had been the first to comfort Mrs. Newman when the Bishop died at Saratoga in 1899, just as Mrs. Newman had stood by her when Ulysses died. Caroline O'Fallon, a link with her early years, had died in St. Louis the year before at the age of ninety-four. Hamilton Fish, General Beale and John Logan had long been dead and Julia moved now in a world of widows. With her indestructible sense of family feeling she always sent them flowers and remembrances on anniversaries.

She spent her last summers in Ontario. Nellie had taken a large red brick house at Cobourg, overlooking the lake, and Julia now said of the Sartoris children: "I take the same interest in them as I used to take in my own, and they are a great comfort to me." She went to New York on a shopping trip in 1901 to help Nellie buy a trousseau for Vivian, who was about to marry Arthur Balfour in England. When interviewed at the Fifth Avenue Hotel "a certain quaint simplicity and a charming, almost childlike candor" were noted in Julia's manner. She was always ready to chat about the past and she made lively observations on the changes she observed in New York.

Trade had moved up the Avenue and Madison Square, with its elms and sycamores, its carriages and playing children, made a pleasing oasis close to her hotel. Mrs. William Astor had moved north from Thirty-fourth Street. Some of the mansions she visited on upper Fifth Avenue were now like art museums, and the Vanderbilt homes suggested French chateaux. Stuyvesant Square was no longer a center of fashion, but Gramercy Park was in its heyday.

Her friends now walked to church through the Easter parade, wearing bunches of violets against their feather boas and with ostrich plumes on their hats. They wore high-buttoned boots of Vici kid and carried chatelaines. Their gigot sleeves were immense. The "Vassar girl" was much discussed and bicyclists went flying past Grant's Tomb. Ethel Barrymore was playing in Captain Jinks of the Horse Marines. Fifi Potter had just become the bride of James A. Stillman in Grace Church and the nuptials of Harry Lehr and Mrs. Elizabeth Drexel Dahlgren were of special interest to Julia because of her old friendship with the Drexel family.

In the end Vivian broke off her engagement with young Balfour and married Roosevelt Scovel, a cousin of Theodore Roosevelt. The ceremony took place at Cobourg and she wore her grandmother's laces. Julia had well developed views on the young by this time. She took note of all the dashing things that girls were doing, but expressed the hope that the domestic arts were not being neglected. "So many men go astray now; there must be something wrong," she commented.

When asked to write a piece for young people for a Lincoln Day celebration she penciled off some homilies:

First of all be obedient and loving sons and daughters. As husbands & wives be loyal and strive to keep the mistletoe ever green in your homes. Wives, keep a bright cheerful fireside, look your prettiest always, let your husband feel that his home is his castle and I will assure you that you will never be alone. Mothers, teach your little ones obedience, honesty and truth. Let these little ones come in full confidence to you with every grief and trouble, knowing they will have your sympathy, advice and help. If you do this wisely we will have a race of brave, noble and true men and women.

In conclusion Julia advised them to vote the Republican ticket. She remained actively interested in political affairs and was a stout champion of Susan Anthony in her suffrage work. She and Mrs. Jefferson Davis were seen together around New York at this time. They had met first at Cranston's in 1893. When Julia heard that the widow of the Confederate leader had arrived at the hotel she called on her. They found much in common and met from time to time after that. On more than one occasion they went together to Grant's Tomb, and Julia told Varina that she thought she would soon be resting there herself.

She was touched when Mrs. Davis, who was then writing for the Sunday World, and living in the Gerard Hotel, off Broadway, made friendly and admiring allusions to Ulysses Grant in her articles. She was one of the three women who wrote tributes to the General for the memorial number of the paper issued at the time Grant's Tomb was dedicated. The other two were Julia and Mrs. Logan. Among topics discussed by the two widows was the abuse that both their husbands had suffered. When Owen Wister's book about Grant came out in 1900 Julia was bitterly hurt, and Varina wrote to her consolingly that if she had not steeled herself against such attacks she would never have known an hour of peace or comfort. "Genl. Grant's and Mr. Davis's record is made up, and posterity will judge for itself if every idle critic in the land, or envious defamer should write from now until the end," Varina wrote. "In another half century when you and I are where we shall 'see clearly' and are having our merited rest the world will judge fairly, and commend justly."

Julia continued to receive distinguished callers, both in New York and Washington, although few of the Generals remained to talk to her about Ulysses. Tuesday was still her reception day and a line of carriages might always be seen along the street when Mrs. Grant was entertaining. She felt rich at the end in the family she and Ulysses had founded. She had twelve grandchildren in all. Buck and Jesse were doing well with real estate in California. Fred was appointed a Brigadier General in the regular army at the turn of the century.

She made her will with care, specifying where each item of her jewelry should go. She had diamonds, pearls and turquoise ornaments to bequeath. Her mother's engagement ring went to Buck and the diamond cross given to her by Ulysses on their twenty-fifth wedding anniversary to little Nell. She willed the thousand-year-old lacquered cabinet given her by the rulers of Japan to the Metropolitan Museum, along with bronze and gold vases. Her estate was divided equally among her children. With characteristic faith in them she wrote that she felt sure "the same harmony and spirit of fairness one to another will exist among my children after my death that has always existed, to my great comfort, during my lifetime."

While at Cobourg in the autumn of 1902 Julia had a severe attack of bronchitis, complicated by heart and kidney disorders. She was taken back to Washington in the middle of October but she never recovered her strength. Realizing her condition, she waited in resignation for the lights to go out. The end came a few minutes after eleven o'clock on the night of December 14, 1902, in her seventy-seventh year. Nellie was with her but her sons were far away. Fred was on an inspection tour of army posts in Texas. Jesse and Ulysses arrived from California. All were present for her burial in Grant's Tomb on December 21. Army and Navy officers in the vicinity assembled to honor the General's widow. Among the mourners were Chauncey Depew, Theodore Roosevelt, Mrs. John A. Logan, Mrs. Alphonso Taft and Mrs. Andrew Carnegie. Her husband's old friend, General Wilson, was one of the few who remained from his intimate group.

Twenty-four hours after her funeral, worshipers in the Metropolitan Methodist Church in Washington, which she had attended for years with Ulysses, heard Dr. Frank Bristol say that Martha Washington and Julia Grant did not shine by reflected light from their distinguished husbands but in their own right. Julia Dent discovered U. S. Grant, he said. "She saw in him, the young lieutenant, power and greatness before anyone else. She said when she married him that she was marrying a future President of the Republic. . . . No man ever owed more to his wife than did Ulysses S.

Grant . . . She helped to lift that genius from oblivion. He knew enough always to appreciate what his wife had done for him."

None could question the fact that Julia had lived a rich and purposeful life. In her own quiet way she had made herself one of the more potent women in American history. She was not conspicuous in her generation, since she was neither a beauty nor a scholar, a siren nor a politician. Her prosaic exterior gave no clue to the bright flame that Julia harbored, to the humor and warmth that infused her generous nature. She was always content to take a back seat and let Ulysses hold the reins, but behind her impulsive manner, her contradictions and her lenient ways, was the optimistic spirit that served him best in moments of crisis and discouragement.

Much wisdom underlay her air of simplicity in the closing years of her life. No American woman of her generation had traveled farther or met more famous people than Julia Grant. She had seen much of war, the world and the ways of government. At the end she had countless friends and few enemies. Above all, she had shared with unerring instinct the mixed fortunes of General Grant. Her faith in him was like a charm throughout his life. His love for her was a shield against destruction.

Made in the USA
Lexington, KY
14 June 2018